The St. Gregory Hymnal And Catholic Choir Book

Nicola A. Montani

Alpha Editions

This Edition Published in 2020

ISBN: 9789354210884

Design and Setting By
Alpha Editions
www.alphaedis.com
Email – info@alphaedis.com

INDEX

The St. Gregory Hymnal

English Hymns

ALPHABETICAL INDEX OF FIRST LINES

III

v

Latin Hymns and Motets
INDEX OF FIRST LINES

                        XI

The Index to the Supplement will be found on page 576

Hark! A Mystic Voice is Sounding
En clara vox

Tr. Rev. E. Caswall   Nicola A. Montani

1. Hark! a mys - tic voice is sound -ing,
2. Lo! the lamb so long ex - pect - ed,

"Christ is nigh," it seems to say,
Comes with par - don down from Heav'n,

"Cast a - way the dreams of dark - ness,
Let us haste, with tears of sor - row,

O ye chil - dren of the day."
One and all to be for - giv'n.

1

Star - tled at the sol - emn warn - ing,
So when next He comes with glo - ry,

Let the earth - bound soul a - rise;
Wrap - ping all the earth in fear,

Christ, her Sun, all sloth dis - pel - ling,
May He then as our De - fen - der,

Shines up - on the morn - ing skies.
On the clouds of Heav'n ap - pear.

2

O Come, O Come, Emmanuel!
Processional

Tr. Dr. J. M. Neale

Traditional Melody
"Veni, O Sapientiae"

Maestoso

1. O come, O come, Em - man - u - el! And
2. O come Thou Rod of Jes - se, free Thine
3. O come, Thou Day-Spring, come and cheer Our
4. O come, O come, Thou Lord of Might, Who

1. ran-som cap-tive Is - ra-el, That mourns in lone-ly
2. own from Sa-tans tyr - an-ny; From depths of hell Thy
3. spir-its by Thine Ad-vent here, Dis-perse the gloom-y
4. to Thy tribes on Si-nai's height, In an - cient times didst

1. ex - ile here, Un - til the Son of God ap-pear.
2. peo-ple save, And give them vic-t'ry o'er the grave.
3. clouds of night, And death's dark shad-ows put to flight.
4. give the law, In cloud, and maj-es-ty and awe.

ff Chorus

Re - joice! Re - - joice! O

rall

Is - ra - el! To thee shall come Em-man-u-el.

3

Behold! behold He cometh

Processional

Translated from the Latin

S. Webbe

Moderato

1. Be - hold! be - hold He com - eth, Who
2. Ho - san - na to the Sav - iour, Who
3. Yea, come in love and meek - ness, Our
4. Soon shalt Thou sit in glo - ry Up -

1. doth sal - va - tion bring; Lift up your heads re -
2. came on Christ-mas morn, And, of a low - ly
3. Sav - iour now to be; Come to be form- ed
4. on the great White Throne, And pun - ish all the

1. joic - ing, And wel - come Zi - on's King; With
2. Vir - gin, Was in a sta - ble born; Em
3. in us, And make us like to Thee, Be -
4. wick - ed, And rec - om - pense Thine own; When

1. hymns of joy we praise the Lord, Ho -
2. man - u - el! dear Je - sus, come, With-
3. fore the Day of Wrath draw near, When
4. ev - 'ry word and deed and thought To

1. san - na to th' In - car - nate Word!
2. in Thy chil - dren make Thy home!
3. as our Judge Thou shalt ap - pear.
4. right - eous judg - ment shall be brought.

4

Ye faithful, with gladness

Adeste Fideles
O Come, All Ye Faithful

Free translation by the
Rt. Rev. Hugh T. Henry, Litt. D., L.L.D.

Traditional Melody

Traditional Text in Italics

1. Ye faith - ful, with glad - ness,
2. Dear Ma - ry, His Moth - er,
3. A - gain sound - ing o'er us,
4. Our voic - es now blend - ing
(1-a) *O come all ye faith - ful,*
(2-a) *God of God*

1. Ban - ish - ing all sad - ness, O
2. Gives to us as Broth - er The
3. Let the An - gel cho - rus The
4. With their songs un - end - ing, All -
(1-a) *Joy - ful and tri - am - phant O*
(2-a) *Light of Light*

1. come ye, O come ye to
2. Lord whom the an - gels are
3. an - them of glad - ness and
4. joy - ful, dear Je - sus, Thy
(1-a) *come ye Oh come ye to*
(2-a) *Lo He ab - hors, not the*

1. Beth - le - hem! 1. See to us giv - en
2. wor - ship - ping: 2. God the e - ter - nal,
3. tri - umph sing; 3. "Glo - ry be giv - en
4. glo - ry sing. 4. Be our en - deav - or
(1-a) *Beth - le - hem. Come and a - dore Him*
(2-a) *Vir - gin's womb. Ve - ry God be -*

1. Christ, the King of Heav - en!
2. Light of Light su - per - nal!" 1.-4.While
3. To the Lord of Heav - en!" (1-4) O
4. Thus to praise Thee ev - er!

(1-a) Born the King of an - gels;
(2-a) got - ten, not cre - a - ted;

mf

an-gels hov-er o'er Him, And shep-herds kneel be-
come let us a - dore Him, Oh, come let us a -

f

fore Him, O come, let us a -
dore Him, O come let us a -

dore Him, Lord___ and___ King!
dore Him, Christ_____ the Lord.

(3-a) Sing choirs of angels,
Sing in exultation,
Sing all ye citizens of Heav'n above:
Glory to God, in the highest;
O come, let us adore Him,
O come, let us adore Him,
O come, let us adore Him, Christ, the Lord

6

See, amid the winter's snow

Rev. E. Caswall   Traditional Melody

Allegretto

1. See, a - mid the win - ter's snow,
2. Lo, with - in a man - ger lies
3. Sa - cred In - fant all di - vine,
4. Teach, oh teach us, ho - ly Child,
5. Vir - gin Moth - er, Ma - ry blest

1. Born for us on earth be - low;
2. He who built the star - ry skies;
3. What a ten - der love was Thine;
4. By Thy Face so meek and mild;
5. By the joys that fill thy breast,

1. See the ten - der lamb ap - pears,
2. He, who throned in heights sub - lime,
3. Thus to come from high - est bliss,
4. Teach us to re - sem - ble Thee
5. Pray for us, that we may prove

1. Prom - ised from e - ter - nal years!
2. Sits a - mid the Cher - u - bim.
3. Down to such a world as this.
4. In Thy sweet hu - mil - i - ty.
5. Wor - thy of the Sav - iour's love.

7

1.-5. Hail, thou ev - er bless - ed morn,

Hail, Re - demp - tion's hap - py dawn!

Sing through all Je - ru - sa - lem,

Christ is born in Beth - le - hem.

O Dear Little Children
Carol

Translated by Sister Jeanne Marie   Traditional Melody
            Arr. by N.A.M.

Moderato semplice

1. O dear lit-tle chil-dren, O
2. O see in the crib low con-
3. He lies there, O chil-dren, on
4. O chil-dren bend low and a-

1. come one and all, Draw near to the
2. ceal-ing His might, See here by the
3. hay and on straw, Dear Ma-ry and
4. dore Him to-day, O lift up your

1. crib, here in Beth-le-hem's stall And
2. rays of the clear shin-ing light, In
3. Jo-seph re-gard Him with awe, The
4. hands like the shep-herds, and pray Sing

1. see what a bright ray of heav-en's de-light Our
2. clean-li-est swad-dle the Heav-en-ly Child More
3. shep-herds, a-dor-ing, bow hum-bly in pray'r, An-
4. joy-ful-ly, chil-dren, with hearts full of love In

1. Fa-ther has sent on this thrice ho-ly night.
2. beau-teous than le-gions of hosts un-de-filed.
3. gel-i-cal choirs with song rend the air
4. ju-bi-lant song join the an-gels a-bove

CHRISTMAS

Angels we have heard on high

Bishop Chadwick   Nicola A. Montani

1. An - gels we have heard on high,
2. Shep - herd, why this ju - bi - lee?
3. Come to Beth - le - hem, and see
4. See Him in a man - ger laid,

1. Sweet - ly sing - ing o'er our plains,
2. Why your rap - turous strains pro - long?
3. Him Whose birth the an - gels sing;
4. Whom the choirs of an - gels praise

1. And the moun - tains in re - ply
2. What may the glad - some tid - ings be
3. Come, a - dore on bend - ed knee
4. Ma - ry, Jo - seph, lend your aid,

1. Ech - o - ing their joy - ous strains.
2. Which in - spire your heav'n - ly song?
3. Christ the Lord, the new - born King.
4. While our hearts in love we raise.

10

The snow lay on the ground
Old English Carol

Rev. Dr. Lingard

Edv. Grieg
Arr. by N. A. M.

Non troppo lento

1. The snow lay on the ground, The
2. 'Twas Ma - ry, daugh - ter pure Of
3. She laid Him in a stall At
4. Saint Jo - seph too was by, To
5. The an - gels hov - ered 'round, And
6. And then that man - ger poor Be -
7. O come then, let us join The

1. stars shone bright, When Christ our Lord was
2. ho - ly Anne, That brought in - to this
3. Beth - le - hem; The ass, and ox - en
4. tend the Child; To guard Him, and pro -
5. sang this song; "Ve - ni - te, ad - o -
6. came a throne; For He whom Ma - ry
7. heav'n - ly host, To praise the Fa - ther,

1. born On Christ - mas night.
2. world The God made Man.
3. shared The roof with them.
4. tect His Moth - er mild.
5. re - mus Do - mi - num."
6. bore Was God the Son.
7. Son And Ho - ly Ghost.

9

Stars of Glory
Carol

Dr. Husenbeth

S. Janowska
Arr. by N. A.M.

Slowly

1. Stars of glo - ry, shine more
2. See a beau - teous an - gel
3. See the shep - herds quick - ly
4. Hark! the swell of heav'n - ly

1. bright - ly, Pur - er be the moon - light's
2. soar - ing In the bright ce - les - tial
3. ris - ing, Hast - 'ning to the hum - ble
4. voic - es Peals a - long the vault - ed

1. beam, Glide, ye hours and mo - ments,
2. blaze, On the shep - herds, low a -
3. stall, And the new - born In - fant
4. sky; An - gels sing while earth re -

1. light - ly, Swift - ly down time's deep - 'ning
2. dor - ing, Rest his mild ef - ful - gent
3. priz - ing, As the might - y Lord of
4. joic - es_ "Glo - ry to our God on

12

1. stream: Bring the hour that ban - ished
2. rays: "Fear not," cries the heav'n - ly
3. all; Low - ly now they bend be -
4. high; Glo - ry in the high - est

1. sad-ness Brought re - demp -tion down to earth;
2. stran-ger,"Him Whom an - cient seers fore-told,
3. fore Him In His help-less in - fant state,
4. heav - en, Peace to hum - ble men on earth;"

1. When the shep - herds heard with glad - ness
2. Weep - ing in a low - ly man - ger
3. Firm - ly faith - ful, they a - dore Him,
4. Joy to these and bliss is giv - en

1. Tid - ings of a Sav - iour's birth.
2. Shep - herds, haste ye to be - hold."
3. And His great -ness cel - e - brate.
4. In the great Re - deem - er's birth.

10

O sing a joyous carol

Sister M. B.

from "Alte Katholische geistliche Kirchengesang" (Köln, 1599)★

Joyously

1. O sing a joy - ous car - ol Un -
2. Who is there meek - ly ly - ing In
3. Who is there near the cra - dle, That

1. to the ho - ly Child, And praise with glad-some
2. yon - der sta - ble poor? Dear chil - dren, it is
3. guards the ho - ly Child? It is our fa - ther

1. voic - es His Moth - er un - de - filed.
2. Je - sus; He bids you now a - dore.
3. Jo - seph Chaste spouse of Ma - ry mild.

1. Our glad - some voic - es greet - ing Shall
2. Who is there kneel - ing by Him In
3. Dear chil - dren, oh, how joy - ful With

1. hail our In - fant King; And our sweet La - dy
2. Vir - gin beau - ty fair? It is our Moth - er
3. them in Heav'n to be! God grant that none be

1. lis - tens When joy - ful voic - es sing.
2. Ma - ry, She bids you all draw near.
3. mis - sing From that fes - tiv - i - ty.

14

★ Catholic melody incorrectly attributed to M. Praetorius.

Silent night, Holy night

Fr. Gruber
Arr. by Nicola A. Montani

Moderato
pp

1. Si - lent night, ho - ly night! Beth-lehem sleeps
2. Si - lent night, ho - ly night! Shep-herds first
3. Si - lent night, ho - ly night! Son of God!

1. yet what light Floats a-round the ho - ly pair:
2. see the light, Hear the Al - le - lu - ias ring
3. oh, what light Ra-diates from Thy man-ger bed

1. Songs of An-gels fill the air Strains of heav-en-ly
2. Which the An-gel cho-rus sing "Christ the Sav-iour has
3. O-ver realms with darkness spread, Thou in Beth-le-hem

pp *rall*

1. peace, Strains of heav - en - ly peace.
2. come, Christ the Sav - iour has come!"
3. born, Thou in Beth - le - hem born.

15

A Virgin most pure,
as the Prophets did tell
Ancient Carol

Traditional Melody
Arr. by N.A.M.

Slowly

1. A Vir - gin most pure, as the
2. In Beth- le - hem cit - y in
3. But when they had en - tered the
4. Then they were con - strained in a
5. The King_____ of glo - ry to this
6. Then God sent an an - gel from
7. Then pres - ent - ly af - ter the

1. Proph - ets did tell, Hath brought forth a
2. Jew - ry it was, Where Jo - seph and
3. cit - y so fair, A num - ber of
4. sta - ble to lie, Where ox - en and
5. world be - ing brought, Small store of fine
6. heav - en so high To cer - tain poor
7. shep - herds did spy A num - ber of

1. Sav - iour, as it hath be - fell, To
2. Ma - ry to - geth - er did pass, And
3. peo - ple so might - y was there That
4. ass - es they used there to tie; Their
5. lin - en to wrap Him was sought; When
6. shep - herds in fields where they lie, And
7. an - gels ap - pear in the sky; Who

16

1. be our Re-deem-er from death,hell and sin, Which
2. there to be tax - ed with man - y one mo? For
3. Ma - ry and Jo-seph,whose substance was small,Could pro-
4. lodg-ing so sim-ple they held it no scorn,But a -
5. Ma - ry had swaddled her young Son so sweet,With -
6.charged them no longer in sor - row to stay, Be -
7. joy-ful-ly talked and sweet-ly did sing, "To

1. Ad-am's trans-gres-sion had wrapped us in.
2. Cæ-sar com-mand-ed the same should be so.
3. cure in the Inn no lodg-ing at all.
4. gainst the next morn-ing a Sav-iour was born.
5. in an ox man-ger she laid Him to sleep.
6. cause that our Sav-iour was born on this day.
7. God be all glo-ry, our heav-en-ly King."

Chorus

1-17. Re-joice and be mer-ry, Set sor-row a-side,Christ

Je-sus our Sav-iour Was born on this tide.

13

Hark! the herald host is singing

E. Humperdinck

Joyously

1. Hark! the her - ald host is
2. And be - hold the stars bright
3. Soft the mes - sen - gers from

1. sing - ing, Thro' the si - lent ho - ly
2. glow - ing, Shed o'er earth their ra - diant
3. Heav - en Wing their flight from home to

1. night, Tid - ings of great joy they're
2. light, While from An - gels' lips are
3. home: Bear - ing les - sons God hath

1. bring - ing, From yon star - ry az - ure
2. flow - ing An - thems thro' the ho - ly
3. giv - en Un - to all on earth that

1. height. And each heart is filled with
2. night. Bright each win - dow now is
3. roam. "Wel - come, wel - come Christ - mas ·

1. glad - ness, At the mes - sage which they
2. glow - ing, Light - ed by . the Christ - mas
3. eve - ning Bring - ing peace and love to

1. bring: "Christ is born, for - get all
2. tree; And each cheek with joy is
3. earth!" Show your grat - i - tude, re -

1. sad - ness, Trust in Him, your Sav - iour King!"
2. glow - ing, And each heart is filled with glee .
3. joic - ing, Christians in your Sav - iour's birth!

19

14

Sleep, Holy Babe

*(For additional Christmas Hymns see Hymns Nos.126 & 127
and Latin Hymns)*

Tr. Rev. E. Caswall   Traditional Melody

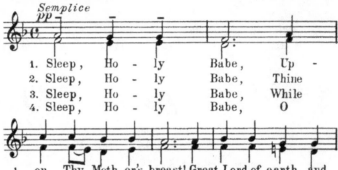

1. Sleep, Ho - ly Babe, Up -
2. Sleep, Ho - ly Babe, Thine
3. Sleep, Ho - ly Babe, While
4. Sleep, Ho - ly Babe, O

1. on Thy Moth-er's breast! Great Lord of earth and
2. An - gels watch a - round; All bend-ing low with
3. I with Ma - ry gaze In joy up - on that
4. snatch Thy brief re - pose; Too quick-ly will Thy

1. sea and sky, How sweet it is to
2. fold - ed wings Be - fore th' In - car - nate
3. Face a - while, Up - on the lov - ing
4. slum - bers break, And Thou to length-ened

1. see Thee lie In such a place of rest!
2. King of Kings, In rev-'rent awe pro - found!
3. In - fant smile, Which there di - vine - ly plays.
4. pains a - wake, That death a - lone shall close.

O Jesus, Thou the beauty art
Jesu, decus Angelicum
St. Bernard

Tr. Rev. E. Caswall   Nicola A. Montani

Andante religioso

1. O   Je - sus,   Thou   the
2. O   my   sweet   Je - sus,

1. beau - ty   art   Of   An - gel   worlds   a -
2. hear   the   sighs   Which   un - to   Thee   I

1. bove; __ Thy   name   is   mu - sic
2. send; __ To   Thee   mine   in - most

1. to   the   heart   In - flam - ing   it   with
2. spir - it   cries,   My   be - ing's   hope   and

21

1. love.___ Ce - les - tial sweet - ness
2. end.___ Stay with us Lord, and

1. un - al - loy'd Who eat Thee hun - ger
2. with Thy light Il - lume the soul's ab -

1. still;___ Who drink of Thee still
2. yss;___ Dis - pel the dark - ness

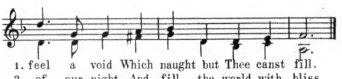

1. feel a void Which naught but Thee canst fill.
2. of our night And fill the world with bliss.

22

To the Name that brings salvation

Processional

Dr. J. M. Neale   Nicola A. Montani

Moderato

1. To the Name that brings sal-va-tion,
2. Name of glad-ness, Name of pleas-ure,
3. 'Tis the Name for a-do-ra-tion,
4. 'Tis the Name that who-so preach-es

1. Hon-or, wor-ship, let us pay, Which for man-y a
2. By this tongue in-ef-fa-ble Name of sweet-ness
3. 'Tis the Name of vic-to-ry, 'Tis the Name for
4. Finds it mu-sic to the ear; Who in pray'r this

1. gen-e-ra-tion Hid in God's fore-knowledge lay.
2. pass-ing meas-ure To the ear de-lec-ta-ble,
3. med-i-ta-tion In this vale of mis-er-y,
4. Name be-seech-es Sweet-est com-fort find-eth near;

1. But with ho-ly ex-ul-ta-tion
2. 'Tis our safe-guard and our treas-ure,
3. 'Tis the Name for ven-e-ra-tion
4. Who its per-fect wis-dom reach-eth

1. We may sing a-loud to-day.
2. 'Tis our help 'gainst sin and hell.
3. By the cit-i-zens on high.
4. Heav'n-ly joy pos-sess-eth here.

17

Jesus the very thought of Thee

Jesu, dulcis memoria

St. Bernard

Tr. Rev. E. Caswall   Traditional Melody

Religioso

1. Je - sus the ver - y thought of Thee,
2. Nor voice can sing, nor heart can frame,
3. O Hope of ev - 'ry con - trite heart,
4. Je - sus, our on - ly joy be Thou,

1. With sweet - ness fills my breast;___
2. Nor can the mem - 'ry find ____
3. O joy of all the meek,___
4. As Thou our prize wilt be ;___

1. But sweet - er far Thy Face to
2. A sweet - er sound than Thy blest
3. To those who fall, how kind Thou
4. O Je - sus, be our glo - ry

1. see And in Thy pres - ence rest.___
2. Name, O Sav - iour of man - kind !___
3. art, How good to those who seek.___
4. now And through e - ter - ni - ty.___

24

He Who once, in righteous vengeance
Ira justa conditoris
(Feast of the Precious Blood)

Tr. Rev. E. Caswall

J. Mohr

Moderato

Arr. by N.A.M.

1. He who once, in right-eous ven-geance,
2. Blest with this all - sav - ing show - er,
3. When be - fore the Judge we trem - ble,

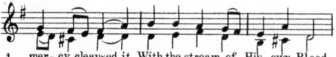

1. Whelm'd the world be-neath the flood, Once a-gain in
2. Earth her beau-ty straight re-sumed; In the place of
3. Con-scious of His brok-en laws, May this Blood in

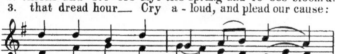

1. mer-cy cleansed it With the stream of His own Blood,
2. thorns and bri-ers Myr-tles sprang and ro-ses bloom'd:
3. that dread hour Cry a - loud, and plead our cause:

1. Com - ing from His throne on high
2. Bit - ter worm-wood of the waste
3. Bid our guil - ty ter - rors cease,

1. On the pain - ful Cross to die.
2. In - to hon - ey changed its taste.
3. Be our par - don and our peace.

25

"Man of Sorrows, wrapt in grief"

M. Bridges

From a Slovak Hymnal
Arr. by N. A. M.

Andante Modᵗᵒ

1. Man of Sor - rows, wrapt in grief,
2. By the gar - den, fraught with woe,
3. By the chal - ice brim - ming o'er
4. Man of Sor - rows! let Thy grief

1. Bow Thine ear to our re - lief:
2. Whith - er Thou full oft wouldst go;
3. With dis - grace and tor - ment sore;
4. Pur - chase for us our re - lief;

1. Thou for us the path hast trod
2. By Thine ag - o - ny of prayer
3. By those lips which fain would pray
4. Lord of mer - cy! bow Thine ear,

1. Of the dread - ful wrath of God;
2. In the des - o - la - tion there;
3. That it might but pass a - way;
4. Slow to an - ger, swift to hear;

26

1. Thou the cup of fire hast drained
2. By the dire and deep dis - tress
3. By the heart which drank it dry,
4. By the Cross - 's roy - al road

1. Till its light a - lone re - mained.
2. Of that mys - t'ry fath - om - less: __
3. Lest a reb - el race should die __ __
4. Lead us to the throne of God, __

1. Lamb of Love! we look to Thee:
2. Lord, our tears in mer - cy see:
3. Be Thy pit - y, Lord, our plea:
4. There for aye to sing to Thee

1. Hear our mourn - ful lit - a - ny.
2. Heark - en to our lit - a - ny.
3. Hear our sol - emn lit - a - ny.
4. Heav'n's tri - umph - ant lit - a - ny.

20
By the Blood that flowed from Thee
Litany of the Passion

C. M. Caddell   Nicola A. Montani

Lento ma non troppo

1. By the Blood that flowed from Thee
2. By the thorns that crowned Thy Head;
3. By the nails and point - ed spear;
4. By the dark - ness thick as night
5. By Thy weep - ing Moth - er's woe;

1. In Thy bit - ter ag - o - ny;
2. By Thy scep - tre of a reed;
3. By Thy peo - ple's cru - el jeer;
4. Blot - ting out the sun from sight;
5. By the sword that pierced her through,

1. By the scourge so meek - ly borne;
2. By Thy Foot - steps faint and slow,
3. By Thy dy - ing pray'r which rose
4. By the cry with which in death
5. When, in an - guish stand - ing by,

rall

1. By Thy pur - ple robe of scorn:
2. Weighed be - neath Thy Cross of woe,
3. Beg - ging mer - cy for Thy foes.
4. Thou didst yield Thy part - ing Breath.
5. On the Cross she saw Thee die.

28

1st Chorus

Maestoso

1-5. Je - sus, Sav - iour, hear our cry!

2d Chorus

Thou wert suf - f'ring once as we;

1st Chorus

Hear the lov - ing lit - a - ny

Tutti

We Thy chil - dren sing to Thee.

Oh come and mourn with me awhile

Father Faber   Jesus Crucified   Nicola A. Montani

Andante religioso

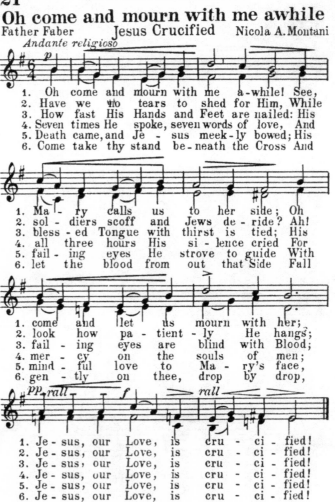

1. Oh come and mourn with me a-while! See,
2. Have we no tears to shed for Him, While
3. How fast His Hands and Feet are nailed: His
4. Seven times He spoke, seven words of love, And
5. Death came, and Je - sus meek-ly bowed; His
6. Come take thy stand be-neath the Cross And

1. Ma - ry calls us to her side; Oh
2. sol - diers scoff and Jews de - ride? Ah!
3. bless - ed Tongue with thirst is tied; His
4. all three hours His si - lence cried For
5. fail - ing eyes He strove to guide With
6. let the blood from out that Side Fall

1. come and let us mourn with her;
2. look how pa - tient - ly He hangs;
3. fail - ing eyes are blind with Blood;
4. mer - cy on the souls of men;
5. mind - ful love to Ma - ry's face,
6. gen - tly on thee, drop by drop,

1. Je - sus, our Love, is cru - ci - fied!
2. Je - sus, our Love, is cru - ci - fied!
3. Je - sus, our Love, is cru - ci - fied!
4. Je - sus, our Love, is cru - ci - fied!
5. Je - sus, our Love, is cru - ci - fied!
6. Je - sus, our Love, is cru - ci - fied!

30

O Sacred Head surrounded
„O Haupt voll Blut und Wunden"

St. Bernard of Clairvaux
(1091–1153)

Melody by H. L. Hassler (1600)
Adaptation as given by J. S. Bach
in his "St. Matthew's Passion"

1. O Sa - cred Head, sur - round - ed, By
2. I see Thy strength and vig - or All
3. In this Thy bit - ter pas - sion, Good

1. crown of pierc - ing thorn! O bleed-ing Head, so
2. fad - ing in the strife, And death, with cru - el
3. Shep - herd, think of me, With Thy most sweet com -

1. wound - ed, Re - viled and put to
2. rig - or, Be - reav - ing Thee of
3. pas - sion, Un - worth - y though I

1. scorn! Death's pal - lid hue comes
2. life; O ag - o - ny and
3. be; Be - neath Thy Cross a -

1. o'er Thee, The glow of life de -
2. dy - ing! O love to sin - ners
3. bid - ing, For - ev - er would I

1. cays, Yet an - gel hosts a -
2. free! Je - sus, all grace sup -
3. rest, In Thy dear love con -

allarg.

1. dore Thee And trem-ble as they gaze.
2. ply - ing, O turn Thy face on me!
3. fid - ing, And with Thy pres-ence blest.

At the Cross her station keeping
Stabat Mater

Jacopone da Todi. XIV Cent.

Traditional Melody from the
Maintzesch Gesangbuch 1661
Harmonized by N. A. M.

Not too slow

1. At the Cross her sta - tion keep - ing,
2. Through her heart, His sor - row shar - ing,
3. O that bless - ed one, grief lad - en,
4. How she stood in des - o - la - tion
5. Who could see, from tears re - frain - ing,
6. Who, un - moved, be - hold her lan - guish
7. For His peo - ple's sins th' All Ho - ly
8. Saw her well - be - lov - ed tak - en,
9. Fount of love and sa - cred sor - row,
10. May my spir - it burn with - in me,

1. Stood the mourn - ful Moth - er, weep - ing,
2. All His bit - ter an - guish bear - ing,
3. Bless - ed Moth - er, Bless - ed Maid - en,
4. Up - ward gaz - ing on the pas - sion
5. Christ's dear Moth - er un - com - plain - ing
6. Un - der - neath His Cross of an - guish,
7. She be - held, a vic - tim low - ly,
8. Saw her Child in death for - sak - en,
9. Moth - er! may my spir - it bor - row
10. Love my God, and great love win me

1. Close to Je - sus to the last.
2. Now at length the sword has passed.
3. Moth - er of the All - blest one.
4. Of that death-less, dy - ing Son.
5. In so great a sor - row bowed?
6. 'Mid the fierce, un-pit-y'ing crowd?
7. Bleed in tor - ments, bleed and die.
8. Heard His last ex - pir - ing cry.
9. Sad - ness from thy ho - ly woe.
10. Grace to please Him here be - low. A - men.

After last stanza

At the Cross her station keeping
Stabat Mater

Jacopone da Todi. XIV Cent.

Traditional Melody from the
Maintzesch Gesangbuch 1661
Harmonized by N. A. M.

Not too slow

11. Those five Wounds on Je - sus smit - ten,
12. Thou, my Sav - iour's Cross who bear - est,
13. In the Pas - sion of my Mak - er
14. Mine with thee be that sad sta - tion,
15. Vir - gin thou of Vir - gins fair - est,
16. Thus Christ's dy - ing may I car - ry,
17. May His Wounds trans - fix me whol - ly,
18. Thus in - flamed with pure af - fec - tion,
19. When in death my limbs are fail - ing,
20. To my part - ing soul be giv - en

11. Moth - er, in my heart be writ - ten,
12. Thou, Thy Son's re - buke who shar - est,
13. Be my sin - ful soul par - tak - er,
14. There to watch the great Sal - va - tion,
15. May the bit - ter woe thou shar - est
16. With Him in His pas - sion tar - ry,
17. May His Cross and Life Blood ho - ly
18. In the Vir - gin's Son pro - tec - tion
19. Let Thy Moth - er's pray'r pre - vail - ing
20. En - trance through the gate of Heav - en,

11. Deep as in thine own they be.
12. Let me share them both with thee.
13. Weep till death, and weep with thee.
14. Wrought up - on th' a - ton - ing Tree.
15. Make on me im - pres - sion deep.
16. And His wounds in mem - 'ry keep.
17. Mor - ti - fy my heart and mind:
18. May I at the judg - ment find.
19. Lift me, Je - sus, to Thy throne;
20. There con - fess me for Thine own. A - men.

*After last
stanza*

I see my Jesus crucified

Nicola A. Montani

1. I see my Je - sus cru - ci - fied, His
2. Those cru - el nails, I drove them in, Each
3. Then to those feet I'll ven - ture near, And
4. Deep grav - en on my sin - ful heart, Oh,

1. wound - ed Hands and Feet and Side, His
2. time I pierced Him with my sin; That
3. wash them with a con - trite tear, And
4. nev - er may that form de - part, That

1. sa - cred Flesh all rent and torn, His
2. crown of thorns 'twas I who wove, When
3. ev - 'ry bleed - ing wound I see, I'll
4. with me al - ways may a - bide The

1. blood - y crown of sharp - est thorn.
2. I de - spised His gra - cious love.
3. think He bore them all for me.
4. thought of Je - sus cru - ci - fied.

O'erwhelmed in depths of woe

Sævo dolorum turbine

Tr Rev. E. Caswall   Nicola A. Montani

1. O'er -whelmed in depths of woe,   Up -
2. See! how the nails those Hands   And
3. Hark! with what aw - ful cry,   His
4. Come, fall be - fore His Cross,   Who
5. Je - su! all praise to Thee,   Our

1. on the Tree of scorn   Hangs
2. Feet so ten - der rend;   See!
3. Spir - it takes its flight;   That
4. shed for us His blood;   Who
5. joy and end - less rest;   Be

1. the Re - deem - er of man - kind,   With
2. down His Face, and Neck, and Breast,   His
3. cry, it smote His Moth-er's heart   And
4. died, the vic - tim of pure love,   To
5. Thou our Guide while pil - grims here,   Our

1. rack - ing an - guish torn.
2. sa - cred Blood de - scend.
3. wrapt her soul in night.
4. make us Sons of God.
5. Crown a - mid the blest.

All glory, laud, and honor
Gloria, laus et honor

From the Latin of St. Theodulph
by Dr. J. M. Neale

M. Haydn

Maestoso con spirito

1. All glo - ry, laud, and hon - or To
2. Thou art the King of Is - ra el, Thou
3. The com - pan - y of an - gels Are
4. The peo - ple of the He - brews With
5. To Thee be - fore Thy Pas - sion They
6. Thou didst ac - cept their prais - es, Ac -

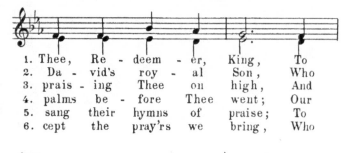

1. Thee, Re - deem - er, King, To
2. Da - vid's roy - al Son, Who
3. prais - ing Thee on high, And
4. palms be - fore Thee went; Our
5. sang their hymns of praise; To
6. cept the pray'rs we bring, Who

1. Whom the lips of chil - dren Made
2. in the Lord's name com - est The
3. mor - tal men and all things Cre -
4. praise and pray'r and an - thems Be -
5. Thee now high ex - alt - ed Our
6. in all good de - light - est, Thou

Jesus Christ is risen to-day

Processional

Surrexit Christus hodie

Translated by the
Rev. J. O' Connor

Nicola A. Montani

Joyously Solo Voices

1. Je - sus Christ is ris'n to day!
2. See the ho - ly wom - en come,
3. Go! tell all his breth - ren dear,
4. Glo - ry, Je - sus, be to Thee!

Chorus   Solo Voices

1. *Al - le - lu - ia!* Sin - ners, wipe your
2. *Al - le - lu - ia!* Bear - ing spi - ces
3. *Al - le - lu - ia!* "He is ris'n, He
4. *Al - le - lu - ia!* Thine own might hath

Chorus

1. tears a - way! *Al - le - lu - ia!*
2. to the tomb; *Al - le - lu - ia!*
3. is not here! *Al - le - lu - ia!*
4. set Thee free. *Al - le - lu - ia!*

1. He Whose death up - on the Cross
2. Hear the white - clad An - gel's voice
3. Seek Him not a - mong the dead;
4. Come, for pri - mal joy re - stored,

Chorus   Solo Voices

1. *Al - le - lu - ia!* Sav - eth us from
2. *Al - le - lu - ia!* Bid the u - ni -
3. *Al - le - lu - ia!* He is ris - en,
4. *Al - le - lu - ia!* Let us bless our

Chorus

1. end - less loss. *Al - le - lu - ia!*
2. verse re - joice! *Al - le - lu - ia!*
3. as He said." *Al - le - lu - ia!*
4. Pas - chal Lord! *Al - le - lu - ia!*

Ye sons and daughters of the Lord
No. 1
O Filii et Filiæ
Processional

Jean Tisserand (1494)   Traditional Melody from
Tr. Rev. E. Caswall   "Airs sur les Hymnes sacres,
Maestoso   Odes et Noels" (Paris 1623)

Al - le - lu - ia!   Al - le - lu -

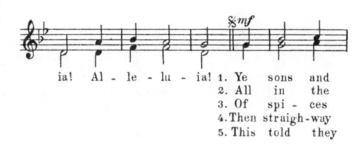

ia! Al - le - lu - ia! 1. Ye   sons   and
2. All   in   the
3. Of   spi - ces
4. Then straigh-way
5. This   told   they

1. daugh-ters   of   the   Lord! The   King   of
2. ear - ly   morn - ing   grey   Went ho - ly
3. pure   a   pre - cious store   In   their pure
4. One   in   white they   see,   Who saith, "Ye
5. Pe - ter, told   they John, Who forth-with

1. glo - ry, King a - dored, This day Him -
2. wom - en on their way, To see the
3. hands those wom - en bore, To a - noint the
4. seek the Lord; but He Is ris'n, and
5. to the tomb are gone; But Pe - ter

1. self from death re - stored. Al - le - lu - ia!
2. tomb where Je - sus lay. Al - le - lu - ia!
3. Sa - cred Bod - y o'er. Al - le - lu - ia!
4. gone to Gal - i - lee." Al - le - lu - ia!
5. is by John out - run. Al - le - lu - ia!

Refrain

Al - le - lu - ia! Al - le - lu - ia! Al - le - lu - ia!

6. That selfsame night, while out of fear
   The doors were shut, their Lord most dear
   To His Apostles did appear. Alleluia!
       Alleluia!   Alleluia!   Alleluia!

7. But Thomas when of this He heard ,
   Was doubtful of his brethren's word;
   Wherefore again there comes the Lord. Alleluia!
       Alleluia!   Alleluia!   Alleluia!

8. "Thomas, behold My Side" saith He;
   "My Hands, My Feet, My Body see,
   And doubt not, but believe in Me." Alleluia!
       Alleluia!   Alleluia!   Alleluia!

9. When Thomas saw that wounded Side ,
   The truth no longer he denied;
   "Thou art my Lord and God," he cried. Alleluia!
       Alleluia!   Alleluia!   Alleluia!

10. Oh, blest are they who have not seen
    Their Lord, and yet believe in Him:
    Eternal life awaiteth them. Alleluia!
        Alleluia!   Alleluia!   Alleluia!

11. Now let us praise the Lord most high,
    And strive His Name to magnify
    On this great day through earth and sky: Alleluia!
        Alleluia!   Alleluia!   Alleluia!

12. Whose mercy ever runneth o'er,
    Whom men and Angel Hosts adore,
    To Him be glory ever more. Alleluia!
        Alleluia!   Alleluia!   Alleluia!

29

Ye sons and daughters of the Lord
No. 2
O Filii et Filiæ

Jean Tisserand (died 1494)
Tr. Rev. E. Caswall

Melody taken from the Gloria
of the Magnificat tertii toni by
Giovanni Pierluigi da Palestrina

Chorus

Al - le - lu - ia! Al-le - lu - ia! Al - le -

Solo Voices or Chanters

lu - ia!   1. Ye sons and daugh - ters
2. All in the ear - ly

1. of the Lord! The King of glo - ry,
2. morn - ing grey Went ho - ly wom - en

1. King a - dored, This day Him - self from
2. on their way, To see the tomb where

Chorus

1. death re - stored.
2. Je - sus lay.   Al - le - lu - ia!

NOTE: *Additional stanzas given in preceding hymn.*

Now at the Lamb's high royal feast
Ad regias Agni dapes

Tr. Rev. E. Caswall   Nicola A. Montani

Allegro moderato

1. Now at the Lamb's high roy - al feast, In
2. And as th' a-veng - ing An - gel pass'd Of
3. Hail, pur - est Vic - tim Heav'n could find The
4. O Je - sus! from the death of sin Keep

1. robes of saint - ly white, we sing, Thro'
2. old the blood - be - sprin - kled door; As
3. pow'rs of Hell to o - ver - throw! Who
4. us, we pray; so shalt Thou be The

1. the Red Sea in safe - ty brought By
2. the cleft sea a pas - sage gave, Then
3. didst the bonds of Death un - bind Who
4. ev - er - last - ing Pas - chal joy Of

1. Je - sus our im - mor - tal King. O
2. closed to whelm th' E - gyp - tians o'er; So
3. dost the prize of Life be - stow. Hail,
4 all the souls new - born in Thee: To

1. depth of love! for us He drains The
2. Christ, our Pas - chal Sac - ri - fice, Has
3. vic - tor Christ! hail, ris - en King! To
4. God the Fa - ther, with the Son Who

1. chal - ice of His ag - o - ny: For
2. brought us safe all per - ils thro', While
3. Thee a - lone be - longs the crown; Who
4. from the grave im - mor - tal rose, And

1. us a Vic - tim on the Cross He
2. for un - leav - ened bread He asks, But
3. hast the heav'n - ly gates un - barred, And
4. Thee, O Par - a - clete be praise, While

1. meek - ly lays Him down to die.
2. heart sin - cere and pur - pose true.
3. cast the Prince of dark - ness down
4. age on end - less a - ges flows.

Christ the Lord is risen today
Victimæ Paschali Laudes

Translated by Miss Leeson   Nicola A. Montani

Allegro Mod[to]

1. Christ the Lord is ris'n to - day:
2. Christ the Vic - tim un - de - filed,
3. Say, O won - d'ring Ma - ry, say,
4. Christ, Who once for sin - ners bled,

1. Chris - tians, haste your vows to pay;
2. Man to God hath rec - on - ciled,
3. What thou saw - est on thy way,
4. Now the first - born from the dead,

1. Of - fer ye your prais - es meet
2. When in strange and aw - ful strife
3. "I be - held, where Christ had lain,
4. Thron'd in end - less might and pow'r,

1. At the Pas - chal Vic - tim's feet;
2. Met to - geth - er death and life;
3. Emp - ty tomb and an - gels twain,
4. Lives and reigns for ev - er more

1. For the sheep the Lamb hath bled,
2. Chris - tians, on this hap - py day
3. I be - held the glo - ry bright
4. Hail, e - ter - nal hope on high!

1. Sin - less in the sin - ners stead,
2. Haste with joy your vows to pay;
3. Of the ris - ing Lord of light:
4. Hail, Thou King of vic - to - ry!

1. Christ the Lord is ris'n on high:
2. Christ the Lord is ris'n on high:
3. Christ my hope is ris'n a - gain;
4. Hail, Thou Prince of life a - dor'd!

1. Now He lives, no more to die.
2. Now He lives, no more to die.
3. Now He lives, and lives to reign?"
4. Help and save us, gra - cious Lord!

48

Lift up, ye princes of the sky
Ps. xxiii

Translated by Father Aylward

From a Slovak Hymnal
Arr. by N. A. M.

With animation

1. Lift up, ye princ - es of the
2. The Lord of strength and match - less

1. sky, Lift up your por - tals, lift them
2. might, The Lord all - con - qu'ring in the

1. high; And you, ye ev - er - last - ing
2. flight, Lift, lift your por - tals, lift them

1. gates, Back on your gold - en hing - es
2. high, Ye princ - es of the con - quered

1. fly: For lo, the King of glo - ry
2. sky; And you, ye ev - er - last - ing

1. waits To en - ter in vic - to - rious -
2. gates, Back on your gold - en hing - es

1. ly. Who is this King of glo - ry?
2. fly: For lo, the King of glo - ry

1. Tell, O ye who sing His praise so well.
2. waits, The Lord of hosts, the Lord most high.

O Thou pure light of souls that love
Salutis humanæ Sator

Translated by Father Caswall

From a Slovak Hymnal
Arr. by N.A.M.

Moderato assai

1. O Thou pure light of souls that love, True joy of ev-'ry hu-man breast, Sow-er of life's im-mor-tal seed, Our Mak-er, and Re-deem-er blest!

2. What won-drous pit-y Thee o'er-came To make our guilt-y load Thine own, And sin-less suf-fer death and shame, For our trans-gres-sions to a-tone!

3. Thou, burst-ing Ha-des o-pen wide, Didst all the cap-tive souls un-chain; And thence to Thy dread Fa-ther's side With glo-rious pomp a-scend a-gain.

4. O still may pit-y Thee com-pel To heal the wounds of which we die; And take us in Thy light to dwell, Who for Thy bliss-ful Pres-ence sigh.

5. Be Thou our guide, be Thou our goal; Be Thou our path-way to the skies; Our joy when sor-row fills the soul; In death our ev-er-last-ing prize.

34

Holy Spirit, Lord of Light
Processional

Tr. Rev. E. Caswall S. Webbe (1740-1816)

Marcato

1. Ho-ly Spir-it, Lord of Light, From the clear ce-
2. Thou, of all con-sol-ers best, Thou, the soul's de-
3. Light im-mor-tal, Light di-vine, Vis-it Thou these
4. Thou, on those who ev-er-more Thee con-fess and

1. les-tial height, Thy pure beam-ing ra-diance give.
2. light-some guest, Dost re-fresh-ing peace be-stow:
3. hearts of Thine, And our in-most be-ing fill:
4. Thee a-dore, In Thy sev'n-fold gifts de-scend:

1. Come, Thou Fa-ther of the poor, Come with treas-ures
2. Thou in toil art com-fort sweet: Pleas-ant cool-ness
3. If Thou take Thy grace a-way, Noth-ing pure in
4. Give them com-fort when they die; Give them life with

1. which en-dure; Come Thou Light of all that live.
2. in the heat; Sol-ace in the midst of woe.
3. man will stay; All his good is turned to ill.
4. Thee on high; Give them joys that nev-er end.

Come Holy Ghost, Creator Come
Veni Creator Spiritus

Translated by Dryden

W. A. Mozart
Arr. from the figured bass by N. A. M.
Melody „O Gottes Lamm" Koch. Verz. No. 343

1. Come, Ho - ly Ghost, Cre - a - tor,
2. Thou who art sev'n - fold in Thy
3. Through Thee may we the Fa - ther

1. come From Thy bright heav'n - ly throne, —
2. grace, Fin - ger of God's right hand; —
3. know, Thro' Thee th' E - ter - nal Son, —

__ 1. Come, take pos - ses - sion of our
__ 2. His prom - ise teach - ing lit - tle
__ 3. And Thee, the Spir - it of them

1. souls, And make them all Thy own. __
2. ones To speak and un - der - stand; __
3. both, Thrice - bless - ed Three in One. __

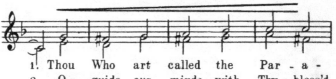

1. Thou Who art called the Par - a -
2. O, guide our minds with Thy bless'd
3. All Glo - ry to the Fa - ther

1. clete, Best gift of God a - bove,___
2. light With love our hearts in - flame;___
3. be, With His co - e - qual Son;___

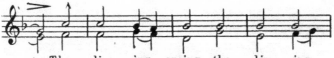

1. The liv - ing spring, the liv - ing
2. And with Thy strength, which ne'er de -
3. The same to Thee, great Par - a -

1. fire, Sweet unc - tion and true love.
2. cays, Con - firm our mor - tal frame.
3. clete, While end - less a - ges run:

O Come, Creator Spirit! Come
Veni Creator Spiritus

Translated by Father Faber   K. Kurpinski

Lento

1. O come Cre - a - tor Spir - it! __ come,
2. Thou that are named the Par - a - clete,
3. The sev'n - fold grace Thou dost ex - pand,
4. To God the Fa - ther let us raise

1. Vouch - safe to make our minds Thy home
2. The Gift of God, His Spir - it sweet;
3. O Fin - ger of the Fa - ther's Hand;
4. And to His on - ly Son, our praise,

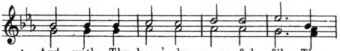

1. And with Thy heav'n - ly grace ful - fil The
2. The liv - ing Foun - tain, Fire, and Love, And
3. True prom - ise of the Fa - ther, rich In
4. Praise to the Ho - ly Spir - it be Now,

1. hearts Thou mad - est at Thy will.
2. gra - cious Unc - tion from a - bove.
3. gifts of tongues and va - rious speech.
4. and for all e - ter - ni - ty.

37

Spirit of Grace and Union

Qui procedis ab utroque

Adam of St. Victor   Nicola A. Montani

Moderato

1. Spir - it   of   grace   and   U - - -
2. The   Fa   ther   and   the   Son   through
3. O   in - ex - haus - tive   Fount   of
4. Lord   of   all   sanc - ti - ty   and

1. nion!   Who   from   the   Fa - ther
2. Thee   Are   linked   in   per - fect
3. light!   How   doth   Thy   ra - diance
4. might!   Im - mense, im - mor - tal,

1. and   the   Son   Dost   e - qual -
2. u - ni - ty,   And   ev - er -
3. put   to   flight   The   dark - ness
4. in - fi - nite!   The   life   of

1. ly pro - ceed. _____ In _ flame our
2. last - ing love ; _____ In - ef - fa -
3. of the mind ! _____ The pure are
4. earth and Heav'n ! _____ Be, through e -

1. hearts with ho - ly fire Our lips with
2. bly Thou dost per - vade All na - ture;
3. on - ly pure through Thee; Thou on - ly
4. ter - nal length of days, All hon - or,

1. el - o - quence in - spire, And
2. and Thy _ self un - sway'd The
3. dost the guilt - y free, And
4. glo - ry, bless - ing, praise, And

rall

1. strength - en us in need. _____
2. whole cre - a - tion move. _____
3. cheer with light the blind. _____
4. a - do - ra - tion giv'n ! _____

38

O God of loveliness
O Bello Dio del Paradiso
St. Alfonso Liguori

Translated by
Rev. E. Vaughan, C. SS. R.

This setting of the text "O God of Loveliness" is the first to be made in connection with the melody "Schönster Herr Jesu." The traditional tune has been modified by N. A. Montani to agree with the text. The harmonization and adaptation are copyrighted.

Andante Maestoso

1. O God of love - li - ness,
2. Thou art blest Three in One,
3. To think Thou art my God,—
4. O love - li - ness su - preme,

1. O Lord of Heav'n a - bove,
2. Yet un - di - vi - ded still;
3. O thought for - ev - er blest!
4. And Beau - ty in - fi - nite;

1. How worth - y to pos - sess My
2. Thou art that One a - lone Whose
3. My heart has o - ver - flowed With
4. O ev - er - flow - ing Stream, And

1. heart's de - vo -ted love! So sweet Thy
2. love my heart can fill. The heav'ns and
3. joy with- in my breast. My soul so
4. O - cean of de - light; O Life by

1. Coun - te - nance, So gra - cious
2. earth be - low, Were fash - ioned
3. full of bliss Is plunged as
4. which I live, My tru - est

1. to be - hold, That one, one
2. by Thy Word; How a - mia -
3. in a sea, Deep in the
4. life a - bove, To Thee a -

1. on - ly glance To me were bliss un - told.
2. ble art Thou, My ev - er - dear - est Lord!
3. sweet a - byss Of ho - ly char - i - ty.
4. lone I give My un - di - vid - ed love.

59

39

Holy God, we praise Thy Name

Te Deum Laudamus

Translated by Rev. Clarence Walworth
(1820–1900)

Melody from the
"Katholisches Gesangbuch"
(1775)

Maestoso

1. Ho - ly God, we praise Thy Name, Lord of
2. Hark! the loud ce - les - tial hymn, An - gel
3. Ho - ly Fa - ther, Ho - ly Son, Ho - ly

1. all, we bow be - fore Thee; All on
2. choirs a - bove are rais - ing! Cher - u -
3. Spir - it, Three we name Thee, While in

(Thy scep-tre ac - claim,)

1. earth Thy scep - tre claim, All in Heav'n a -
2. bim and Ser - a - phim In un - ceas - ing
3. es - sence on - ly One, Un - di - vid - ed

(Bound-less is)

1. bove a - dore Thee, In - fi - nite Thy vast do -
2. cho - rus prais - ing; Fill the Heav'ns with sweet ac -
3. God we claim Thee: And a - dor - ing bend the

1. main, Ev - er - last - ing is Thy reign.
2. cord: Ho - ly, ho - ly, ho - ly Lord!
3. knee, While we own the mys - ter - y.

Full of Glory, full of wonders

Processional

Father Faber　　　　　　　　　　　　　　　　Nicola A. Montani

1. Full of glo - ry, full of won - ders,
2. Time - less, space - less, sin - gle, lone - ly,
3. Splen - dors up - on splen - dors beam - ing

1. Maj - es - ty Di - vine! 'Mid Thine ev - er -
2. Yet sub - lime - ly Three, Thou art grand - ly,
3. Change and in - ter - twine! Glo - ries o - ver

1. last - ing thun - ders How Thy light-nings shine!
2. al - ways, on - ly God in U - ni - ty!
3. glo - ries stream - ing All trans - lu - cent shine!

1. Shore - less O - cean! who shall sound Thee?
2. Lone in gran - deur, lone in glo - ry,
3. Bless - ings, prais - es, a - do - ra - tions

1. Thine own e - ter - ni - ty is round Thee,
2. Who shall tell Thy won - drous sto - ry,
3. Greet Thee from the trem - bling na - tions

1. Maj - es - ty Di - vine! Maj - es - ty Di - vine!
2. Aw - ful Trin - i - ty? Aw - ful Trin - i - ty?
3. Ma - jes - ty Di - vine! Ma - jes - ty Di - vine!

41

I need Thee, Precious Jesus
(Communion Hymn)

For additional Communion Hymns see Nos. 44, 47, 49, 51, 53, 54, 122.

From a Slovak Hymnal
Arr. by N. A. M.

With devotion

1. I need Thee, pre - cious Je - sus, I
2. I need Thy Blood, sweet Je - sus, To
3. I need Thee, sweet-est Je - sus, In Thy

1. need a friend like Thee; A friend to soothe and
2. wash each sin - ful stain: To cleanse this sin - ful
3. Sac - ra -ment of Love; To nour - ish this poor

1. sym- pa-thize, A friend to care for me. I
2. soul of mine, And make it pure a - gain. I
3. soul of mine, With the treas-ures of Thy Love. I'll

1. need Thy Heart, sweet Je - sus, To
2. need Thy Wounds, sweet Je - sus, To
3. need Thee, sweet-est Je - sus, When

1. feel each anx - ious care; I
2. fly from per - ils near, To
3. death's dread hour draws nigh, To

1. long to tell my ev - 'ry want, And
2. shel - ter in these hal - lowed clefts, From
3. hide me in Thy Sa - cred Heart, Till

1. all my sor - rows share.
2. ev - 'ry doubt and fear.
3. waft - ed safe on high.

63

When morning gilds the skies
(May Jesus Christ be praised)

Translated by   Processional   Traditional Melody
Father Caswall   (1678)

Moderato (Solo Voices ad lib.)

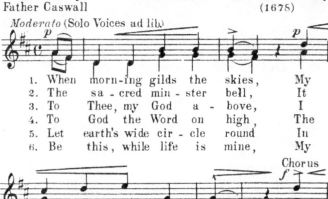

1. When morn-ing gilds the skies,   My
2. The sa - cred min - ster bell,   It
3. To Thee, my God a - bove,   I
4. To God the Word on high,   The
5. Let earth's wide cir - cle round   In
6. Be this, while life is mine,   My

Chorus

1. heart a - wak - ing cries: May
2. peals o'er hill and dell: May
3. cry with glow - ing love: May
4. host of an - gels cry: May
5. joy - ful notes re - sound: May
6. can - ti - cle di - vine: May

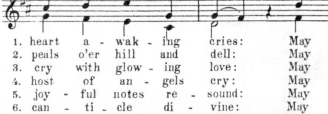

Solo Voices

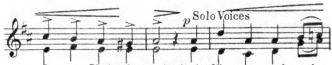

1. Je-sus Christ be praised! A - like at work and
2. Je-sus Christ be praised! Oh! hark to what it
3. Je-sus Christ be praised! The fair-est gra - ces
4. Je-sus Christ be praised! Let mor-tals, too up -
5. Je-sus Christ be praised! Let air, and sea, and
6. Je-sus Christ be praised! Be this th'e - ter - nal

1. prayer: To   Je - sus I re -
2. sings: As   joy - ous - ly it
3. spring   In   hearts that ev - er
4. raise   Their voice in hymns of
5. sky,   From depth to height re -
6. song,   Through all the a - ges

1. pair: May Je - sus Christ be
2. rings: May Je - sus Christ be
3. sing: May Je - sus Christ be
4. praise: May Je - sus Christ be
5. ply: May Je - sus Christ be
6. on: May Je - sus Christ be

Chorus

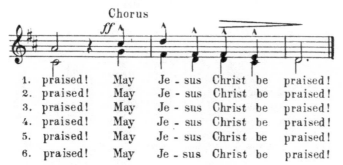

1. praised! May Je - sus Christ be praised!
2. praised! May Je - sus Christ be praised!
3. praised! May Je - sus Christ be praised!
4. praised! May Je - sus Christ be praised!
5. praised! May Je - sus Christ be praised!
6. praised! May Je - sus Christ be praised!

43

Crown Him with many Crowns
Processional

Matthew Bridges　　　　　　　　　　　　Nicola A. Montani

With expression

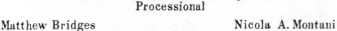

1. Crown Him with man - y crowns, The
2. Crown Him the Vir - gin's Son, The
3. Crown Him the Lord of Love: Be -
4. Crown Him the Lord of peace, Whose
5. Crown Him the Lord of heaven, One

1. Lamb up - on His throne; Hark, how the heav'n-ly
2. God In - car-nate born; Whose arm those crim-son
3. hold His Hands and Side, Rich Wounds, yet vis - i -
4. pow'r a scep-tre sways From pole to pole, that
5. with the Fa - ther known, And the blest Spir-it

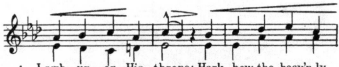

1. an - them drowns All mu - sic but its own; A -
2. tro-phies won, Which now His brow a - dorn! Fruit
3. ble a - bove In beau-ty glo - ri - fied; No
4. wars may cease, Ab-sorbed in pray'r and praise: His
5. through Him giv'n From yon-der Tri - une throne: All

1. wake,   my   soul,   and   sing _____   Of
2. of   the   Mys - tic   Rose, _____   As
3. An - gel   in   the   sky _____   Can
4. reign   shall know   no   end, _____   And
5. hail,   Re - deem - er,   hail! _____   For

1. Him Who died for thee, And hail Him as thy
2. of that Rose the Stem; The Root whence Mer-cy
3. ful - ly bear that sight, But down-ward bends his
4. round His pierc - éd Feet Fair flow'rs of Par - a -
5. Thou hast died for me; Thy praise shall nev - er,

1. match-less King Thro' all e - ter - ni - ty.
2. ev - er flows, The Babe of Beth - le - hem.
3. burn - ing eye At mys - ter - ies so bright.
4. dise ex - tend Their fra - grance ev - er sweet.
5. nev - er fail Thro'-out e - ter - ni - ty.

67

44

Jesus, Lord, be Thou mine own

Mondo, piú per me non sei
Communion Hymn

St. Alphonsus
Tr. Rev. E. Vaughan, C. SS. R.

Don Lorenzo Perosi
Adapted by N. A. M.

Moderato

1. Je - sus Lord, be Thou mine own;
2. Life with - out Thy Love would be
3. Thou, O God, my heart in - flame,
4. God of beau - ty, Lord of Light,

1. Thee I long for, Thee a - lone;
2. Death, O Sov'r - eign Good, to me;
3. Give that love which Thou dost claim;
4. Thy good will is my de - light;

1. All my self I give to Thee;
2. Bound and held by Thy dear chains
3. Pay - ment I will ask for none;
4. Now hence - forth Thy will di - vine

1. Do what - e'er Thou wilt with me.
2. Cap - tive now my heart re - mains.
3. Love de - mands but love a - lone.
4. Ev - er shall in all be mine.

Loving Shepherd of Thy sheep

The Good Shepherd

Processional

Pastor Amans

Miss J. E. Leeson
(1807-1882)

Adaptation of a Litany Melody
from Catholic Hymntunes
(publ. 1819; J. M. Capes)

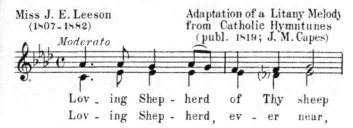

Lov _ ing Shep - herd of Thy sheep
Lov - ing Shep - herd, ev _ er near,

Keep me, Lord, in safe - ty keep;
Teach me still Thy voice to hear;

Noth - ing can Thy pow'r with - stand,
Suf _ fer not my step to stray

None can pluck me from Thy Hand.

From the strait and nar - row way.

Lov - ing Shep-herd,Thou didst give Thine own life that

Where Thou lead-est may I go, Walk-ing in Thy

I might live; May I love Thee day by day,

steps be - low; Then be-fore Thy Fa-ther's throne,

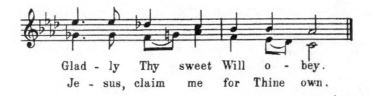

Glad - ly Thy sweet Will o - bey.

Je - sus, claim me for Thine own.

The Very Angels' Bread
Panis Angelicus

Tr. by Rt.Rev.Msgr H.T. Henry, Litt.D. P. Meurers

The ver-y An-gels' Bread Doth food to
men af-ford; The types have van-ish-éd, Re-
mains the Truth a-dored: O won-drous
mys-ter-y Their ban-quet is the Lord The
poor and low-ly, bond and free.

O God for-ev-er blest, O Three in
One, we pray: Vis-it the long-ing breast Enter this house of clay, And lead us
through the Night Un-to the per-fect Day Where
dwell-est Thou in end-less light.

Soul of my Saviour
Anima Christi

L. Dobici
Adapted by N.A.M.

Slowly: with devotion
pp

1. Soul of my Sav - iour sanc - ti - fy my
2. Strength and pro - tec - tion may His Pas - sion
3. Guard and de - fend me from the foe ma -

1. breast, Bod - y of Christ, be
2. be, O bles - sèd Je - sus,
3. lign; In death's drear mo - ments

1. Thou my sav - ing guest; Blood of my
2. hear and an - swer me; Deep in Thy
3. make me on - ly Thine; Call me and

1. Sav - iour bathe me in Thy Tide;
2. Wounds, Lord, hide and shel - ter me;
3. bid me come to Thee on high,

1. Wash me, ye wa - ters gush - ing from His Side.
2. So shall I nev - er, nev - er part from Thee.
3. Where I may praise Thee with Thy Saints for aye.

Thee prostrate I adore
(Adoro Te devote)

Translated by St. Thomas Aquinas
Father Aylward, O. P.
          Nicola A. Montani

Moderato devoto

1. Thee pros-trate I a - dore, the
2. The sight, the touch, the taste, In
3. I see not with mine eyes, Thy
4. Me - mo - rial sweet, that shows the

1. De - i - ty that lies Be - neath these hum-ble
2. Thee are here de-ceived; But by the ear a -
3. Wounds, as Thomas saw; Yet own Thee for my
4. death of my dear Lord; Thou liv - ing bread, that

1. veils, __ con-cealed from hu - man eyes: My
2. lone __ this truth is safe be - lieved; I
3. God __ with e - qual love and awe; Oh
4. life __ dost un - to man af - ford; Oh

cresc

1. heart doth whol-ly yield, sub-ject-ed to Thy
2. hold what-e'er the Son of God hath said to
3. grant me, that my faith may ev - er firm-er
4. grant, that this my soul may ev - er live on

1. sway, For con-tem-plat-ing Thee it
2. me; Than this blest word of truth no
3. be, That all my hope and love may
4. Thee, That Thou mayst ev-er - more its

Refrain

1. whol-ly faints a-way.
2. word can tru-er be.
3. still re-pose in Thee.
4. on-ly sweet-ness be.

1-4. Hail, Je-sus, hail; do

Thou, good Shep-herd of the sheep, In-

crease in all true hearts the faith they fond-ly keep.

74

THE BLESSED SACRAMENT   **49**
Jesus, gentlest Saviour
Thanksgiving after Communion
For additional Communion Hymns see Nos. 41, 44, 51, 54, 128 to 131.

Father Faber   Nicola A. Montani

Andante semplice

1. Je - sus, gen - tlest Sav - iour!
2. Out be - yond the shin - ing
3. Oh, how can we thank Thee
4. Now at least we'll keep Thee

1. God of might and pow'r! Thou Thy-self art
2. Of the fur - thest star, Thou art ev - er
3. For a gift like this,— Gift that tru - ly
4. All the time we may;— But Thy grace and

1. dwell - ing In us at this hour.
2. stretch - ing In - fi - nite - ly far.
3. mak - eth Heav'ns e - ter - nal bliss!
4. bless - ing We will keep al - way.

1. Na-ture can-not hold Thee, Heav'n is all too strait
2. Yet the hearts of chil-dren Hold what worlds can-not,
3. Ah! when wilt Thou al-ways Make our hearts Thy home?
4. When our hearts Thou leavest, Worth-less tho' they be,

1. For Thine end-less glo - ry And Thy roy - al state.
2. And the God of won-ders Loves the low-ly spot.
3. We must wait for Heav-en— Then the day will come.
4. Give them to Thy Moth-er To be kept for Thee.

Copyright 1920 by N. A. M.

The Word, descending from above
Verbum supernum prodiens

Translated by   St. Thomas Aquinas
the Rev. E. Caswall
                                     Nicola A. Montani

Non troppo lento

1. The Word de-scend-ing from a-bove, Though
2. He short-ly to a death ac-cursed By
3. Him-self in ei-ther kind He gave; He
4. At birth our broth-er He be-came; At
5. O sav-ing Vic-tim! o-pen wide The
6. To Thy great Name be end-less praise, Im-

1. with the Fa-ther still on high, Went forth up-on His
2. a dis-ci-ple shall be giv'n; But, to His twelve dis-
3. gave His Flesh, He gave His Blood; Of flesh and blood all
4. meat Him-self as food He gives; To ran-som us He
5. gate of Heav'n to man be-low! Sore press our foes from
6. mor-tal God-head, One in Three! Oh, grant us end-less

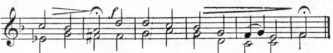

1. work of love; And soon to life's last eve drew nigh.
2. ci-ples, first He gives Him-self, the Bread from Heav'n.
3. men are made; And He of man would be the Food.
4. died in shame; As our re-ward, in bliss He lives.
5. ev-'ry side; Thine aid sup-ply, Thy strength be-stow.
6. length of days, In our true na-tive land, with Thee!

Hail to Thee! true Body

Translated by
Father Caswall

Ave Verum Corpus

J. F. Kloss
Arr by N. A. M.

Con anima

Hail to Thee! true Bod - y, sprung

From the Vir - gin Ma - ry's womb!

The same that on the Cross was hung,

And bore for man the bit - ter doom!

Thou, Whose Side was pierc'd, and flow'd

Both with wa - ter and with blood;

Suf - fer us to taste of Thee,

In our life's last ag - o - ny.

Slower
pp
Son of Ma - ry, Je - sus blest!

rall
Sweet - est, gen - tlest, ho - li - est!

78

Sing, my tongue. the Saviour's glory
Pange Lingua gloriosi

Tr. Rev. E. Caswall

M. Haydn

1. Sing, my tongue, the Sav-iour's glo-ry,
2. Of a pure and spot-less Vir-gin
3. On the night of that Last Sup-per,
4. Word made Flesh, the bread of na-ture

Tantum ergo Sacramentum

5. Down in a-do-ra-tion fall-ing,
6. To the Ev-er-last-ing Fa-ther,

1. Of His Flesh the mys-t'ry sing;
2. Born for us on earth be-low,
3. Seat-ed with His chos-en band,
4. By His word to Flesh He turns;
5. Lo! the sa-cred Host we hail;
6. And the Son Who reigns on high,

1. Of the Blood all price ex-ceed-ing,
2. He, as Man, with man con-vers-ing,
3. He the Pas-chal vic-tim eat-ing,
4. Wine in-to His Blood He chang-es:—
5. Lo! o'er an-cient forms de-part-ing,
6. With the Ho-ly Ghost pro-ceed-ing

1. Shed   by   our   im - mor - tal   King,
2. Stayed, the   seeds of   truth to   sow;
3. First   ful - fils   the   Law's com - mand;
4. What   though sense no   change dis - cerns?
5. New - er rites of   grace pre - vail;
6. Forth   from   Each   e -   ter - nal - ly,

1. Des - tined, for   the   world's re - demp - tion,
2. Then   He   closed in   sol - emn or - der
3. Then,   as   Food   to   His   A - pos - tles
4. On - ly   be   the   heart in   ear - nest,
5. Faith   for   all   de - fects sup - ply - ing,
6. Be   sal - va - tion, hon - or,   bless - ing,

1. From   a   no - ble womb   to   spring.
2. Won - drous - ly His   Life   of   woe.
3. Gives   Him - self with His   own   Hand.
4. Faith   her   les - son quick - ly learns.
5. Where   the   fee - ble sens - es fail.
6. Might,   and   end - less maj - es - ty.   A - men.

Jesus, my Lord, my God, my All!

Father Faber

Nicola A. Montani

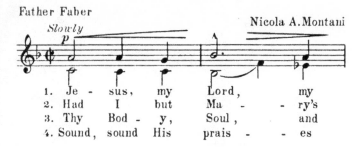

1. Je - sus, my Lord, my
2. Had I but Ma - ry's
3. Thy Bod - y, Soul, and
4. Sound, sound His prais - - es

1. God, my All! How can I love Thee
2. sin - less heart To love Thee with, my
3. God - head, all! O mys - ter - y of
4. high - er still, And come, ye an - gels,

1. as I ought? And how re - vere this
2. dear - est King! Oh, with what bursts of
3. love di - vine! I can - not com - pass
4. to our aid; 'Tis God! 'tis God! the

1. won - drous gift, So far sur -
2. fer - vent praise Thy good - ness,
3. all I have, For all Thou
4. ver - y God, Whose pow'r both

1. pass - ing hope or thought?
2. Je - sus! would I sing!
3. hast and art are mine.
4. man and an - gels made!

Refrain
1st time pp 2d time f

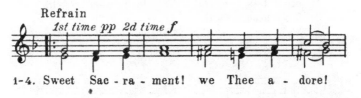

1-4. Sweet Sac - ra - ment! we Thee a - dore!

(Repeat Refrain ad lib.)

Oh! make us love Thee more and more.

82

THE BLESSED SACRAMENT 54

Jesus, Food of Angels

Communion Hymn

Partendo dal Mondo

Translated by Father
E. Vaughan, C.S.S.R.

Ch. Gounod
Arr. by N.A.M.

Andante Religioso

1. Je - sus, food of an - gels, Mon - arch
2. Soon I hope to see Thee, And en -

of the heart; Oh, that I could
joy Thy love, Face to face, sweet

nev - er From Thy face de - part! Yes, Thou ev - er
Je - sus, In Thy Heav'n a - bove. But on earth an

dwell - est Here for love __ of me, __
ex - ile My de - light __ shall be __

Hid-den Thou re - main-est, God of Maj - es - ty.
Ev - er to be near Thee Veiled for love of me.

55

O Jesus Christ, remember
Gesù Sacramentato

Father Caswall

Nicola A. Montani

With devotion

1. O Je - sus Christ, re - mem - ber, When
2. Re - mem - ber then, O Sav - iour, I
3. Ac - cept Di - vine Re - deem - er, The

1. Thou shalt come a - gain, Up -
2. sup - pli - cate of Thee, That
3. hom - age of my praise; Be

1. on the clouds of Heav - en, With
2. here I bowed be - fore Thee Up -
3. Thou the light and hon - or And

1. all Thy shin - ing train; When
2. on my bend - ed knee; That
3. glo - ry of my days; Be

1. ev - 'ry eye shall see Thee In
2. here I owned Thy Pres - ence, And
3. Thou my con - so - la - · tion When

1. De - i - ty re - vealed, Who
2. did not Thee de - ny; And
3. death is draw - ing nigh; Be

1. now up - on this al - tar In
2. glo - ri - fied Thy great - ness, Though
3. Thou my on - ly treas - ure Through

1. si - lence art con - cealed;
2. hid from hu - man eye.
3. all e - ter - ni - ty.

Wondrous love that cannot falter

(Hymn of the Association of Perpetual Adoration)

Tr. Rt.Rev. Msgr. H.T. Henry

Ch. Gounod
Arr. by N.A.M.

1. Won - drous love that can - not
2. An - gel hosts are hushed in
3. Tho' the Heav'n - ly choir re -
4. All He hath in high - est
5. Bread of An - gels! who can
6. Bend - ing low in a - do -

1. fal - ter! Je - sus in the Host doth
2. won - der And a - dore with fold - ed
3. joic - es Praise to sing... His lov - ing
4. Heav - en Veil - éd in the Host we
5. meas - ure All it means? this dai - ly
6. ra - tion, Ev - er con - stant let us

1. dwell Day and night up - on the
2. wings: For the low - ly Spe - cies
3. ear Seeks the trib - ute of our
4. see: And to us the care is
5. food? And the dai - ly grant - ed
6. be, Mak - ing Je - sus Rep - a -

1. Al - tar Near to those He loves so
2. un - der, Hid - den lies the King of
3. voic - es: 'Tis for us He wait - eth
4. giv - en Of His won - drous pov - er -
5. treas - ure Of His sac - ri - fi - cial
6. ra - tion For the worlds in con - stan -

Refrain

1. well.
2. Kings.
3. here! 1-6. Low in end - less wor - ship
4. ty.
5. Blood?
6. cy.

(Upper notes optional)

bent, Praise the Bless - ed Sac - ra - ment!

57

O Food to Pilgrims Given
O Esca Viatorum

17th Century
Translated by Rt. Rev.
Msgr. H. T. Henry, Litt. D.

H. Isaak (1493)
Harmonized by J. S. Bach

Slowly

1. O Food to pil-grims giv-en, Bread of the hosts of Heav-en Thou Man-na of the sky! Feed with the bless-ed sweet-ness, Of Thy di-vine com-plete-ness The hearts that for Thee sigh.

2. O Foun-tain ru-by glow-ing, O stream of love out-flow-ing From Je-sus' pierc-ed Side! This thought a-lone shall bless us This one de-sire pos-sess us, To drink of Thy sweet tide.

3. We love Thee, Je-su ten-der Who hid'st Thine aw-ful splen-dor Be-neath these veils of grace: O let the veils be riv-en, And our clear eye in heav-en Be-hold Thee face to face!

rall

O Heart of Jesus, Heart of God

Lady G. Fullerton   Nicola A. Montani

Moderato

1. O Heart of Je - sus, Heart of God, O
2. The hearts of men are of - ten hard And
3. The world is cold, and life is sad, I

1. source of bound - less love ; By
2. full of self - ish care ; But
3. crave this bless - ed rest Of

1. an - gels praised, by saints a - dored From
2. in the Sa - cred Heart we find A
3. those who lay their wea - ry heads Up -

1. their bright throne a - bove. The
2. ref - uge from de - spair. To
3. on Thy sa - cred Breast. For

1. .poor - est, sad - dest heart on earth, May
2. Thee, my Je - sus, then I come, A
3. love is strong - er far than ,death, And

1. claim Thee for its own ; O
2. poor and help _ less child ; And
3. who can love like Thee, My

1. burn - ing, throb - bing Heart of Christ, Too
2. on Thine own words "Come to Me," My
3. Sav - iour, Whose ap - peal - ing Heart Broke

1. late, too lit - tle known.
2. on - ly hope I build.
3. on the Cross for me?

90

Sacred Heart of Jesus, fount of love

From a Slovak Hymnal
Arr. by N. A. M.

Slowly
p

1. Sa - cred Heart of Je - sus,
2. Sa - cred Heart of Je - sus!
3. Sa - cred Heart of Je - sus!
4. Sa - cred Heart of Je - sus!

1. fount of love and mer - cy, To -
2. make us know and love Thee, Un -
3. make us pure and gen - tle, And
4. bless all hearts that love Thee, And

1. day we come Thy bless-ing to im - plore;
2. fold to us the treas-ures of Thy grace,
3. teach us how to do Thy bless - ed will;
4. may Thine own Heart ev - er bless - ed be;

1. Oh, touch our hearts, so cold and so un -
2. That so our hearts, from things of earth up -
3. To fol - low close the print of Thy dear
4. Bless us, dear Lord, and bless the friends we

1. grate - ful, And make them, Lord, Thine
2. lift - ed, May long a - lone to
3. foot - steps, And when we fall— Sa-cred
4. cher - ish, And keep us true to

Refrain

1. own for - ev - er more.
2. gaze up - on Thy Face.
3. Heart, oh, love us still. 1-4. Sa-cred Heart of
4. Ma - ry and to Thee.

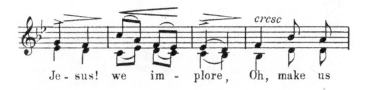

cresc

Je - sus! we im - plore, Oh, make us

love Thee more and more.

92

Jesus, Creator of the world
(Auctor beate sæculi)
Unison or two-part chorus

Translated by Father Caswall J. d' Hooghe

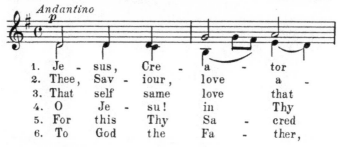

1. Je - sus, Cre - a - tor
2. Thee, Sav - iour, love a -
3. That self same love that
4. O Je - su! in Thy
5. For this Thy Sa - cred
6. To God the Fa - ther,

1. of the world! Of all man -
2. lone con - strain'd To make our
3. made the sky, Which made the
4. Heart di - vine May that same
5. Heart was pierced, And both with
6. and the Son, All praise, and

1. kind Re - deem - er blest!
2. mor - tal flesh Thine own;
3. sea, and stars, and earth,
4. love for - ev - er glow, -
5. Blood and Wa - ter ran;
6. pow'r, and glo - ry be;

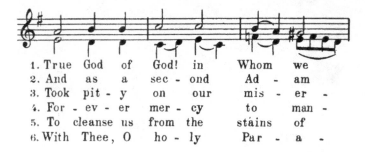

1. True God of God! in Whom we
2. And as a sec - ond Ad - am
3. Took pit - y on our mis - er -
4. For - ev - er mer - cy to man -
5. To cleanse us from the stains of
6. With Thee, O ho - ly Par - a -

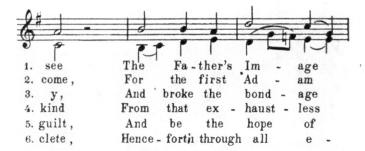

1. see The Fa - ther's Im - age
2. come, For the first Ad - am
3. y, And broke the bond - age
4. kind From that ex - haust - less
5. guilt, And be the hope of
6. clete, Hence - forth through all e -

1. clear _____ ex - press'd! _____
2. to _____ a - tone. _____
3. of _____ our birth. _____
4. foun - tain flow. _____
5. strength _____ of man. _____
6. ter - ni - ty. _____

To Jesus' Heart all burning

J.A. Christie S.J.(Trans.)
Aloys Schlör

Nicola A.Montani

Slowly

1. To   Je - sus' Heart, all burn - ing With
2. Too   true I   have for - sak - en Thy
3. As   Thou art meek and low - ly, And
4. O   that to me   were giv - en The
5. When life a - way   is   fly - ing, And

1. fer - vent love   for   men,   My
2. love by   wil - ful   sin;   Yet
3. ev - er   pure   of   heart, So
4. pin - ions of   a   dove,   I'd
5. earth's false glare is   done;   Still,

1. heart with   fond - est   yearn - ing Shall
2. now   let   me   be   tak - en   Back
3. may   my   heart be   whol - ly   Of
4. speed a - loft to   Heav - en,   My
5. Sa - cred Heart, in   dy - ing   I'll

Refrain

1. raise   its   joy - ful   strain.
2. by   Thy   grace a - gain.
3. Thine   the   coun - ter - part.   1 - 5. While
4. Je - sus'   love   to   prove.
5. say   I'm   all   Thine   own.

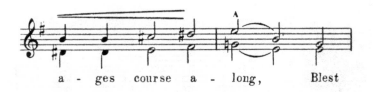

a - ges   course a - long,   Blest

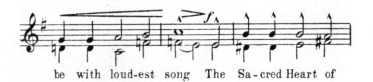

be with loud-est song The Sa - cred Heart of

Je - sus By ev - 'ry heart and tongue!

96

Heart of Jesus! golden chalice

Processional

Bishop Casartelli

Ch. Gounod
Arr. by N. A. M.

Slowly and with devotion

1. Heart of Je - sus! gold - en chal - ice
2. Heart of Je - sus! Comb of hon - ey
3. Heart of Je - sus! Rose of Shar - on
4. Heart of Je - sus! brok - en Vi - al

1. Brim - ming with the rud - dy Wine,
2. From the cleft of Cal - vary's rock,
3. Glist - 'ning with the dew of tears,
4. Full of pre - cious spik - en - ard!

1. Trod - den in the press of fu - ry,
2. Sweet - ness com - ing from the Strong One,
3. All a - mong the thorn - y prick - les
4. Al - a - bas - ter vase of oint - ment!

1. Pur-est juice of tru-est vine, From the Vine-yards
2. Dripping from the green-wood stock; Fam-ish-ing of
3. Lo! Thy blood-stained Head ap-pears! Spread Thy fra-grance
4. See, our souls are sore and hard: Let Thy heal-ing

1. of En - ged-di, Quench this thirst-y heart of mine!
2. death is on us: Feed, oh, feed Thy hun-gry flock!
3. all a-round us, Sweet-ly lul - ling all our fears!
4. vir-tue touch them, And from sin's cor-rup-tion guard!

63

To Christ, the Prince of Peace

Processional

Tr. Rev. E. Caswall   *Summi Parentis filio*   Nicola A. Montani

With Spirit
mf

1. To Christ, the Prince of Peace, And
2. O Je - sus! Vic - tim blest! What
3. Hide me in Thy dear Heart, For

1. Son of God most high, The Fa-ther of the
2. else but love di - vine Could Thee con-strain to
3. thith- er do I fly; There seek Thy grace thro'

1. world to come, Sing we with ho - ly joy. Deep
2. o - pen thus That Sa-cred Heart of Thine? O
3. life, in death Thine im-mor-tal - i - ty. Praise

1. in His Heart for us! The
2. Fount of end - less life! O
3. to the Fa - ther be, And

1. wound of love He bore; That love, where-with He
2. Spring of wa - ter clear! O Flame ce - les-tial,
3. sole - be-got - ten Son, Praise, Ho - ly Par- a -

1. still in-flames The hearts that Him a - dore.
2. cleans- ing all Who un - to Thee draw near.
3. clete, to Thee, While end-less a - ges run.

98

O Heart of Jesus, purest Heart
(Cor Jesu, Cor purissimum)

Translated by
Father M. Russell, S.J.

Traditional Melody

Con anima

1. O Heart of Je - sus, pur - est Heart, A
2. Take from me, Lord, this tep - id will, Which
3. Most hum - ble Heart of all that beat, Heart
4. But, ah, were e'en my heart on fire With

1. Shrine of ho - li - ness Thou art; Cleanse
2. doth Thy Heart with loath - ing fill; And
3. full of good - ness, meek and sweet, Give
4. all the Ser - a - phim's de - sire, Till

1. Thou, my heart, so sor - did cold, And
2. then in - fuse a spir - it new, A
3. me a heart more like to Thine, And
4. love a con - fla - gra - tion proved, Not

1. stained by sins so man - i - fold.
2. fer - vent spir - it, deep and true.
3. light the flame of love in mine.
4. yet wouldst Thou e - nough be loved.

65

O dearest Love divine

Rt. Rev. Msgr. H. T. Henry, Litt. D.   Nicola A. Montani

Andante devoto

1. O dear - est Love di - vine, My
2. Who can re - quite the love Shown
3. Thy Heart is o - pened wide That,
4. Here in Thy Heart I find A,

1. heart to Thee I give, Ex - chang-ing it for
2. in the won - drous plan, Where-by the God a -
3. free-ly en - t'ring in, I may Thy guest a -
4. hav-en of sweet rest, An ev - er - qui - et

1. Thine, That Thou in me may'st live. Most
2. bove For me be - came a Man? Thou
3. bide, And new - er life be - gin. This
4. mind, A man - sion of the Blest. Rock

1. lov-ing and most meek, Hearts on-ly dost Thou seek: O
2. say'st "Give Me thy heart!" With it I free-ly part, Hop-
3. do-est Thou, to gain My love, and e'er re - tain: O
4. that was cleft for me, Be - hold, I fly to Thee, Like

1. may my heart but prove A love like Thine, sweet Love!
2. ing that it may prove A love like Thine, sweet Love!
3. may my an - swer prove A love like Thine, sweet Love!
4. a world-wea - ry dove, Home to its mat - ed Love!

Sacred Heart! in accents burning

Sacred Song

Eleanor C. Donnelly ★

Ch. Gounod
Adapted and arr. by N. A. Montani

1. Sa-cred Heart in ac-cents burn-ing Pour we
2. Heart of boun-ty Thou art bring-ing All Thy

forth our love of Thee; Here our hopes and here our
thirst-ing chil-dren here, Where the liv-ing wa-ters

yearn-ings Meet and min-gle ten-der-ly. Heart of
spring-ing Tell of hope and com-fort near. O Thou

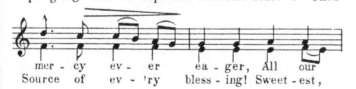

mer-cy ev-er ea-ger, All our
Source of ev-'ry bless-ing! Sweet-est,

woes and wounds to heal! Heart, most pa-tient, Heart most
strong-est, ho-liest, blest! Be our treasure here on

pure! To our souls, Thy depths re-veal. Sa - cred
earth, And in Heav'n be Thou our rest.

Heart of our Re - deem - er! Pierced with

love on Cal - va - ry! Heart of

Je - sus ev - er lov - ing, Make us burn with love of

Thee! Praise to Thee! O Sa - cred Heart!

All ye who seek a comfort sure
(Old Office of the Sacred Heart)

Translated by Father Caswall   Nicola A. Montani

1. All ye who seek a com - fort sure In
2. Ye hear how kind - ly He in - vites; Ye
3. O Heart! Thou joy of Saints on high, Thou

1. trou - ble and dis - tress,   What -
2. hear His words ·so blest: "All
3. Hope of sin - ners here!   At -

1. ev - er sor - row vex the mind, Or
2. ye that la - bor, come to Me, And
3. tract - ed by those lov - ing words, To

1. guilt the soul op - press: Je -
2. I will give you rest."   What
3. Thee I lift my pray'r.   Wash

1. sus, who gave Him - self for you Up -
2. meek - er than the Sav - iour's Heart? As
3. Thou my wounds in that dear Blood Which

1. on the Cross to die, O -
2. on the Cross He lay; It
3. forth from Thee doth flow, New

1. pens to you His Sa - cred Heart; Oh,
2. did His mur - der - ers for - give, And
3. grace, new hope, in - spire; a new And

1. to that Heart draw nigh!
2. for their par - don pray.
3. bet - ter heart be - stow.

104

A Message from the Sacred Heart

Father M. Russell   Nicola A. Montani

1. A mes-sage from the Sa-cred Heart; What
2. A mes-sage to the Sa-cred Heart; Oh,

may its mes-sage be? "My Child, My Child, give
bear it back with speed: "Come, Je-sus, reign with-

Me thy heart_My Heart has bled for thee." This
in my heart_Thy Heart is all I need." Thus,

is the mes-sage Je-sus sends To
Lord, I'll pray un-til I share That

my poor heart to-day, And ea-ger from His
home whose joy Thou art; No mes-sage, dear-est

Throne He bends To hear what I shall say.
Je-sus, there, For heart will speak to heart

There is an everlasting home

M. Bridges   M. Mattoni

Slowly

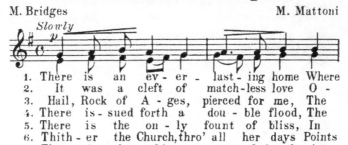

1. There is an ev - er - last - ing home Where
2. It was a cleft of match-less love O -
3. Hail, Rock of A - ges, pierced for me, The
4. There is-sued forth a dou - ble flood, The
5. There is the on - ly fount of bliss, In
6. Thith - er the Church, thro' all her days Points
7. There is the gold-en gate of heav'n, An

1. con-trite souls may hide, Where death and dan - ger
2. pen'd when He had died: When mer - cy hailed in
3. grave of all my pride; Hope, peace and heav'n are
4. sin a - ton-ing tide, In streams of wa - ter
5. joy and sor-row tried; No ref - uge for the
6. as a faith-ful guide; And cel - e - brates with
7. en-trance for the Bride, Where the sweet crown of

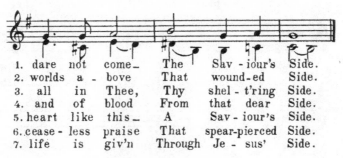

1. dare not come_ The Sav - iour's Side.
2. worlds a - bove That wound-ed Side.
3. all in Thee, Thy shel - t'ring Side.
4. and of blood From that dear Side.
5. heart like this_ A Sav - iour's Side.
6. cease - less praise That spear-pierced Side.
7. life is giv'n Through Je - sus' Side.

Hail, Rock of Ages
(From the Hymn "There is an everlasting home" Nº 69)

M. Bridges   Nicola A. Montani

Moderato (alla breve)

1. Hail, Rock of A - ges, pierced for
2. There is - sued forth a dou - ble
3. There is the on - ly fount of
4. There is the gold - en gate of

1. me, The grave of all my pride: ___
2. flood, The sin a - ton - ing tide, ___
3. bliss, In joy and sor - row tried; ___
4. heav'n, An en - trance for the Bride, ___

1. Hope, peace and heav'n are all in ___
2. In streams of wa - ter and of ___
3. No ref - uge for the heart like ___
4. Where the sweet crown of life is ___

1. Thee, Thy shel - t'ring Side. ___
2. blood From that dear Side. ___
3. this ___ A Sav - iour's Side. ___
4. giv'n, Through Je - sus' Side. ___

71

Hail, Jesus, hail!
(Viva! Viva! Gesù)

From the Italian by Father Faber   Nicola A. Montani

Con Spirito

1. Hail, Je-sus, hail! Who for my sake Sweet
2. To end-less a-ges let us praise The
3. Oh, to be sprin-kled from the wells Of
4. Ah! there is joy a-mid the saints, And

1. Blood from Ma-ry's veins didst take, And
2. Pre-cious Blood, whose price could raise The
3. Christ's own Sa-cred Blood, ex-cels Earth's
4. hell's des-pair-ing cour-age faints When

1. shed it all for me; Oh,
2. world from wrath and sin; Whose
3. best and high-est bliss; The
4. this sweet song we raise: Oh

1. bless _ ed   be   my   Sav _ iour's Blood, My
2. streams our   in _ ward thirst ap - pease, And
3. min - is - ters   of   wrath di - vine Hurt
4. loud _ er   then, and   loud - er   still, Earth

1. life, my   light, my   on - ly   good, To
2. heal   the   sin - ner's worst dis - ease, If
3. not   the   hap - py   hearts that shine With
4. with   one   might - y   cho - rus   fill, The

1. all   e - ter - ni - ty,   To
2. he   but   bathe   there - in,   If
3. those red   drops   of   His,   With
4. Pre - cious Blood   to   praise, The

1. all   e - ter - ni - ty.
2. he   but   bathe   there - in.
3. those red   drops   of   His!
4. Pre - cious Blood   to   praise!

72
Glory be to Jesus

See also Hymn No. 18 (Viva! Viva! Gesu)

Tr. Rev. E. Caswall   Nicola A. Montani

1. Glo - ry be to Je - sus,
2. Blest thro' end - less a - ges
3. A - bel's Blood for ven - geance
4. Oft as earth ex - ult - ing

1. Who in bit - ter pains Poured for me the
2. Be the pre - cious stream, Which from end - less
3. Plead - ed to the skies; But the Blood of
4. Wafts its praise on high, Hell with ter - ror

1. life-blood From His Sa-cred Veins. Grace and life e -
2. tor-ment Doth the world re-deem! There the faint-ing
3. Je - sus For our par-don cries. Oft as it is
4. trem-bles, Heav'n is filled with joy. Lift ye, then, your

1. ter - nal In that Blood I find; Blest be His com-
2. spir - it Drinks of life her fill; There, as in a
3. sprin-kled On our guilt-y hearts, Sa - tan in con-
4. voic - es, Swell the might-y flood; Loud-er still, and

1. pas - sion, In - fi - nite - ly kind!
2. foun - tain, Laves her - self at will.
3. fu - sion Ter - ror - struck de - parts.
4. loud - er Praise the Pre - cious Blood.

Hail, thou Star of ocean!

Ave Maris Stella

Translated by Father Caswall   M. Taddei

Andante religioso

1. Hail, thou star of o | - cean! Por - tal
2. Oh! by Ga - briel's A - ve, Ut - tered
3. Break the cap - tive's fet - ters; Light on
4. Show thy - self a Moth - er; Of - fer
5. Vir - gin of all Vir - gins! To thy
6. Still as on we jour - ney, Help our
7. Thro' the high - est Heav - en, To the Al -

1. of the sky, ___ Ev - er - Vir - gin
2. long a - go, ___ E - va's name re -
3. blind - ness pour; ___ All our ills ex -
4. Him our sighs, ___ Who for us In -
5. shel - ter take us; Gen - tlest of the
6. weak en - deav - or; Till with thee and
7. might - y Three, ___ Fa - ther, Son, and

1. Moth - er, Of the Lord most high! ___
2. vers - ing, 'Stab - lish peace be - low. ___
3. pel - ling, Ev - 'ry bliss im - plore. ___
4. car - nate Did not thee de - spise. ___
5. gen - tle! Chaste and gen - tle make us.
6. Je - sus We re - joice for - ev - er.
7. Spir - it, One same glo - ry be. ___

74

Ave Maria! O Maiden, O Mother
Star of the Sea

Sister M.

From a Slovak Hymnal
Arr. by N.A.M.

Slowly: with expression

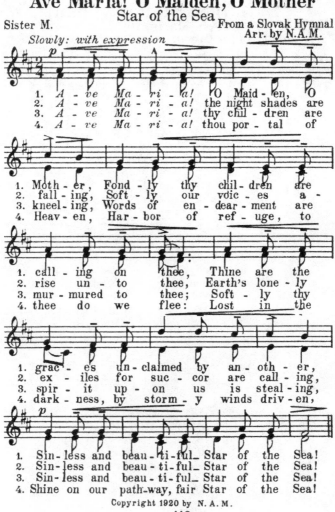

1. A - ve Ma - ri - a! O Maid - en, O
2. A - ve Ma - ri - a! the night shades are
3. A - ve Ma - ri - a! thy chil - dren are
4. A - ve Ma - ri - a! thou por - tal of

1. Moth - er, Fond - ly thy chil - dren are
2. fall - ing, Soft - ly our voic - es a -
3. kneel - ing, Words of en - dear - ment are
4. Heav - en, Har - bor of ref - uge, to

1. call - ing on thee, Thine are the
2. rise un - to thee, Earth's lone - ly
3. mur - mured to thee; Soft - ly thy
4. thee do we flee: Lost in the

1. grac - es un - claimed by an - oth - er,
2. ex - iles for suc - cor are call - ing,
3. spir - it up - on us is steal - ing,
4. dark - ness, by storm - y winds driv - en,

1. Sin - less and beau - ti - ful_ Star of the Sea!
2. Sin - less and beau - ti - ful_ Star of the Sea!
3. Sin - less and beau - ti - ful_ Star of the Sea!
4. Shine on our path-way, fair Star of the Sea!

Refrain

Ma_ ter A - ma - bi - lis, o - ra pro

no - bis! pray for thy chil - dren who

call up - on thee; A - ve San -

ctis - si - ma! A - ve pu - ris - si - ma!

Sin _ less and beau _ ti _ ful _ Star of the Sea!

Daily, daily sing to Mary (A)
Omni die dic Mariæ

St. Casimir
Translated by Father Bittlestone

Traditional Melody
Arr. by N.A.M.

With spirit

1. Dai - ly dai - ly sing to Ma - ry,
2. She is might - y to de - liv - er;
3. Sing my tongue, the Vir - gin's tro - phies,
4. All my sens - es, heart, af - fec - tions,

1. Sing, my soul, her prais - es due;
2. Call her, trust her lov - ing - ly:
3. Who for us our Mak - er bore;
4. Strive to sound her glo - ry forth:

1. All her feasts, her ac - tions wor - ship
2. When the tem - pest rag - es round thee,
3. For the curse of old in - flict - ed,
4. Spread a - broad the sweet mem - o - rials

1. With the hearts de - vo - tion true.
2. She will calm the troub - led sea.
3. Peace and bless - ing to re - store.
4. Of the Vir - gin's price - less worth:

1. Lost in won - d'ring con - tem - pla - tion,
2. Gifts of Heav - en she has giv - en
3. Sing in songs of praise un - end - ing,
4. Where the voice of mu - sic thrill - ing,

1. Be her maj - es - ty con - fest!
2. No - ble la - dy! to our race:
3. Sing the world's ma - jes - tic Queen.
4. Where the tongue of el - o - quence,

1. Call her Moth- er, call her Vir - gin,
2. She, the Queen, who decks her sub - jects
3. Wea - ry not nor faint in tell - ing
4. That can ut - ter hymns be - seem- ing

1. Hap - py Moth - er, Vir - gin blest!
2. With the light of God's own grace.
3. All the gifts she gives to men.
4. All her match - less ex - cel - lence?

76

Daily, daily sing to Mary (B)

St. Casimir
Processional

Tr. Father Bittlestone   Nicola A. Montani

Allegro modto

1. Dai - ly, dai - ly, sing to Ma - ry,
2. She is might - y to de - liv - er,

Sing, my soul, her prais - es due;
Call her, trust her lov - ing - ly:

All her feasts, her ac - tions wor - ship,
When the tem - pest rag - es round thee,

With the heart's de - vo - tion true.
She will calm the troub - led sea.

Lost in won - d'ring con - tem - pla - tion,
Gifts of Heav - en she has giv - en,

Be her maj - es - ty con - fest:
No - ble La - dy! to our race;

Call her Moth - er, call her Vir - gin,
She, the Queen who decks her sub - jects

Hap - py Moth - er, Vir - gin blest,
With the light of God's own grace,

Call her Moth - er, call her Vir - gin,
She, the Queen who decks her sub - jects

Hap - py Moth - er, Vir - gin blest.
With the light of God's own grace.

(*Additional Stanzas given in previous Hymn, with repetition of last two lines.*)

Mother of Mercy

Mater Misericordiæ

Father Faber   S. M. Yenn

1. Moth - er of mer - cy, day by
2. Though pov - er - ty and work and
3. But scorn - ful men have cold - ly
4. They know but lit - tle of Thy

1. day, My love of thee grows more and
2. woe The mas - ters of my life may
3. said Thy love was lead - ing me from
4. worth Who speak these heart - less words to

1. more; Thy gifts are strewn up - on my
2. be, When times are worst who does not
3. God; And yet in this I did but
4. me, For what did Je - sus love on

1. way   Like   sands   up - on   the
2. know   Dark-ness is   light   with
3. tread   The   ver - y   path   my
4. earth   One   half   so   ten - der -

1. great   sea - shore.   Thy   gifts   are
2. love   of   thee? When   times   are
3. Sav - iour   trod.   And   yet   in
4. ly   as   thee?   For   what   did

1. strewn   up - on   my   way   Like
2. worst   who   does   not   know
3. this   I   did   but   tread   The
4. Je - sus   love   on   earth   One

1. sands   up - on   the   great   sea - shore.
2. Dark-ness is   light   with   love   of   thee?
3. ver - y   path   my   Sav - iour   trod.
4. half   so   ten - der - ly   as   thee?

78

Hail, all hail, great Queen of Heaven!
Our Lady of Lourdes
Processional

(The melody of Hymn No. 76 "Daily, Daily" may also be used with this text, with repetition of the last two lines of the refrain.)

Text by S.N.D.

Traditional Melody (1750)
"Pone luctum"

With spirit

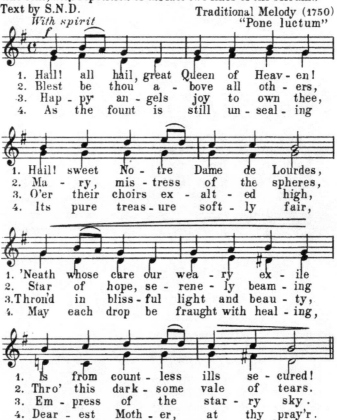

1. Hail! all hail, great Queen of Heav - en!
2. Blest be thou a - bove all oth - ers,
3. Hap - py an - gels joy to own thee,
4. As the fount is still un - seal - ing

1. Hail! sweet No - tre Dame de Lourdes,
2. Ma - ry, mis - tress of the spheres,
3. O'er their choirs ex - alt - ed high,
4. Its pure treas - ure soft - ly fair,

1. 'Neath whose care our wea - ry ex - ile
2. Star of hope, se - rene - ly beam - ing
3. Thron'd in bliss - ful light and beau - ty,
4. May each drop be fraught with heal - ing,

1. Is from count - less ills se - cured!
2. Thro' this dark - some vale of tears.
3. Em - press of the star - ry sky.
4. Dear - est Moth - er, at thy pray'r.

NOTE: For Congregational singing it is suggested that the hymn be transposed a full tone lower. Copyright 1920 by N A. M.

1-4. Then let men and An - gels praise thee

For each bless - ing thou'st pro - cured,

While in glad - some strains we're sing - ing,

Hail! sweet No - tre Dame de Lourdes!

79

O purest of creatures
The Immaculate Conception

Father Faber   Nicola A. Montani

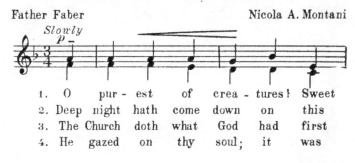

1. O pur - est of crea - tures! Sweet
2. Deep night hath come down on this
3. The Church doth what God had first
4. He gazed on thy soul; it was

1. Moth - er, sweet Maid! The   one spot - less
2. rough - spok- en world, And the ban - ners of
3. taught her to do; He looked o'er the
4. spot - less and fair; For the em - pire of

1. womb where - in Je - sus was laid! Dark
2. dark - ness are bold - ly un - furl'd: And the
3. world to find hearts that were true; Thro' the
4. sin- it had nev - er been there; None

cresc

1. night hath come down on us Moth - er! and
2. tem - pest - tost Church all her eyes are on
3. a - ges He looked, and He found none but
4. had ev - er owned thee, dear Moth - er, but

1. we Look out for thy shin_ing, sweet
2. Thee, They look to thy shin - ing, sweet
3. thee, And He loved thy clear shin - ing, sweet
4. He, And He bless'd thy clear shin_ing, sweet

ff

1. Star of the Sea! Look out for thy
2. Star of the Sea! They look to thy
3. Star of the Sea! And He loved thy clear
4. Star of the Sea! And He bless'd thy clear

1. shin - ing, sweet Star of the Sea!
2. shin - ing, sweet Star of the Sea!
3. shin - ing, sweet Star of the Sea!
4. shin - ing, sweet Star of the Sea!

80 Whither thus, in holy rapture?

Quo sanctus ardor te rapit
The Visitaton

Translated by the Rev. E. Caswall　　　　From a Slovak Hymnal
Arr. by N. A. M.

1. Whith - er thus in ho - ly rap - ture,
2. Lo thine a - ged cous - in claims thee,
3. As the sun, his face con-ceal - ing,

1. Roy - al maid - en, art thou bent?
2. Claims thy sym - pa - thy and care;
3. In a cloud with- draws from sight,

1. Why so fleet - ly art thou speed - ing
2. God her shame from her hath tak - en,
3. So in Ma - ry then lay hid - den

1. Up the moun - tain's rough as - cent?
2. He hath heard her fer - vent pray'r.
3. He Who is the world's true light.

1. Filled with th' E - ter - nal God - head!
2. Blessed Moth - ers! joy - ful meet - ing!
3. Hon - or, glo - ry, vir - tue, mer - it,

1. Glow - ing with the Spir - it's flame!
2. Thou in her, the hand of God,
3. Be to Thee, O Vir - gin's Son!

1. Love it is that bears thee on - ward,
2. She in thee, with lips in - spir - ed,
3. With the Fa - ther, and the Spir - it,

1. And sup - ports thy ten - der frame.
2. Owns the Moth - er of her Lord.
3. While e - ter - nal a - ges run.

81

Hail Virgin, dearest Mary
Queen of May

S. M. Yenn

1. Hail Vir - gin, dear - est Ma - ry! Our love - ly Queen of May! O spot - less, bless - ed La - dy, Our love - ly Queen of May. Thy chil - dren, hum - bly bend - ing, Sur - round thy shrine so dear; With heart and voice as - cend - ing, Sweet Ma - ry, hear our pray'r.

2. Be - hold earth's blos - soms spring - ing In beau - teous form and hue. All na - ture glad - ly bring - ing Her sweet - est charms to you. We'll gath - er fresh, bright flow - ers, To bind our fair Queen's brow; From gay and ver - dant bow - ers, We haste to crown thee now.

3. Hail Vir - gin, dear - est Ma - ry! Our love - ly Queen of May, O spot - less, bless - ed La - dy, Our love - ly Queen of May. And now, our bless - ed Moth - er, Smile on our fes - tal day; Ac - cept our wreath of flow - ers, And be our Queen of May.

Copyright 1919 by S. M. Yenn
126

This is the image of the Queen
Month of Mary
Crowning Hymn

Tr. Rev. E. Caswall

From a Slovak Hymnal
Arr. by N. A. M.

Joyously: marcato

1. This is the im-age of the Queen Who
2. This hom-age of-fered at the feet Of
3. How fair so-ev-er be the form Which
4. Sweet are the flow'-rets we have culled This

1. reigns in bliss a - bove; Of
2. Ma - ry's im - age here To
3. here your eyes be - hold, Its
4. im - age to a - dorn; But

1. her who is the hope of men, Whom
2. Ma - ry's self at once as - cends A -
3. beau - ty is by Ma - ry's self Ex -
4. sweet - er far is Ma - ry's self, That

1. men and an-gels love! Most ho-ly Ma - ry!
2. bove the star-ry sphere. Most ho-ly Ma - ry!
3. cell'd a thou-sand-fold. Most ho-ly Ma - ry!
4. rose with-out a thorn! Most ho-ly Ma - ry!

1. at thy feet I bend a sup - pliant
2. at thy feet I bend a sup - pliant
3. at thy feet I bend a sup - pliant
4. at thy feet I bend a sup - pliant

1. knee; In this thy own sweet
2. knee; In all my joy, in
3. knee; In my temp - ta - tions
4. knee; When on the bed of

1. month of May, Dear Moth - er of my
2. all my pain, O Vir - gin born with -
3. each and all, From Eve de - rived in
4. death I lie, By Him who did for

1. God, I pray, Do thou re - mem - ber me!
2. out a stain, Do thou re - mem - ber me!
3. Ad - am's fall, Do thou re - mem - ber me!
4. sin - ners die, Do thou re - mem - ber me!

Hail! Holy Queen, enthroned above

Salve Regina
Mater Misericordiæ

Traditional Melody
Salve Regina Coelitum

Andante moderato

1. Hail, ho - ly Queen, en - thron'd a - bove,
2. Our life, our sweet - ness here be - low,
3. To thee we cry, poor sons of Eve,
4. This earth is but a vale of tears,
5. Turn then, most gra - cious Ad - vo - cate,
6. When this our ex - ile is com - plete,
7. O clem - ent, gra - cious, Moth - er sweet,

1. O Ma - ri - a! Hail, Moth - er of Mer - cy
2. O Ma - ri - a! Our hope in sor - row
3. O Ma - ri - a! To thee we sigh, we
4. O Ma - ri - a! A place of ban - ish -
5. O Ma - ri - a! T'wards us thine eyes com -
6. O Ma - ri - a! Show us thy Son, our
7. O Ma - ri - a! O Vir - gin Ma - ry,

1. and of love! O Ma - ri - a!
2. and in woe, O Ma - ri - a!
3. mourn, we grieve, O Ma - ri - a!
4. ment, of fears, O Ma - ri - a!
5. pas - sion - ate, O Ma - ri - a!
6. Je - sus sweet, O Ma - ri - a!
7. we en - treat, O Ma - ri - a!

Refrain

1-7. Tri - umph, all ye Cher - u - bim,

Sing with us, ye Ser - a - phim,

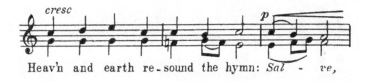

Heav'n and earth re-sound the hymn: Sal - ve,

sal - ve, sal - ve Re - gi - na!

Hail, Queen of heaven
Ave, Regina cœlorum

Rev. Dr. Lingard   Traditional Melody

1. Hail, Queen of heav'n, the o - cean star, Guide
2. O gen - tle, chaste, and spot - less Maid, We
3. So - jour - ners in this vale of tears, To
4. And while to Him Who reigns a - bove, In

1. of the wan-derer here be - low, Thrown on life's
2. sin-ners make our pray'rs thro' thee; Re - mind thy
3. thee, blest Ad - vo - cate, we cry, —— Pit - y our
4. God-head One, in Per - sons Three, The Source of

1. surge, we claim thy care, Save us from per - il
2. Son that He has paid The price of our in -
3. sor - rows, calm our fears, And soothe with hope our
4. life, of grace, of love, —— Homage we pay on

1. and from woe. Moth-er of Christ, Star of the
2. iq - ui - ty. Vir - gin, most pure, Star of the
3. mis - er - y. Ref - uge in grief, Star of the
4. bend-ed knee—Do thou, bright Queen, Star of the

1. Sea, Pray for the wan - derer, pray for me.
2. Sea, Pray for the sin - ner, pray for me.
3. Sea, Pray for the mourn-er, pray for me.
4. Sea, Pray for the chil - dren, pray for me.

85

Remember, holy Mary
Memorare
St. Bernard

Tr. Rev. M. Russell, S.J.

From a Slovak Hymnal
Adapted by N.A.M.

1. Re - mem - ber, ho - ly Ma - ry, 'Twas
2. And so to thee, my Moth - er, With
3. See at thy feet a sin - ner, Groan-
4. All, all His love re - mem - ber, And,

1. nev - er heard or known____ That
2. fil - ial faith I call,____ For
3. ing and weep - ing sore_____ Ah!
4. oh! re - mem - ber too____ How

1. an - y one who sought thee___ And
2. Je - sus dy - ing gave thee___ As
3. throw thy man - tle o'er me,___ And
4. prompt I am to pur - pose,___ How

1. made to thee his moan,___ That
2. Moth - er to us all.___ To
3. let me stray no more.___ Thy
4. slow and frail to do.___ Yet

1. an - y one who hast - ened ___ For
2. thee, O Queen of vir - gins, ___ O
3. Son has died to save me, ___ And
4. scorn not my pe - ti - tions, ___ But

1. shel - ter to thy care, ___ Was
2. Moth - er meek, to thee ___ I
3. from His throne on high ___ His
4. pa - tient - ly give ear, ___ And

1. ev - er yet a - ban - doned ___
2. run with trust - ful fond - ness, ___
3. Heart this mo - ment yearn - eth ___
4. help me, O my Moth - er, ___

1. ___ And left to his de - spair. ___
2. ___ Like child to moth - er's knee. ___
3. ___ For ev - en such as I. ___
4. ___ Most lov - ing and most dear. ___

Hail, full of grace and purity
The Rosary
The Joyful Mysteries

Father Conway, O.P.   Isabella Montani

Moderato

1. *The Anunciation: Humility.*
   Hail   full   of   grace   and
2. *The Visitation: Charity to our neighbors.*
   By   that   pure   love   which
3. *The Birth of our Lord: Poverty.*
   This   bless - ing   beg ,   O
4. *Presentation in the Temple: Obedience.*
   Most   Ho - ly   Vir - gin,
5. *The finding of Our Lord: Love of Him and of His service.*
   By   thy   dear   Son,   re -
6. *Concluding Verse.*
   Queen   of   the   Ho - ly

1. pu - ri - ty! Meek Hand-maid of the
2. prompt-ed thee To seek thy cous-in
3. Vir - gin Queen, From Je - sus through His
4. Maid-en mild, Ob-tain for us, we
5. stored to thee, This grace for us im -
6. Ro - sa - ry, With ten-der love look

1. Lord, Hail mod - el of hu -
2. blest, Pray that the fires of
3. birth, By ho - ly pov - er -
4. pray, To im - i - tate thy
5. plore, To serve our Lord most
6. down, And bless the hearts that

1. mil - i - ty! Chaste Moth-er of the Word.
2. char - i - ty May burn with-in our breast.
3. ty to wean Our hearts from things of earth.
4. Ho - ly Child, By striv-ing to o - bey.
5. faith-ful-ly, And love Him more and more.
6. of - fer thee This chap-let for thy crown.

87

Hear thy children, gentlest Mother

Children's Hymn to Our Lady

Father Stanfield

M. Haydn
Arr. by N.A.M.

1. Hear thy chil-dren, gen-tlest Moth-er, Pray'r-ful hearts to thee a-rise; Hear us while our eve-ning A-ve Soars be-yond the star-ry skies. Dark-ling shad-ows fall a-round us, Stars their si-lent watch-es keep; Hush the heart op-press'd with sorrow, Dry the tears of those who weep.

2. Hear, sweet Moth-er, hear the wear-y, Borne up-on life's troubled sea; Gen-tle guid-ing Star of O-cean, Lead thy chil-dren home to thee. Still watch o'er us, dear-est Moth-er, From thy beau-teous throne a-bove; Guard us from all harm and dan-ger, 'Neath thy shelt'ring wings of love.

O most holy one
O Sanctissima

Tr. by Rev. J. M. Raker

Sicilian Melody
Arr. by N. A. M.

Slowly, with devotion

1. O most ho-ly one, O most low-ly one, Dear-est Vir-gin Ma-ri-a! Moth-er of fair Love, Home of the Spir-it Dove, O-ra, o-ra pro no-bis.
2. Help in sad-ness drear, Port of glad-ness near, Vir-gin Moth-er, Ma-ri-a! In pit-y heed-ing, Hear thou our plead-ing, O-ra, o-ra pro no-bis.
3. Call we fear-ful-ly, Sad-ly, tear-ful-ly, Save us now O Ma-ri-a! Let us not lan-guish, Heal thou our an-guish, O-ra, o-ra pro no-bis.
4. Moth-er, Maid-en fair, Look with lov-ing care, Hear our pray'r, O Ma-ri-a! Our sor-row feel-ing, Send us thy heal-ing, O-ra, o-ra pro no-bis.

Mother of Christ

S.N.D.

Nicola A. Montani

Not too slow (alla breve)

1. Moth-er of Christ, Moth-er of Christ, What shall I
2. Moth-er of Christ, Moth-er of Christ, What shall I
3. Moth-er of Christ, Moth-er of Christ, I toss on a

ask of thee? I do not sigh for the
do for thee? I will love thy Son with the
storm-y sea, O lift thy Child as a

wealth of the earth, For the joys that fade and flee;
whole of my strength, My on-ly King shall He be.
bea-con light 'To the port where I fain would be,

But, Moth-er of Christ, Moth-er of Christ,
Yes, Moth-er of Christ, Moth-er of Christ,
Then, Moth-er of Christ, Moth-er of Christ;

This do I long to see, The Bliss un-told which thine
This will I do for thee, Of all that are dear or
This do I ask of thee, When the voy-age is o'er, O

arms en-fold, The treas-ure up-on thy knee.
cher-ished here, None shall be dear as He.
stand on the shore And show Him at last to me.

Copyright 1920 by N.A. Montani

Raise your voices, vales and mountains

Causa nostra laetitiae

St. Alphonsus Liguori

Translated by Rev. E. Vaughan   William Schultes (1815-1879)

Arr. by N.A.M.

Joyfully (alla breve)

1. Raise your voic - es, vales and moun - tains,
2. Murm-'ring brooks your trib - ute bring - ing,
3. Like a sun with splen - dor glow - ing
4. Like the rose and lil - y bloom - ing,

1. Flow - 'ry mead - ows, streams and foun - tains,
2. Lit - tle birds with joy - ful sing - ing,
3. Gleams thy heart with love o'er - flow - ing,
4. Sweet - ly heav'n and earth per - fum - ing

1. Praise, O praise the love - liest Maid - en
2. Come with mirth - ful prais - es lad - en
3. Like the moon in star - ry heav - en
4. Stain - less, spot - less thou ap - pear - est:

1. The Cre - a - tor ev - er made.
2. To your Queen be hom - age paid.
3. Shines thy peer - less pu - ri - ty.
4. Queen - ly beau - ty grac - es thee.

O Mother! most afflicted
Our Mother of Sorrows

Anonymous   Traditional Melody (1638)
Arr. by N. A. M.

1. O Moth-er! most af-flict-ed, Stand-
2. Thy heart is well-nigh break-ing, Thy
3. His liv-id Form is bleed-ing, His
4. O Ma-ry! Queen of Mar-tyrs, The
5. O dear and lov-ing Moth-er! En-

1. ing be-neath that tree, Where
2. Je-sus thus to see, De-
3. Soul with sor-row wrung, Whilst
4. sword has pierced thy heart, Ob-
5. treat that we may be Near

1. Je-sus hangs re-ject-ed On the
2. rid-ed, wound-ed, dy-ing, In
3. thou, af-flict-ed Moth-er, Shar'st the
4. tain for us of Je-sus In thy
5. thee and thy dear Je-sus Now

1. hill   of   Cal - va - ry:
2. great - est   ag - o - ny.
3. tor - ments   of   thy   Son.   1-5. O
4. grief   to   bear   a - part.
5. and   e - ter - nal - ly.

Ma - ry! sweet - est   Moth - er,   We

love to pit - y   thee;   O! for the sake of

Je - sus Let   us   thy   chil - dren   be.

92

St. Joseph

O blessed Saint Joseph
The Patronage of St. Joseph

Father Faber

Melody from the
Trier Gesangbuch (1872)

Moderato

1. O blless-ed Saint Jo-seph, how great was thy worth, The one chos-en shad-ow of God up-on earth, The fa-ther of Je-sus!—Ah, then, wilt thou be, Sweet spouse of our La-dy! a fa-ther to me?

2. For thou to the pil-grim art fa-ther and guide, And Je-sus and Ma-ry felt safe by thy side; Ah, bless-ed Saint Jo-seph, how safe I should be, Sweet spouse of our La-dy! if thou wert with me!

3. When the treas-ures of God where un-shel-tered on earth, Safe keep-ing was found for them both in thy worth; O fa-ther of Je-sus, be fa-ther to me, Sweet spouse of our La-dy! and I will love thee.

St. Joseph

Great Saint Joseph! Son of David

Du aus David's

Translated by
Bishop Casartelli

From a Slovak Hymnal
Arr. by N. A. M.

Con Spirito

1. Great Saint Jo - seph! Son of Da - vid,
2. Three long days in grief and an - guish
3. Clasped in Je - sus' arms and Ma - ry's,

1. Fos - ter - fa - ther of our Lord,
2. With His Moth - er sweet and mild,
3. When death gen - tly came at last,

1. Spouse of Ma - ry ev - er Vir - gin,
2. Ma - ry Vir - gin, didst thou wan - der
3. Thy pure spir - it sweet - ly sigh - ing

1. Keep - ing o'er them watch and ward!
2. Seek - ing the be - lov - ed Child.
3. From its earth - ly dwell - ing passed.

1. In the sta - ble thou didst guard them
2. In the tem - ple thou didst find Him:
3. Dear Saint Jo - seph! by that pass - ing

1. With a fa - ther's lov - ing care;
2. Oh! what joy then filled thy heart!
3. May our death be like to thine;

1. Thou by God's com - mand didst save them
2. In thy sor - rows, in thy glad - ness
3. And with Je - sus, Ma - ry, Jo - seph,

1. From the cru - el Her - od's snare.
2. Grant us, Jo - seph, to have part.
3. May our souls for - ev - er shine.

144

Joseph, pure Spouse
of that Immortal Bride

Te Joseph Celebrent

Translated by Father Caswall   M. Mattoni

Devoto (alla breve)

1. Jo - seph, pure spouse of that im - mor - tal
2. Thine arms em - braced thy Mak - er new - ly
3. Not un - til af - ter death their bliss - ful
4. Grant us great Trin - i - ty, for Jo - seph's

1. Bride, Who shines in ev - er - vir - gin glo - ry
2. born: With Him to E - gypt's des - ert didst thou
3. crown Oth - ers ob - tain, but un - to thee was
4. sake Un - to the star - ry man - sions to at -

1. bright, Thro' all the Chris-tian climes thy praise be
2. flee: Him in Je - ru - sa - lem didst seek and
3. giv'n, In thine own life-time to en - joy thy
4. tain; There, with glad tongues, thy praise to cel - e -

1. sung, Thro' all the realms of light.
2. find; O grief, O joy for thee.
3. God As do the blest in Heav'n.
4. brate In one e - ter - nal strain.

95

Hail! Holy Joseph, Hail!

Father Faber

Con Spirito

From the Catholic Songbook
(St. Gall 1863)

1. Hail, ho-ly Jo-seph, hail! Chaste spouse of Ma - ry,
2. Hail, ho-ly Jo-seph, hail! Com - rade of An -.gels,
3. Hail, ho-ly Jo-seph, hail! Teach us our flesh to

1. hail! Pure as the lil - y flow'r In
2. hail! Cheer thou the hearts that faint, And
3. tame, And, Ma - ry, keep the hearts That

1. E-den's peace -ful vale. Hail! ho - ly Jo - seph,
2. guide the steps that fail. Hail! ho - ly Jo - seph,
3. love thy hus - band's name. Moth.er of Je - sus!

1. hail! Prince of the house of God ! May
2. hail ! God's choice wert thou a - lone! To
3. bless, And bless, ye saints on high, All

1. His best grac-es be By thy sweet hands be-stowed.
2. thee the Word made flesh, Was sub-ject as a Son.
3. meek and sim -ple souls That to Saint Jo-seph cry.

Hail, glorious Saint Patrick (No. 1)

Sister Agnes

Arr. by N.A.M.

Maestoso

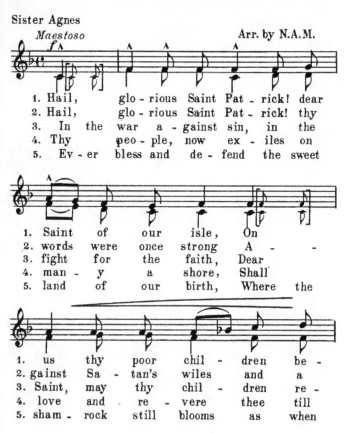

1. Hail, glo - rious Saint Pat - rick! dear Saint of our isle, On us thy poor chil - dren be -
2. Hail, glo - rious Saint Pat - rick! thy words were once strong A - - gainst Sa - tan's wiles and a
3. In the war a - gainst sin, in the fight for the faith, Dear Saint, may thy chil - dren re -
4. Thy peo - ple, now ex - iles on man - y a shore, Shall love and re - vere thee till
5. Ev - er bless and de - fend the sweet land of our birth, Where the sham - rock still blooms as when

1. stow   a   sweet   smile;   And
2. her - e - tic   throng; Not
3. sist   to   the   death;   May   their
4. time   be   no   more;   And   the
5. thou wert on   earth, And   our

1. now thou art high in the man-sions a-bove, On
2. less is thy might where in Heav-en thou art; Oh,
3. strength be in meek-ness, in pen-ance, and pray'r,Their
4. fire thou hast kin-dled shall ev - er burn bright,Its
5. hearts shall yet burn,where-so - ev - er we roam, For

1. E - rin's green val- leys look down in thy love.
2. come to our aid, in our bat - tle take part!
3. ban -ner the Cross,which they glo - ry to bear.
4. warmth un-di - min-ished, un - dy - ing its light.
5. God and Saint Pat-rick and our na - tive home.

Hail, glorious Saint Patrick (No. 2)

Sister Agnes

Ancient Irish Melody
Arr. by N.A.M.

Moderato

1. Hail,   glo - rious Saint Pat - rick, dear
2. Hail,   glo - rious Saint Pat - rick, thy
3. In the   war   a - gainst sin, in   the
4. Thy   peo - ple,   now ex - iles   on
5. Ev - er bless and   de - fend the sweet

1. Saint   of   our   isle!   On   us   thy   poor
2. words were once strong A - gainst Sa - tan's
3. fight   for   the   faith, Dear Saint, may thy
4. man - y   a   shore, Shall love and   re -
5. land   of   our   birth, Where the sham - rock still

1. chil - dren, be - stow   a   sweet smile; And
2. wiles and   a   her - e - tic   throng; Not
3. chil - dren re - sist   to   the   death; May their
4. vere thee till time   be   no   more: And   the
5. blooms as when thou wert on   earth, And   our

1. now   thou   art   high   in   the
2. less   in   thy   might   now   in
3. strength be   in   meek - ness,   in
4. fire   thou   hast   kin - dled   shall
5. hearts shall yet   burn, where - so -

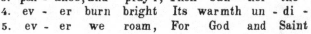

1. man - sions a - bove, On   E - rin's green
2. heav - en thou art   Oh, come to   our
3. pen - ance, and pray'r, Their ban - ner the
4. ev - er burn bright Its warmth un - di -
5. ev - er we   roam, For God and Saint

1. val - leys look down in   thy   love.
2. aid,   in   our bat - tle take part.
3. Cross, which they glo - ry to   bear.
4. min - ished, un - dy - ing its light.
5. Pat - rick and our na - tive home.

Seek ye a Patron to defend

Si vis Patronum quaerere

Translated by Father Caswall   Nicola A. Montani

1. Seek ye a Pa - tron to de - fend Your
2. By pen - i - ten - tial tears thou didst The
3. The An - gel touch'd thee and forth-with Thy
4. Firm Rock whereon the Church is based Pil -

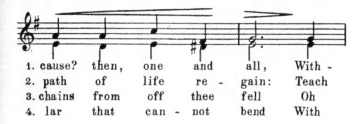

1. cause? then, one and all, With -
2. path of life re - gain: Teach
3. chains from off thee fell Oh
4. lar that can - not bend With

1. out de - lay up - on the Prince Of
2. us with thee to weep our sins And
3. loose us from the sub - tle coils That
4. strength en - due us; and the Faith From

1. the   A - pos - tles   call.
2. wash   a - way   their   stain.
3. link   us   close   with   Hell.
4. her - e - sy   de - fend.

1-4. Blest

hold - er   of   the   heav'n - ly   Keys!   Thy

pray'rs we all im - plore; Un - lock to us the

sa - cred bars Of Heav'n's e - ter - nal door.

152

Lead us, great teacher Paul

Translated from the Latin   From a Slovak Hymnal

Slowly

1. Lead us, great teach-er Paul, in wis-dom's ways,
2. Praise, bless-ing, maj - es - ty, thro' end-less days,

And lift our hearts with thine to Heav'n's high throne,
Be to the Trin - i - ty im-mor-tal giv'n,

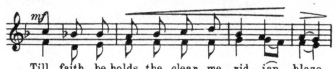

Till faith be-holds the clear me - rid - ian blaze,
Who in pure u - ni - ty pro-found-ly sways,

And in the soul reigns char-i - ty a - lone.
E - ter-nal - ly all things in earth and Heav'n.

SAINTS
St. Anthony of Padua

If great wonders thou desirest
(Si quæris)

Translated by
Father Aylward, O. P.

Melody from a
Slovak Hymnal

Andante moderato

1. If great won - ders thou de -
2. Young and old are ev - er
3. Pa - du - a has been the
4. Glo - ry be to God the

1. sir - est, Hope - ful to Saint An - thon - y
2. sing - ing, Prais - es to Saint An - thon - y
3. wit - ness Of these deeds six hun - dred
4. Fa - ther And to His co - e - qual

1. pray; Er - ror, Sa - tan, wants the
2. bring - ing; Storm - y o - cean calms its
3. years; Dan - gers flee and need must
4. Son, To the Ho - ly Ghost re -

1. dir _ est, Death and pest his will o -
2. pas - sion, Bonds and fet _ ters break in
3. per - ish, Grief and sor - row dis - ap -
4. splen-dent; One in Three_ Three in

1. bey, And the sick, who beg his
2. twain, Treas - ures lost and limbs dis -
3. pear, Fill - ing all the world with
4. One; Praise we Fa - ther, Son and

1. pit - y, From their couch_es haste a - way.
2. a - bled, These his pow'r re - stores a - gain.
3. won-der, While the de - mons quake with fear.
4. Spir- it While e - ter - nal a - ges run.

Glorious Patron

Sr. Mercedes   J. Lewis Browne

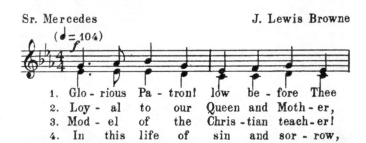

1. Glo - rious Pa - tron! low be - fore Thee
2. Loy - al to our Queen and Moth - er,
3. Mod - el of the Chris - tian teach - er!
4. In this life of sin and sor - row,

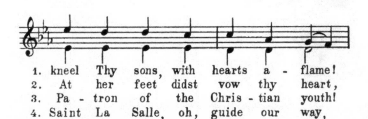

1. kneel Thy sons, with hearts a - flame!
2. At her feet didst vow thy heart,
3. Pa - tron of the Chris - tian youth!
4. Saint La Salle, oh, guide our way,

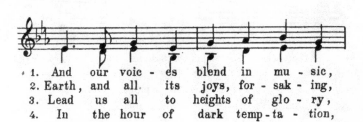

1. And our voic - es blend in mu - sic,
2. Earth, and all. its joys, for - sak - ing,
3. Lead us all to heights of glo - ry,
4. In the hour of dark temp - ta - tion,

1. Sing - ing prais - es to thy name,
2. Thou didst choose the bet - ter part.
3. As we strive in ear - nest ruth.
4. Fa - ther! be our spir - its' stay!

1. Saint John Bap - tist! glo - rious Pa - tron!
2. Saint La Salle, our glo - rious Fa - ther,
3. Saint La Salle! oh, guard and guide us,
4. Take our hand and lead us home - ward,

1. Saint La Salle we sound thy fame.
2. Pierce our souls with love's own dart.
3. As we spread a - far the Truth!
4. Saint La Salle, to Heav'n's bright day!

SAINTS
St. Francis of Assisi

Blessed Francis, holy Father
Patron of Franciscan Tertiaries

From the Fransciscan Manual

From a Slovak Hymnal
Arr by N. A. M.

Con anima

1. Bless - ed Fran - cis, ho - ly fa - ther,
2. By thy love so deep and burn - ing,
3. Hum - ble fol - low - er of Je - sus,
4. Teach us al - so, dear Saint Fran - cis,

1. Now our hearts to thee we raise,
2. For thy Sav - iour cru - ci - fied;
3. Lik - ened to Him in thy birth,
4. How to mourn for ev - 'ry sin;

1. As we gath - er 'round thine al - tar,
2. By the tok - ens which He gave thee
3. In thy way thro' life de - spis - ing,
4. May we walk in thy dear foot - steps

1. Pour - ing forth our hymns of praise.
2. On thy hands and feet and side:
3. For His sake the goods of earth:
4. Till the crown of life we win.

1. Bless thy chil - dren, ho - ly Fran - cis,
2. Bless thy chil - dren, ho - ly Fran - cis,
3. Make us love the price - less vir - tue
4. Bless thy chil - dren, ho - ly Fran - cis,

1. Who thy might - y help im - plore,
2. With those wound - ed hands of thine,
3. By our hid - den God es - teemed,
4. With those wound - ed hands of thine,

1. For in heav - en thou re - main - est,
2. From thy glo - rious throne in heav - en
3. Make it val - ued, ho - ly Fran - cis,
4. From thy glo - rious throne in heav - en

1. Still the fa - ther of the poor.
2. Where re - splen - dent - ly they shine.
3. By the souls of the re - deemed.
4. Where re - splen - dent - ly they shine.

103

Saint of the Sacred Heart

Father Faber   Nicola A. Montani

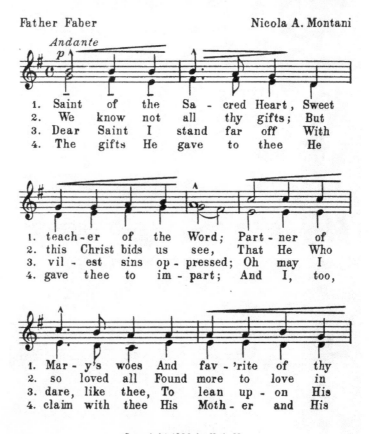

1. Saint of the Sa - cred Heart, Sweet
2. We know not all thy gifts; But
3. Dear Saint I stand far off With
4. The gifts He gave to thee He

1. teach - er of the Word; Part - ner of
2. this Christ bids us see, That He Who
3. vil - est sins op - pressed; Oh may I
4. gave thee to im - part; And I, too,

1. Mar - y's woes And fav - 'rite of thy
2. so loved all Found more to love in
3. dare, like thee, To lean up - on His
4. claim with thee His Moth - er and His

1. Lord! Thou to whom grace was giv'n To
2. thee. When the last eve - ning came, Thy
3. Breast? His touch could heal the sick, His
4. Heart. Ah teach me, then, dear Saint! The

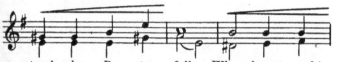

1. stand where Pe - ter fell, Whose heart could
2. head was on His Breast, Pil - lowed on
3. voice could raise the dead! Oh that my
4. se - crets Christ taught thee, The beat - ings

rall

1. brook the Cross Of Him it loved so well!
2. earth where now In heav'n the Saints find rest.
3. soul might be Where He al - lows thy head.
4. of His Heart, And how it beat for me.

104

St. Jeanne d' Arc

The Maid of France, with visioned eyes

Rt.Rev.Msgr. H. T. Henry ★   ★★ Ancient French Melody
Arr. by N. A.M.

Andante maestoso

1. The Maid of France, with vis - ioned
2. The Vi - sions and the Voic - es
3. The Maid be - lieved the great com -
4. O who shall dare her glo - ry

1. eyes, Saw mes - sen - gers from Par - a -
2. spoke A won - drous mes - sage:"Break the
3. mand, And fought for God and na - tive
4. paint? She lived a he - ro, died a

1. dise And Voic - es bore a hid - den
2. yoke That bur - dens France, and crown your
3. land: Her · love was like a liv - ing
4. Saint: A mod - el she shall ev - er

★ Written expressly for the St. Gregory Hymnal (all rights reserved)

★★ A traditional Catholic melody (Provencal Noel) known as the "Marche dei Rei" words of which are attributed to King Rene. The Noel, over two centuries old, was utilized by Bizet in his incidental music to "L' Arlessienne."

1. word That on - ly by her ear was
2. King, Sweet Her - ald of his tri - umph -
3. lamp To guide her feet in court or
4. stand Of love for God and Fa - ther -

Refrain

1. heard.
2. ing!"
3. camp.   1-4. O bless - ed Maid, the chant we
4. land.

raise That tells the mean-ing of thy praise:Thou teachest

us the les-son grand Of love for God and Fa-ther-land.

105

SAINTS

St. Cecilia

Let the deep organ swell the lay

Rev. C. Pise   Nicola A. Montani

Marcato

1. Let the deep or - gan swell the lay, In
2. Then from the world's be - wil- d'ring strife, In

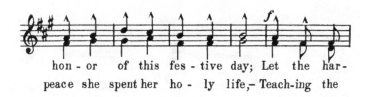

hon - or   of this fes - tive day; Let the har-
peace she spent her ho - ly life,— Teach-ing the

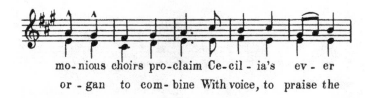

mo - nious choirs pro-claim Ce-cil - ia's   ev - er
or - gan   to com- bine With voice, to praise the

bless - ed name.   Rome gave the   vir - gin
Lamb di - vine. Ce - cil - ia,   with a

mar-tyr birth, Whose ho - ly name hath filled the
two - fold crown A - dorned in Heav'n, we pray look

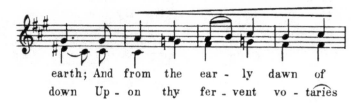

earth; And from the   ear - ly   dawn   of
down   Up - on   thy   fer - vent   vo - taries

youth, She fixed her heart on God and   truth.
here, And heark-en   to their hum - ble   pray'r.

106

Sweet Agnes, Holy Child

S.N.D.

Melody from a Slovak Hymnal
Arr. by N.A.M.

Andante religioso

1. Sweet Ag_nes, ho - ly child, All pu - ri - ty,
2. O gen-tle pa - tron - ess Of ho - ly youth,
3. Look down and hear our pray'r From realms a-bove,

1. Oh, may we un - de - filed, Be pure as thee:
2. Ask God all those to bless Who love the truth:
3. Show us thy ten - der care, Thy guid - ing love:

1. Read-y our blood to shed Forth as the mar-tyrs led,
2. Oh, guide us on our way Un-to th'e-ter-nal day,
3. Oh, keep us in thy sight, Till in th'un-cloud-ed light

1. The path of pain to tread, And die like thee.
2. With hearts all pure and gay, Dear Saint, like thine.
3. Of Heav'n's pure vi - sion bright We dwell with thee.

St. Ursula

Afar upon a foreign shore

Ancient Breton Melody
Arr. by N.A.M.

Andante religioso

mf

1. A - far up - on a for-eign shore A
2. O hap - py Saint! up - on whose way God's
3. To God the Fa - ther with the Son, And

1. mar - tyr's crown thy love did win, Thy
2. spe - cial love a glo - ry cast, Thy
3. Ho - ly Spir - it, Three in One, Be

1. life, thy death to Je - sus giv'n, With
2. sor - rows o'er, thy tem - pest past, Thou
3. glo - ry while the a - ges flow, From

Refrain
rall *a tempo*

1. Him to reign for - ev - er - more.
2. shar - est His e - ter - nal day. 1-3. Hail
3. all a - bove and all be - low

Bless-ed Saint, hail Ur-su-la! Ob-

tain for us, we pray,——— That

love may make us mar-tyrs too, And

in our hearts hold sway.

O blessed Father sent by God

Father Faber   Nicola A. Montani

Moderato

1. O bless-éd Fa-ther! sent by God His
2. Thy mir - a - cles are works of love; Thy
3. Dear Saint not in the wil - der-ness Thy
4. For char - i - ty a -noint-ed thee O'er

1. mer - cy to dis - pense, Thy
2. great - est is to make Room
3. fra - grant vir - tues bloom, But
4. want and woe, and pain; And

1. hand is out o'er all the earth, Like
2. in a day for toil that weeks In
3. in the cit - y's crowd - ed haunts, The
4. she hath crowned thee em - per - or Of

1. God's own prov - 'i - dence . There
2. oth - er men would take . All
3. al - ley's cheer - less gloom. When
4. all her wide do - main. Vin -

Copyright 1920 by N.A.M.

169

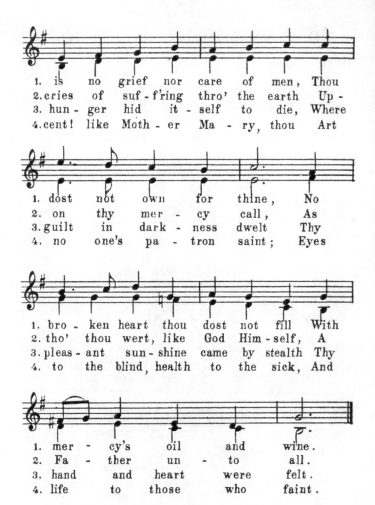

1. is   no   grief nor   care   of   men, Thou
2. cries of   suf - f'ring thro' the earth Up -
3. hun - ger hid   it - self   to   die, Where
4. cent! like Moth - er Ma - ry, thou Art

1. dost   not   own   for   thine,   No
2. on   thy   mer - cy   call,   As
3. guilt in   dark - ness dwelt   Thy
4. no   one's pa - tron saint;   Eyes

1. bro - ken heart thou dost not fill With
2. tho' thou wert, like God Him - self, A
3. pleas - ant sun - shine came by stealth Thy
4. to   the blind, health to the sick, And

1. mer - cy's oil   and   wine.
2. Fa - ther un - to   all.
3. hand   and   heart were felt.
4. life   to   those who   faint.

Feasts of Virgins

Dear Crown of all the Virgin-choir

Jesu, corona Virginum

For Unison, or Two-Part Chorus of Equal Voices

Translated by Father Caswall   P. Piel

Moderato

1. Dear Crown of all the Vir-gin choir! That ho-ly
2. En- cir-cled by Thy Vir-gin band, A- mid the
3. And still wher-ev- er Thou dost bend Thy love -ly
4. Keep us, O Pur- i - ty di - vine, From ev-'ry
5. To God the Fa-ther, and the Son, All hon-or,

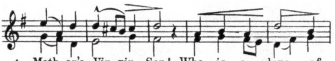

1. Moth-er's Vir-gin Son! Who is, a - lone of
2. lil - ies Thou art found; For Thy pure brides with
3. steps, O glo - rious King, Vir-gins up - on Thy
4. least cor-rup-tion free; Our ev-'ry sense from
5. glo - ry, praise be giv'n; With Thee, co - e - qual

1. wom-an- kind, Moth-er and Vir-gin both in one .
2. lav-ish hand Scat-t'ring im-mor-tal grac-es round.
3. steps at-tend, And hymns to Thy high glo - ry sing.
4. sin re-fine, And pu - ri - fy our souls for Thee.
5. Par - a-clete! For- ev- er-more in earth and Heav'n

SAINTS
Feasts of Apostles
Now let the earth with joy resound
Exsultet orbis gaudiis
Processional

Translated by Father Caswall   Lachmannov Spevniček

Joyously and with animation(alla breve) **Arr. by N.A.M.**

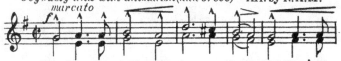

1. Now let the earth with joy re-sound; And Heav'n the
2. O ye who, throned in glo-ry dread, Shall judge the
3. So when the world is at its end, And Christ to
4. Praise to the Fa-ther, with the Son, And Ho-ly

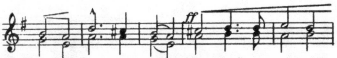

1. chant re-ech-o round; Nor Heav'n nor earth too
2. liv-ing and the dead! Lights of the world for
3. judg-ment shall de-scend, May we be called these
4. Spir-it, Three in One; As ev-er was in

1. high can raise The great A-pos-tles' glo-rious praise.
2. ev-er-more! To you the suppliant pray'r we pour.
3. joys to see Pre-pared from all e-ter-ni-ty.
4. a-ges past, And so shall be while a-ges last.

Hark! hark! my soul
The Pilgrims of the Night

Father Faber   Nicola A. Montani

Moderato (alla breve)

1. Hark! hark! my soul! an - gel - ic songs are
2. Dark - er than night life's shad-ows fall a -
3. Far, far a - way, like bells at ev' - ning
4. An - gels! sing on, your faith-ful watch-es

1. swell - ing O'er earth's green fields and
2. round us, And, like be - night - ed
3. peal - ing, The voice of Je - sus
4. keep - ing, Sing us sweet frag - ments

1. o - cean's wave -beat shore; How sweet the
2. men, we miss our mark; God hides Him -
3. sounds o'er land and sea; And lad - en
4. of the songs a - bove; While we toil

1. truth those bless-ed strains are tell-ing   Of
2. self, and grace hath scarce-ly found us,   Ere
3. souls, by thou-sands meek-ly steal-ing,   Kind
4. on, and soothe our-selves with weep-ing,   Till

1. that new life where sin shall be no more!
2. death finds out his vic-tims in the dark.
3. Shep-herd! turn their wea-ry steps to Thee.
4. life's long night shall break in end-less love.

Refrain

1-4. An-gels of Je-sus! An-gels of light!

Sing-ing to wel-come The pil-grims of the night.

Dear Angel! ever at my side
The Guardian Angel

Father Faber   Nicola A. Montani

1. Dear An-gel! ev-er at my side, How
2. Thy beau-ti-ful and shin-ing face, I
3. But when, dear Spir-it, I kneel down, Both
4. Oh! when I pray thou pray-est too, Thy
5. Then, for thy sake, dear An-gel! now More
6. Then love me, love me, An-gel dear! And

1. lov-ing must thou be, To leave thy home in
2. see not, tho' so near; The sweetness of thy
3. morn and night to pray'r, Something there is with-
4. pray'r is all for me; But when I sleep, thou
5. hum-ble will I be: But I am weak, and
6. I will love thee more; And help me when my

1. heav'n to guide A lit-tle child like me.
2. soft low voice Too deaf am I to hear.
3. in my heart, Which tells me thou art there.
4. sleep-est not, But watch-est pa-tient-ly.
5. when I fall, O wea-ry not of me.
6. soul is cast Up-on th'e-ter-nal shore.

113

Help, Lord, the Souls which Thou hast made

The Faithful departed

Cardinal Newman

From a Slovak Hymnal
Arr. by N. A. M.

1. Help, Lord, the souls which Thou hast made, The
2. Those ho - ly souls, they suf - fer on, Re -
3. For dai - ly falls, for par - doned crime, They
4. Oh, by their pa - tience of de - lay, Their
5. Oh, by their fire of love, not less In
6. Good Je - sus, help! sweet Je - sus, aid The

1. souls to Thee so dear,___ In pris - on for the
2. signed in heart and will,___ Un - til Thy high be-
3. joy to un - der - go ___ The shadow of Thy
4. hope a - mid their pain,___ Their sa - cred zeal to
5. keen-ness than the flame,___ Oh, by their ver - y
6. souls to Thee most dear,___ In pris - on for the

1. debt un - paid, Of sins com - mit - ted here.
2. hest is done, And jus - tice has its fill.
3. Cross sub - lime, The rem - nant of Thy woe.
4. burn a - way Dis - fig - ure - ment and stain;
5. help - less-ness, Oh, by Thy own great Name:
6. debt un - paid Of sins com - mit - ted here.

Ye Souls of the Faithful

O vos fideles animæ

Tr. by Father Caswall

From an Italian Hymn Book
Arr. by N. A. M.

1. Ye souls of the faith-ful, who sleep in the Lord, Who
2. O Fa-ther of mer-cies, Thine an-ger with-hold; These
3. O tender Re-deem-er, their mis-er-y see: De-
4. O Spir-it of Grace, Thou Con-sol-er di-vine, See

1. yet are shut out from your fin-al re-ward: O!
2. works of Thy Hand in Thy mer-cy be-hold: Too
3. liv-er the souls that were ransomed by Thee: Be-
4. how for Thy pres-ence they long-ing-ly pine, To

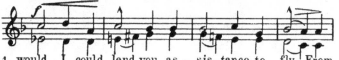

1. would I could lend you as-sis-tance to fly From
2. oft from Thy path they have wan-dered a-side, But
3. hold how they love Thee, de-spite of their pain: Re-
4. lift, to en-liv-en their sad-ness, de-scend; And

1. pris-on be-low! to your pal-ace on high!
2. Thee, their Cre-a-tor, they nev-er de-nied.
3. store them, re-store them to fa-vor a-gain.
4. fill them with peace and with joy in the end.

115

O turn to Jesus, Mother, turn

Father Faber

From a Slovak Hymnal
Arr. by N. A. M.

1. O turn to Je-sus, Moth-er! turn, And
2. Ah! they have fought a gal-lant fight; In
3. They are the chil-dren of thy tears; Then
4. O Ma-ry, let thy Son no more His
5. Pray, then, as thou hast ev-er prayed; An-

1. call Him by His ten-derest names; Pray for the Ho-ly
2. death's cold arms they per-se-vered; And af-ter life's un-
3. hast-en, Moth-er, to their aid; In pit-y think each
4. lin-gering Spouses thus ex-pect: God's children to-their
5. gels and souls, all look to thee; God waits thy pray'rs, for

1. Souls that burn This hour a-mid the cleans-ing flames.
2. cheer-y night, The ar-bour of their rest is neared.
3. hour ap-pears An age while glo-ry is de-layed.
4. God re-store, And to the Spir-it His e-lect.
5. He hath made Those pray'rs His law of char-i-ty.

178

Unto him, for whom this day
Recessional

Rt.Rev. Msgr. H.T. Henry, Litt.D.   Nicola A. Montani

1. Un-to him, for whom, this day; ___ Juste ju-
2. When at Judg-ment he shall stand,___ Rex tre-
3. He hath fought the gal - lant fight___ In - ter

1. dex ___ ul - ti - o _ nis, We in love and
2. men-dæ maj - es - ta - tis, Grant him what Thy
3. o - ves lo - cum præ - sta, Lead Him on to

1. pit - y pray; Do-num fac re-mis-si - o - nis.
2. love hath planned, Qui sal-van-dos sal-vas gra - tis.
3. Heav-en's light Sta-tu-ens in par-te dex - tra.

Refrain
1-3. Pi - e Je - su Do-mi - ne, ___ Do - na

e - i re - qui - em.   re - qui - em.

Out of the depths
De Profundis

S. Webbe

With devotion

1. Out of the depths to Thee, O Lord, I cry,
2. Oh, hear our pray'rs and sighs, Re-deem-er blest,
3. To be ap-peased in wrath, dear Lord, is Thine;
4. This God Him-self shall come from Heav'n a - bove,

1. Lord! gra-cious turn Thine ear to supp-liant sigh;
2. And grant Thy ho - ly souls e - ter - nal rest
3. Thou mer-cy with Thy jus-tice canst com-bine;
4. The Christ! the God of mer-cy and of love!

f

1. If sins of man Thou scann'st, who may stand
2. And let per-pet - ual light up - on them shine;
3. Thy blood our count-less stains can wash a - way:
4. He comes_ He comes! the God In - car - nate He!

cresc molto

rall

1. That search-ing eye of Thine, and chast'n - ing hand?
2. For tho' not spot - less, still these souls are Thine.
3. This is Thy, law our hope and stead - fast stay.
4. And by His glo-rious death makes all men free!

Jerusalem the Golden

Urbs Sion aurea

Bernard of Cluny
Translated by J. M. Neale

J. Grabowski
Arr. by N. A. M.

Con moto

1. Je - ru - sa - lem the Gold - en, With
2. They stand, those Halls of Si - on, All
3. There is the throne of Da - vid, And
4. O sweet and bless - ed coun - try, The

1. milk and hon - ey blest, Be -
2. ju - bi - lant with song, And
3. bliss with - out al - loy; The
4. home of God's e - lect! O

1. neath thy con - tem - pla - tion Sink
2. bright with man - y an An - gel, And
3. shout of them that tri - umph, The
4. sweet and bless - ed coun - try That

1. heart and voice op - prest; I
2. all the Mar - tyr throng; The
3. song of fes - tal joy; And
4. ea - ger hearts ex - pect! Je -

181

1. know not— Oh, I know not Wha
2. Prince is ev - er in them, His
3. they, who with their Lead - er Have
4. su, in mer - cy bring us To

1. joys a - wait us there; What
2. light is al - ways seen; The
3. con - quered in the fight, For
4. that dear land of rest; Who

1. ra - dian - cy of glo - ry, What
2. pas - tures of the bless - ed Are
3. ev - er and for ev - er Are
4. art, with God the Fa - ther, And

1. bliss be - yond com pare.
2. decked in glo - rious sheen.
3. clad in robes of white.
4. Spir - it, ev - er blest.

Jerusalem, my happy home

L. Anderson, S. J.   From an Italian Hymnal

Moderato (alla breve)

1. Je - ru - sa - lem, my hap - py
2. O hap - py har - bor of the
3. There lust and lu - cre can - not
4. Je - ru - sa - lem, Je - ru - sa -

1. home, When shall I come to thee?— When
2. Saints, O sweet and pleas - ant soil:— In
3. dwell, There en - vy bears no sway,— There
4. lem, God grant I once may see— Thy

1. shall my sor - rows have an end? Thy
2. thee no sor - row may be found, No
3. is no hun - ger, heat or cold But
4. end - less joys, and of the same, Par -

1. joys when shall I see?—
2. grief, no care, no toil.—
3. pleas - ure ev - 'ry way.—
4. tak - er, aye to be.—

120

O Paradise! O Paradise!

Father Faber

From a Slovak Hymnal
Arr. by N. A. M.

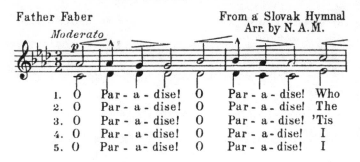

1. O Par - a - dise! O Par - a - dise! Who
2. O Par - a - dise! O Par - a - dise! The
3. O Par - a - dise! O Par - a - dise! 'Tis
4. O Par - a - dise! O Par - a - dise! I
5. O Par - a - dise! O Par - a - dise! I

1. doth not crave for rest? Who
2. world is grow - ing old; Who
3. wea - ry wait - ing here; I
4. want to sin no more; I
5. great - ly long to see The

1. would not seek the hap - py land, Where
2. would not be at rest and free Where
3. long to be where Je - sus is, To
4. want to be as pure on earth As
5. spe - cial place my dear - est Lord In

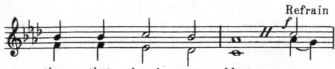

Refrain

1. they that loved are blest:
2. love is nev - er cold;
3. feel, to see Him near; 1-5. Where
4. on thy spot - less shore;
5. love pre - pares for me;

loy - al hearts, and true, Stand

ev - er in the light, All rap -ture thro' and

thro' In God's most ho - ly sight?

185

121

Faith of our Fathers
Fideles ad mortem

Father Faber

Nicola A. Montani

Maestoso, ben marcato

1. Faith of our Fa - thers! liv - ing
2. Our Fa - thers, chained in pris - ons
3. Faith of our Fa - thers! we will

1. still In spite of dun - geon,
2. dark, Were still in heart and
3. love Both friend and foe in

1. fire, and sword; Oh, how our
2. con - science free: How sweet would
3. all our strife: And preach thee

1. hearts   beat   high   with   joy
2. be   their   chil - dren's   fate,
3. too,   as   love   knows   how

(A)
Optional Version:

(B)

1. When - e'er   we   hear   that   glo - rious   word.
2. If   they, like   them, could   die   for   thee!
3. By   kind - ly   words   and   vir - tuous   life:

Refrain

1-3. Faith   of   our   Fa - thers!   Ho - ly   Faith!

We will   be   true   to   thee   till   death.

187

122

Long Live the Pope
Hymn for the Pope

Rt. Rev. Msgr. Hugh T. Henry, Litt. D.   H. G. Gauss

Maestoso

1. Long live the Pope! His prais-es sound A-
2. Be-lea-guered by the foes of earth, Be-
3. His sig-net is the Fish-er-man's; No
4. Then raise the chant, with heart and voice, In

1. gain and yet a-gain: His rule is o-ver
2. set by hosts of hell, He guards the loy-al
3. scep-tre does he bear; In meek and low-ly
4. church and school and home: "Long live the Shep-herd

1. space and time; His throne the hearts of men: All
2. flock of Christ, A watch-ful sen-ti-nel: And
3. maj-es-ty He rules from Pe-ter's Chair: And
4. of the Flock! Long live the Pope of Rome!" Al-

1. hail! the Shep-herd King of Rome, The
2. yet, a-mid the din and strife, The
3. yet from ev-'ry tribe and tongue, From
4. might-y Fa-ther, bless his work, Pro-

By permission   Copyright 1908 by J. Fischer & Bro.

1. theme of lov-ing song: Let all the earth his
2. clash of mace and sword, He bears a - lone the
3. ev - 'ry clime and zone, Three hun-dred mil - lion
4. tect him in his ways, Re-ceive his pray'rs, ful -

1. glo - ry sing, And heav'n the strain pro
2. shep - herd staff, This cham - pion of the
3. voic - es sing, The glo - ry of his
4. fil his hopes And grant him "length of

1. long, Let all the earth his
2. Lord, He bears a - lone the
3. throne, Three hun - dred mil - lion
4. days," Re - ceive his pray'rs, ful -

1. glo - ry sing, And heav'n the strain pro - long.
2. shep-herd staff, This cham-pion of the Lord.
3. voic - es sing, The glo - ry of his throne.
4. fil his hopes And grant him "length of days".

Blest is the Faith

Father Faber   Nicola A. Montani

Maestoso

1. Blest is the Faith, di - vine and strong, Of
2. Blest is the Hope that holds to God, In
3. Blest is the Love that can - not love Aught

1. thanks and praise and end - less foun - tain,
2. doubt and dark - ness still un - shak - en,
3. that earth gives of best and bright - est;

1. Whose life is one per - pet - ual song,
2. And sings a - long the heav'n - ly road,
3. Whose rap - tures thrill like saints' a - bove,

1. High up the Sav - iour's ho - ly moun - tain.
2. Sweet - est when most it seems for - sak - en.
3. Most when its earth - ly gifts are light - est.

Refrain

1-3. Oh, Si - on's songs are sweet to sing, With

mel - o - dies of glad - ness lad - en;

Hark! how the harps of an - gels ring,

allargando

Hail! Son of Man! Hail! Moth - er Maid- en!

124

Hear Thy Children, gentle Jesus

Father Stanfield

M. Haydn
Arr. by N. A. M.

Hear Thy chil-dren, gen - tle Je - sus,
Gen - tle Je - sus, look in pit - y,

While we breathe our dai - ly prayer,
From Thy great white throne a - bove;

Save us from all harm and dan - ger,
All the night Thy Heart is wake-ful,

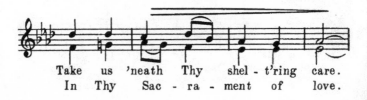

Take us 'neath Thy shel - t'ring care.
In Thy Sac - ra - ment of love.

Save us from the wiles of Sa - tan,—
Shades of e - ven fast are fall - ing,—

— 'Mid the lone and sleep - ful night,
— Day is fad - ing in - to gloom,

Sweet - ly may bright Guar - dian An - gels
When the shades of death fall 'round us,

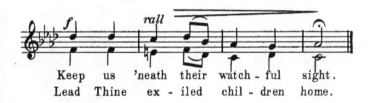

Keep us 'neath their watch - ful sight.
Lead Thine ex - iled chil - dren home.

Little King, so fair and sweet
School Hymn

S. N. D.

From a Slovak Hymnal
Arr. by N. A. M.

1. Lit - tle King, so fair and sweet,
2. Raise Thy lit - tle hand to bless
3. Be our Teach - er when we learn,
4. And when hol - i - days have come,

1. See us gath - ered at Thy feet:
2. All our child - hood's hap - pi - ness;
3. All the hard to ea - sy turn;
4. Call Thy chil - dren to Thy home,

1. Be Thou Mon - arch of our school,
2. Bless our sor - row and our pain,
3. Be our Play - mate when we play,
4. In that gen - tle voice of Thine,

1. It shall pros - per 'neath Thy rule,
2. That each cross may be our gain.
3. So we shall in - deed be gay.
4. Which we know, sweet Child Di - vine.

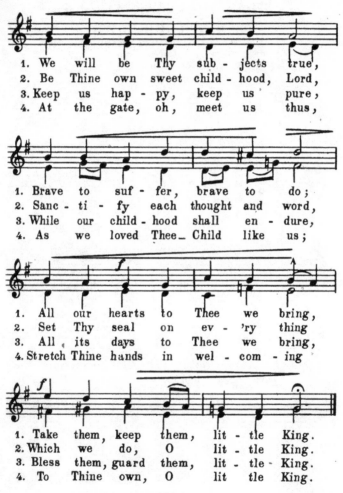

1. We will be Thy sub - jects true,
2. Be Thine own sweet child - hood, Lord,
3. Keep us hap - py, keep us pure,
4. At the gate, oh, meet us thus,

1. Brave to suf - fer, brave to do;
2. Sanc - ti - fy each thought and word,
3. While our child - hood shall en - dure,
4. As we loved Thee_ Child like us;

1. All our hearts to Thee we bring,
2. Set Thy seal on ev - 'ry thing
3. All its days to Thee we bring,
4. Stretch Thine hands in wel - com - ing

1. Take them, keep them, lit - tle King.
2. Which we do, O lit - tle King.
3. Bless them, guard them, lit - tle - King.
4. To Thine own, O lit tle King.

195

126 FOR CHILDREN
The Infant Jesus
When Blossoms flowered
'mid the snows
A Christmas Carol
For Unison Chorus
Frederick H. Martens *(Gesu Bambino)*   Pietro A. Yon *

1. When

1. blos - soms flow-ered 'mid the snows Up -
2. gain the heart with rap - ture glows To

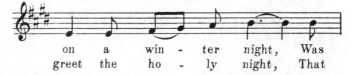

on a win - ter night, Was
greet the ho - ly night, That

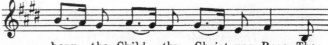

born the Child, the Christ-mas Rose, The
gave the world its Christ-mas Rose, Its

King of Love and Light. The
King of Love and Light. Let

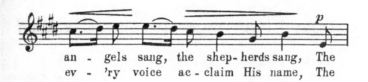

an - gels sang, the shep- herds sang, The
ev - 'ry voice ac - claim His name, The

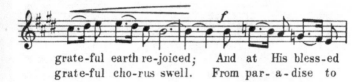

grate-ful earth re-joiced; And at His bless-ed
grate-ful cho-rus swell. From par- a-dise to

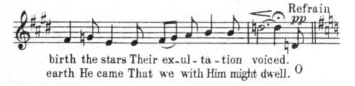

birth the stars Their ex-ul- ta -tion voiced.
earth He came That we with Him might dwell. O

come let us a-dore Him, O come let us a-

dore Him, O come let us a - dore Him

Christ the Lord. 2. A-

127 FOR CHILDREN

The Infant Jesus

Dear little One! how sweet Thou art
Christmas

For additional Children's Hymn see No. 87

Father Faber   Nicola A. Montani

Andante

1. Dear lit - tle One! how sweet Thou art, Thine
2. How faint and fee-ble is Thy cry, Like
3. When Ma - ry bids Thee sleep Thou sleep'st, Thou
4. Saint Jo - seph takes Thee in his arms, And
5. Yes! Thou art what Thou seem'st to be, A

1. eyes, how bright they shine; So bright, they al-most
2. plaint of harm-less dove, When Thou dost mur-mur
3. wak-est when she calls; Thou art con-tent up -
4. smoothes Thy lit - tle cheek, Thou look-est up in
5. thing of smiles and tears; Yet Thou art God, and

1. seem to speak When Ma - ry's look meets Thine!
2. in Thy sleep Of sor - row and of love.
3. on her lap, Or in the rug - ged stalls.
4. to his face So help - less and so meek.
5. Heav'n and earth A - dore Thee with their fears.

Acts of Faith, Hope, Love and Contrition

Great God, whatever through Thy Church

From a Slovak Hymnal
Arr. by N. A. M.

Maestoso

Faith 1. Great God, what-ev-er thro' Thy Church
Hope 2. My God, I firm-ly hope in Thee,
Love 3. With all my heart and soul and strength,
Contrition 4. Most Ho-ly God, my ver-y soul

1. Thou teach-est to be true, I
2. For Thou art great and good; Thou
3. I love Thee, O my Lord, For
4. With grief sin-cere is mov'd, Be-

1. firm-ly do be-lieve it all,
2. gav-est us Thine on-ly Son
3. Thou art per-fect, and all things
4. cause I have of-fend-ed Thee,

1. And will con-fess it, too. Thou
2. To die up-on the Rood. I
3. Were made by Thy blest Word. Like
4. Whom I should e'er have lov'd. For

1. nev - er canst de - ceiv - ed be,
2. hope thro' Him for grace to live
3. me to Thine own im - age made,
4. give me, Fa - ther; I am now

1. Thou nev - er canst de - ceive, For
2. As Thy com - mand - ments teach, And
3. My neigh - bor Thou didst make, And
4. Re - solved to sin no more, And

1. Thou art truth it - self, and Thou
2. thro' Thy mer - cy, when I die
3. as I love my - self, I love
4. by Thy ho - ly grace to shun

1. Dost tell me to be - lieve.
2. The joys of Heav'n to reach.
3. My neigh - bor for Thy sake.
4. What made me sin be - fore.

O Lord, I am not worthy

Nicola A. Montani

Lento con espressione

1. O Lord, I am not wor - thy That
2. And hum - bly I'll re - ceive Thee, The
3. O Might - y E - ter - nal Spir - it Un -

1. Thou should'st come to me; But
2. Bride - groom of my soul, No
3. wor - thy tho' I be, Pre -

1. speak the words of com - fort, My
2. more by sin to grieve Thee, Or
3. pare me to re - ceive Him And

1. spir - it healed shall be.
2. fly Thy sweet con - trol.
3. trust the Word to me.

Jesus, Thou art coming

Acts before Communion

Moderato   From a Slovak Hymnal

1. Je - sus, Thou art com - ing,
2. Who am I, my Je - sus,
Trust
3. Put Thy kind arms round me,
Love and Desire
4. Dear - est Lord, I *love* Thee,
Offering and petition
5. Ah! what gift or pres - ent,
6. Take my bod - y, Je - sus,

1. Ho - ly as Thou art, Thou, the God who
2. That Thou com'st to me? I have sinned a -
3. Fee - ble as I am; Thou art my Good
4. With my whole, whole heart, Not for what Thou
5. Je - sus, can I bring? I have noth - ing
6. Eyes, and ears, and tongue; Nev - er let them,

1. made me, To my sin - ful heart.
2. gainst Thee, Of - ten, griev - ous - ly;
3. Shep - herd, I, Thy lit - tle lamb;
4. giv - est, But for what Thou art.
5. wor - thy Of my God and King;
6. Je - sus, Help to do Thee wrong.

202

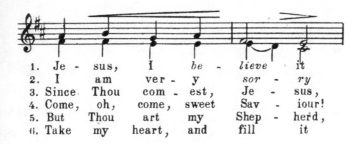

1. Je - sus, I *be - lieve* it
2. I am ver - y *sor - ry*
3. Since Thou com _ est, Je - sus,
4. Come, oh, come, sweet Sav - iour!
5. But Thou art my Shep - herd,
6. Take my heart, and fill it

1. On Thy on - ly word; Kneel-ing, I *a -*
2. I have caused Thee pain; I will nev - er,
3. Now to be my Guest, I can *trust* Thee
4. Come to me, and stay, For I *want* Thee,
5. I, Thy lit - tle lamb; Take *my - self,* dear
6. Full of love for Thee; All I have I

rall

1. *dore* Thee As my King and Lord.
2. nev - er, Wound Thy Heart a - gain.
3. al - ways, Lord, for all the rest.
4. Je - sus, More than I can say.
5. Je - sus, All I have and am.
6. give Thee, Give Thy - self to me.

131   HOLY COMMUNION

Jesus, Jesus come to me
Hymn before Communion

For additional Communion Hymns see Nos. 49, 51, 54, and
Hymns in honor of the Blessed Sacrament. See also "Acts,"
Nos. 128, 129, 130, 145.

Tr. Sister Jeanne Marie   Traditional Melody

1. Je - sus, Je - sus, come to me,
2. Je - - sus, I live for Thee,
3. Com - fort my poor soul dis - tressed,

All my long - ing is for Thee,
Je - - sus, I die for Thee,
Come and dwell with - in my breast,

Of all friends the best Thou art,
I be - - long to Thee,
Oh how oft I long for Thee,

Make of me Thy coun - ter - part.
For - - e'er in life and death.
Je - sus, Je - sus, come to me.

My God, accept my heart this day

M. Bridges

Nicola A. Montani

Slowly with devotion

1. My God, ac-cept my heart this day, And
2. Be-fore the cross of Him who died, Be -
3. A-noint me with Thy heav'n-ly grace, A -
4. May the dear blood, once shed for me, My
5. Let ev- 'ry thought, and work, and word, To

1. make it al-ways Thine, That I from Thee no
2. hold I pros-trate fall; Let ev-'ry sin be
3. dopt me for Thine own,- That I may see Thy
4. best a-tone-ment prove;-That I from first to
5. Thee be ev- er giv'n— Then life shall be Thy

1. more may stray, No more from Thee de-cline.
2. cru - ci - fied, Let Christ be all in all.
3. glo-rious face And wor-ship at Thy throne.
4. last may be The pur-chase of Thy love!
5. ser - vice, Lord, And death the gate of heav'n!

133

Jesus, my Lord!
behold at length the time
Act of Contrition

Bishop Chadwick   Traditional Melody

Moderato

1.   Je - sus, my Lord! be - hold   at   length the   time
2. Since my poor soul Thy precious Blood has cost
3. Kneel-ing in tears, be - hold me at   Thy   Feet,

Refrain

1. When   I   re - solve to turn a -way from crime.
2.   Suf - fer it not for- ev - er to be   lost. 1-3. Oh,
3.   Like Magda-lene, for-give-ness I   en - treat.

par-don me, Je-sus: Thy mer-cy I im-plore; I will

nev-er more of-fend Thee; Oh, fend Thee; no, never more.

God of mercy and compassion

Rev. E. Vaughan　　　　　　　　　　Nicola A. Montani

Moderato

1. God of mer-cy and com-pas-sion! Look with
2. By my sins I have a-ban-doned Right and
3. See our Sav-iour, bleed-ing, dy-ing, On the

1. pit-y up-on me; Fa-ther! let me call Thee
2. claim to Heav'n a-bove, Where the Saints re-joice for
3. Cross of Cal-va-ry; To that Cross my sins have

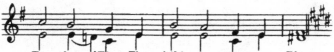

1. Fa-ther; 'Tis Thy child re-turns to Thee.
2. ev-er In a bound-less sea of love.
3. nailed Him, Yet He bleeds and dies for me.

Refrain

1-3. Je-sus, Lord, I ask for mer-cy; Let me not implore in

vain; All my sins I now detest them, Never will I sin a-gain

Jesus, ever-loving Saviour
Hymn for a Happy Death

Franz Schubert
Arr. by N. A. M.

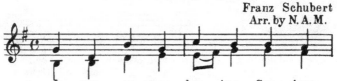

1. Je - sus,   ev - er   lov - ing   Sav - iour,
2. When the   last   dread   hour   ap - proach - ing
3. Ma - ry,   thou   canst   not   for - sake   me,
4. Je - sus,   when   in   cru - el   an - guish
5. Then, by   all   that   Thou   didst   suf - fer,

1. Thou   didst   live   and   die   for   me,
2. Fills   my   guilt - y   soul   with   fear;
3. Vir - gin - moth - er   un - de - filed;
4. Dy - ing   on   the   shame - ful   tree,
5. Grant   me   mer - cy   in   that   day;

1. Liv - ing,   I   will   live   to   love   Thee,
2. All   my   sins   rise   up   be - fore   me,
3. Thou   didst   not   a - ban - don   Je - sus,
4. All   a - ban - doned   by   Thy   Fa - ther,
5. Help   me,   Ma - ry,   my   sweet   Moth - er,

1. Dy - ing, I will die for Thee. Je _ sus!
2. All my vir-tues dis-ap-pear. Je _ sus!
3. Dy - ing, tor-tured,and re - viled. Je _ sus!
4. Thou didst writhe in ag-o-ny. Je _ sus!
5. Ho - ly Jo-seph, near me stay. Je - sus!

1. Je _ sus! By Thy life and death and sor-row,
2. Je - sus! Turn not Thou in an- ger from me,
3. Je - sus! Send Thy Moth-er to con -sole me:
4. Je - sus! By those three long hours of sor-row
5. Je - sus! Let me die, my lips re-peat-ing,

1. Help me in my ag - o - ny.
2. Ma - ry, Jo - seph, then be near!
3. Ma - ry, help Thy guilt - y child!
4. Thou didst pur - chase hope for me.
5. Je - sus, mer - cy! Ma - ry, pray!

The Holy Family

Happy we who thus united

Rev. E. Vaughan

"Ave Virgo" 15th Century melody
Arr. by N. A. M.

Allegro moderato

1. Hap-py we, who thus u - nit - ed
2. Je - sus, whose al - might-y bid - ding
3. Ma - ry! thou a - lone wert chos - en
4. Jo - seph! thou wert called the fa - ther

1. Join in cheer - ful mel - o - dy;
2. All cre - at - ed things ful - fil,
3. Vir - gin Moth - er of thy Lord:
4. Of thy Mak - er and thy Lord;

1. Prais - ing Je - sus, Ma - ry, Jo - seph,
2. Lives on earth in meek sub - jec - tion
3. Thou didst guide the ear - ly foot - steps
4. Thine it was to save thy Sav - iour

1. In the "Ho - ly Fam - i - ly."
2. To His earth - ly par - ents' will.
3. Of the Great In - car - nate Word.
4. From the cru - el Her - od's sword.

1. Je - sus, Ma - ry, Jo - seph, help us,
2. Sweet - est In - fant, make us pa - tient
3. Dear - est Moth - er! make us hum - ble;
4. Suf - fer us to call thee fa - ther;

1. That we ev - er true may be,
2. And o - be - dient for Thy sake,
3. For thy Son will take His rest
4. Show to us a fa - ther's love;

1. To the prom - is - es that bind us
2. Teach us to be chaste and gen - tle,
3. In the poor and low - ly dwell - ing
4. Lead us safe thro' ev - 'ry dan - ger

1. To the "Ho - ly Fam - i - ly."
2. All our storm - y pas - sions break.
3. Of a hum - ble sin - ner's breast.
4. Till we meet in heav'n a - bove.

137 GENERAL
The Rosary
The Glorious Mysteries

By the first bright Easter Day

For the Joyful Mysteries see Hymn No. 86

C. M. Caddell

From a Slovak Hymnal
Arr. by N. A. M.

Allegro moderato

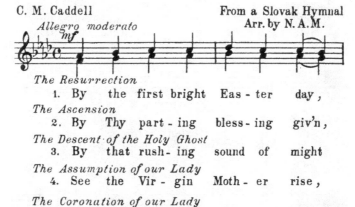

The Resurrection
1. By the first bright Eas - ter day,
The Ascension
2. By Thy part - ing bless - ing giv'n,
The Descent of the Holy Ghost
3. By that rush - ing sound of might
The Assumption of our Lady
4. See the Vir - gin Moth - er rise,

The Coronation of our Lady
5. Ma - ry reigns up - on the throne

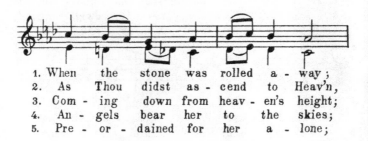

1. When the stone was rolled a - way;
2. As Thou didst as - cend to Heav'n,
3. Com - ing down from heav - en's height;
4. An - gels bear her to the skies;
5. Pre - or - dained for her a - lone;

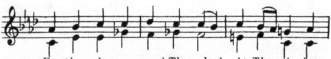

1. By the glo-ry round Thee shed At Thy ris-ing
2. By the cloud of liv-ing light That received Thee
3. By the clo-ven tongues of fire, Ho-ly Ghost, our
4. Mount a-loft, im-pe - rial Queen, Plead on high the
5. Saints and an-gels round her sing, Moth-er of our

Chorus

1. from the dead.
2. out of sight.
3. hearts in-spire! 1-5. King of Glo-ry, hear our cry;
4. cause of men!
5. God and King.

Make us soon Thy joy to see, Where enthroned in

ma -jes - ty Count-less an-gels sing to Thee.

GENERAL
Evening Hymn

Sweet Saviour! bless us ere we go

Father Faber   Nicola A. Montani

Andante ma non troppo

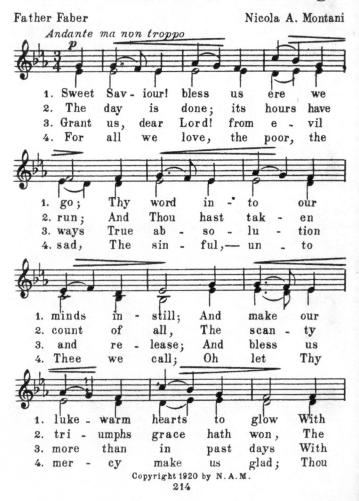

1. Sweet Sav - iour! bless us ere we
2. The day is done; its hours have
3. Grant us, dear Lord! from e - vil
4. For all we love, the poor, the

1. go; Thy word in - to our
2. run; And Thou hast tak - en
3. ways True ab - so - lu - tion
4. sad, The sin - ful,— un - to

1. minds in - still; And make our
2. count of all, The scan - ty
3. and re - lease; And bless us
4. Thee we call; Oh let Thy

1. luke - warm hearts to glow With
2. tri - umphs grace hath won, The
3. more than in past days With
4. mer - cy make us glad; Thou

1. low - ly   love   and   fer - vent   will.
2. bro - ken   vow,   the   fre - quent   fall.
3. pur - i - ty   and   in - ward   peace.
4. art   our   Je - sus   and   our   All.

Refrain

1-4. Thro' life's long day   and death's dark night,

O gen - tle Je - sus! be   our light;

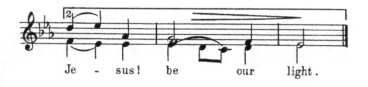

Je - sus! be   our   light.

139

GENERAL
Evening Hymn

As fades the glowing orb of day
Jam sol recedit igneus

Translated by T. J. Potter   S. Webbe (1740-1816)

Moderato

1. As fades the glow-ing orb of day, To
2. At ear - ly dawn, at close of day, To

Thee, great source of light, we pray; Blest
Thee our vows we hum - bly pay; May

Three in One, to ev - 'ry heart Thy
we, 'mid joys that nev - er end, With

beams of life and love im - part.
Thy bright saints in hom - age bend.

When day's shadows lengthen

Mane nobiscum, quoniam ad vesperascit

Dr. F. G. Lee

Traditional Melody
Arr. by N.A.M.

Andante

1. When   day's   shad - ows   length - en,
2. When   the   night   grows   dark - est,
3. Come,   Thou   Food   of   an - gels,
4. Then   be   near   me,   Je - sus,
5. So   shall   no   fears   chill   me
6. Bless - éd   war - fare   o - ver,

1. Je - sus,   be   Thou   near:
2. And   the   stars   are   pale,
3. Source   of   ev - 'ry   grace,
4. En - e - mies   shall   flee:
5. On   that   un - known   shore;
6. End - less   rest   a - lone;

1. Par - don,   com - fort,   strength - en,
2. When   the   foe - men   gath - er
3. In   Thy   Fa - ther's   man - sions
4. Hid - den   God   and   Sav - iour,
5. For   in   death   He   con - quered,
6. Tears   no   more,   nor   sor - row,

1. Chase   a - way   my   fear;
2. In   death's   mist - y   vale,
3. Give   me   soon   a   place;
4. Thou   my   com - fort   be:
5. And   can   die   no   more.
6. Neith - er   sigh   nor   moan,

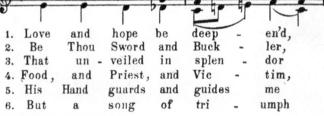

1. Love   and   hope   be   deep - en'd,
2. Be   Thou   Sword   and   Buck - ler,
3. That   un - veiled   in   splen - dor
4. Food,   and   Priest,   and   Vic - tim,
5. His   Hand   guards   and   guides   me
6. But   a   song   of   tri - umph

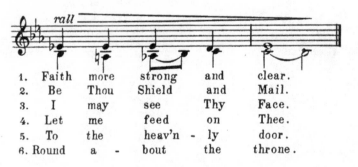

1. Faith   more   strong   and   clear.
2. Be   Thou   Shield   and   Mail.
3. I   may   see   Thy   Face.
4. Let   me   feed   on   Thee.
5. To   the   heav'n - ly   door.
6. Round   a - bout   the   throne.

Praise we our God with joy

The Praise of God
Processional

Canon Oakeley   Nicola A. Montani

Allegro maestoso (with well-marked rhythm)

1. Praise we our God with joy
2. He is our Shep - herd true,
3. Bleed - ing, we lay, but He
4. His Word our lan - tern is,

1. And glad - ness nev - er end - ing;
2. With watch - ful care un - sleep - ing;
3. With sooth - ing bands hath bound us;
4. His Peace our con - so - la - tion;

1. An - gels and Saints with us
2. On us, His err - ing sheep, __
3. Dark was our path, but He __
4. His Sweet - ness all our rest, __

1. Their grate-ful voic-es blend-ing.
2. An eye of pit-y keep-ing.
3. Hath poured His | Light a-round us;
4. Him-self our great Sal-va-tion!

1. He is our Fa-ther dear, O'er-filled with
2. He with a might-y arm The bonds of
3. Grac-es in co-pious streams From that pure
4. Then live we all to God, Re-ly on

1. Fa-ther's love; Mer-cies un-
2. sin doth break, And to our
3. foun-tain come, Down to our
4. Him in faith, Be He our

1. sought, un-known He show-ers from a-bove.
2. bur-den'd hearts In words of peace doth speak.
3. heart of hearts, Where God hath set His home.
4. guide in life, Our joy, our hope, in death.

Praise to the Holiest in the height
Dream of Gerontius
Processional

Cardinal Newman

Nicola A. Montani

With spirit

1. Praise to the Ho - li - est in the height, And in the depth be praise; _____ In
2. O lov - ing wis - dom ____ of our God! When all was sin and shame, _____ A
3. O wis - est love! that ____ flesh and blood Which did in Ad - am fail, _____ Should
4. And that a high - er ____ gift than grace Should flesh and blood re - fine, _____ God's
5. O gen - 'rous love! that ____ He who smote In man for man the foe, _____ The
6. And in the gar - den ____ se - cret - ly, And on the Cross on high, _____ Should

1. all His words most
2. sec - ond Ad - am
3. strive a - fresh a -
4. Pres - ence and His
5. dou - ble ag - o -
6. teach His breth - ren

1. won - der - ful, Most sure in
2. to the fight And to the
3. gainst the foe; Should strive and
4. ver - y Self, And Es - sence
5. ny in man For man should
6. and in - spire To suf - fer

1. all His ways! _____
2. res - cue came. _____
3. should pre - vail; _____
4. all di - vine. _____
5. un - der - go ; _____
6. and to die. _____

Lord, for tomorrow and its needs
("Just for today")

Sister M. Xavier S.N.D. Nicola A. Montani

Slowly

1. Lord, for to-mor-row and its needs I do not
2. Let me be slow to do my will, Prompt to o-
3. Let me in sea-son, Lord, be grave, In sea-son,
4. In Pur-ga-to-ry's cleansing fires Brief be my

1. pray: Keep me, my God, from stain of sin,
2. bey: Help me to mor-ti-fy my flesh,
3. gay; Let me be faith-ful to Thy grace,
4. stay; Oh, bid me, if to-day I die,

1. Just for to-day. Let me both di-li-
2. Just for to-day. Let me no wrong or
3. Just for to-day. And if to-day my
4. Go home to-day. So, for to-mor-row

1. gen-tly work, And du-ly pray: Let
2. i-dle word Un-think-ing say; Set
3. tide of life Should ebb a-way, Give
4. and its needs, I do not pray; But

1. me be kind in word or deed, Just for to-day.
2. Thou a seal up-on my lips, Just for to-day.
3. me Thy Sac-ra-ments di-vine, Sweet Lord, to-day.
4. keep me, guide me, love me, Lord, Just for to-day.

144
Why art thou sorrowful?
The Remembrance of Mercy

Father Faber   S. M. Yenn

Moderato

1. Why art thou sor - row - ful, ser - vant of
2. Oh, is there a thought in the wide world so
3. Oh, then, when the spir - it of dark-ness comes
4. That God hath once whis-pered a word in thine

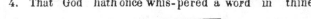

1. God? And what is this dul - ness that
2. sweet, As that God has so cared for us,
3. down With clouds and un - cer - tain - ties
4. ear, Or sent thee from Heav - en one

1. hangs o'er thee now? Sing the prais - es of
2. bad as we are, That He thinks for us,
3. in - to thy heart, One look to thy
4. sor - row for sin, Is e - nough for a

cresc

1. Je - sus, and sing them a - loud, And the
2. plans for us, stoops to en - treat, And
3. Sav - iour, one thought of thy crown, And the
4. life both to ban - ish all fear, And to

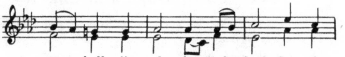

1. song   shall dis - pel   the dark cloud from thy
2. fol - lows us, wan - der we   ev - er   so
3. tem - pest is   o - ver, the   shad - ows de -
4. turn in - to peace all the   trou - bles with-

Poco piu mosso

1. brow. Sing the prais - es   of   Je - sus, and
2. far? That He thinks for us, plans for us,
3. part.   One   look   to thy Sav - iour, one
4. in.   Is e - nough for a   life both to

Meno

1. sing them a - loud, And the song shall dis -
2. stoops   to en - treat, And   fol - lows us,
3. thought of thy crown, And the tem - pest is
4. ban - ish all . fear, And to turn in - to

allargando   *rit*

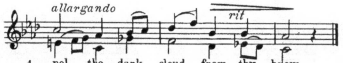

1. pel the dark cloud from thy brow.
2. wan - der we   ev - er   so   far?
3. o - ver, the shad - ows de - part.
4. peace all the trou - bles with - in.

225

145 Acts of Faith, Hope and Charity

For acts of Contrition etc. see Nos. 128, 133, and Hymns
for Holy Communion.

(A) *ACT OF FAITH*

Anon.
St. Patrick's Hymn Book

Moderato (Recitativo libero)

My God, I be-lieve in Thee, And

all Thy Church doth teach, Because Thou hast

said it And Thy word is true.

(B) *ACT OF HOPE*

My God, I hope in Thee, For

Grace and for glo - ry, Because of Thy

prom - is - es, Thy mer - cy, and Thy pow'r.

(C) *ACT OF CHARITY*

My God, because Thou art so good, I

love Thee with all my heart, And for Thy

sake, I love my neigh-bor as my - self.

What a Sea of Tears and Sorrows
O quot undis lacrymarum

Tr. by Rev. F. Campbell

Ch. Gounod
Arr. by N. A. M.

Andante religioso

1. What   a   sea   of   tears   and   sor - rows,
2. Oh,   that   mourn - ful   Vir - gin - Moth - er,
3. Oft,   and   oft   His   Arms   and   Bos - om,
4. Gen - tle   Moth - er,   we   be - seech   thee,

1. Did   the   soul   of   Ma - ry   toss
2. See   her   tears   how   fast   they   flow
3. Fond - ly   strain - ing   to   her   own ;
4. By   thy   tears   and   trou - bles   sore ;

1. To   and   fro   up - on   its   bil - lows
2. Down   up - on   His   man - gled   Bod - y
3. Oft,   her   pal - lid   lips   im - print - ing
4. By   the   death   of   thy   dear   Off - spring,

1. While she wept her bit - ter loss;
2. Wound - ed Side and thorn - y Brow;
3. On each Wound of her dear Son:
4. By the blood - y Wounds He bore;

1. In her arms her Je - sus hold - ing,
2. While His Hands and Feet she kiss - es,
3. Till at last in swoons of an - guish,
4. Touch our hearts with that true sor - row

1. Torn so new - ly from the Cross.
2. Pic - ture of im - mor - tal woe.
3. Sense and con - scious - ness are gone.
4. Which af - flict - ed thee of yore.

147

The Divine Praises

Organ sustains chords in recitations   J. Lewis Browne

Bless-ed be God! Bless-ed be His Ho-ly Name!

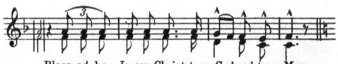

Bless-ed be Je-sus Christ, true God and true Man;

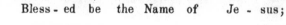

Bless - ed be the Name of Je - sus;

Bless-ed be His most Sa-cred Heart, Bless-ed be

Je - sus in the most Ho - ly Sa - cra - ment

By permission

of the Al - tar! Bless - ed be the great

Moth - er of God, Ma - ry most ho - ly!

Bless-ed be her Holy and Im - ma-cu-late Con-cep-tion;

(a) Bless- ed be the Name of Ma -ry, Vir-gin and Moth-er.
(b) Bless- ed be Saint Jo-seph her most chaste spouse.

Bless -ed be God in His an-gels, and in His Saints.

148 GENERAL
The Lord's Prayer
Our Father, Who Art in Heaven
Nicola A. Montani

Andante religioso

Our Fa-ther Who art in heav_en, hal-lowed be Thy
Name; Thy King-dom come; Thy will be done on
earth, as it is in heav-en. Give us this day our
dai - ly bread; And for-give us our tres-pass-es, as
we for-give those who tres-pass a-gainst us. And
lead us not in - to temp-ta - tion; but de -
liv - er us from e - vil. A - men.

Hail, Mary, full of Grace
The Angelical Salutation

Nicola A. Montani

Hail, Ma - ry, full of grace; the Lord is

with thee: bless-ed art thou a-mongst wom-en, and

bless - ed is the fruit of thy womb, Je - sus.

Ho-ly Ma-ry, Moth-er of God, pray for us sin-ners,

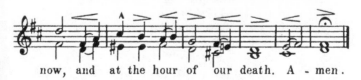

now, and at the hour of our death. A - men.

150

Lord, Who at Cana's Wedding Feast

A. Thrupp   J. Lewis Browne

Moderato

1. Lord, Who at Ca-na's wed-ding feast Didst
2. For Thou, O Christ dost ho-ly prove The
3. The ho-liest vow that man can make, The
4. Which blest by Thee, what-e'er be-tides, No
5. On those who at Thine al-tar kneel, O
6. Oh grant them here in peace to live, In

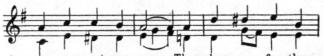

1. as a guest ap-pear, Thou, dear-er far than
2. mar-riage vow to be, Pro-claim-ing it a
3. gold-en thread in life, The bond that none may
4. e-vil shall de-stroy, Thro' care-worn days each
5. Lord, Thy bless-ing pour, That each may wake the
6. pu-ri-ty and love, And, this world leav-ing,

1. earth-ly guest, Vouchsafe Thy presence here;
2. type of love Between the Church and Thee.
3. dare to break, That bindeth man and wife;
4. care di-vides, And doubles ev-'ry joy.
5. oth-er's zeal To love Thee more and more:
6. to re-ceive A crown of life a-bove! A - men.

By permission   234

Creator Alme Siderum

D. Thermignon

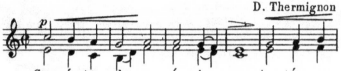

1. Cre - á - tor al - me sí - de - rum, Ae - tér - na
2. Qui dǽ-mo - nis ne fraú - di - bus Per - í - ret
3. Com - mú - ne qui mun - di ne - fas Ut ex - pi -
4. Cu - jus po - té - stas gló - ri - æ, No - mén-que
5. Te de - pre - cá - mur, úl - ti - mae Ma-gnum di -
6. Vir - tus, ho - nor, laus, gló - ri - a De - o Pa -

1. lux cre - dén - ti - um, Je - su, Re - dém-ptor ó - mni -
2. or - bis ím - pe - tu A - mó - ris a - ctus, lán - gui -
3. á - res, ad cru - cem E Vír - gi - nis sa - crá - ri -
4. cum pri -mum so - nat, Et cœ - li - tes et ín - fe -
5. é - i Jú - di - cem, Ar - mis su - pér - næ grá - ti -
6. tri cum Fí - li - o, Sán - cto si - mul Pa - rá - cli -

After last verse

1. um, In - tén - de vo - tis súp - pli - cum.
2. di Mun - di me - dé - la fa - ctus es.
3. o In - tá - cta pro - dis ví - cti - ma.
4. ri Tre - mén - te cur - ván - tur ge - nu.
5. æ De - fén - de nos ab hó - sti - bus.
6. to, In sæ - cu - ló - rum sæ - cu - la. A - men.

152
Veni, Veni Emmanuel

Ancient Chant

1. Ve-ni, ve-ni Em-mán-nu el! Cap-tí-vum sol-ve
2. Ve-ni, O Jes-se Vír-gu-la! Ex hos-tis tu-os
3. Ve-ni, ve-ni O O-ri-ens! So-lá-re nos ad-
4. Ve-ni Cla-vis Da-vi-di-ca! Re-gna, re-clu-de

1. Ís - ra-el   Qui ge-mit in e-xí - li-o
2. ún - gu-la   De spe-cu tu-os tár-ta-ri,
3. vé - ni-ens: No-ctis de-pél-le né-bu-las,
4. coe-li-ca   Fac i-ter tu-tum su-pér-num

1. Pri-vá-tus De-i Fi-li-o.
2. E-duc, et an-tro bá-rath-ri.
3. Di-rás-que no-ctis té-ne-bras.
4. Et clau-de vi-as ín-fe-rum.

1-4. Gáu-de, Gáu-de,

Em-mán-nu-el Nas-cé-tur pro te, Ís-ra-el.

236

O Emmanuel

Antiphonæ Majores

Second Mode

O Em‿má‿nu‿el, Rex et lé‿gi‿fer no‿ster,

ex ‿ spe ‿ ctá ‿ ti ‿ o gén ‿ ti ‿ um, _____

Et Sal ‿ vá ‿ tor e ‿ á ‿ rum: ve ‿ ni

rall

Ad Sal ‿ ván ‿ dum nos. Do ‿ mi ‿ ne De ‿ us no ‿ ster.

154 En Clara Vox Redarguit

First Mode   Antiphoale (Vatican Edition)

1. En clá - ra vox re - dár - gu - it
2. Mens jam re - súr - gat tór - pi - da,
3. En A - gnus ad nos mít - ti - tur
4. Ut cum se - cún - do fúl - se - rit,
5. Vir - tus, ho - nor, laus, glo - ri - a

1. Ob - scú - ra quae - que pér - so - nans:
2. Non ám - pli - us ja - cens hu - mi:
3. Lax - á - re gra - tis dé - bi - tum:
4. Me - tú - que mun - dum cín - xe - rit,
5. De - o Pa - tri cum Fi - li - o,

1. Pro - cul fu - gén - tur só - mni - a,
2. Si - dus re - fúl - get jam no - vum,
3. O - mnes si - mul cum lá - cri - mis
4. Non pro re - á - tu pú - ni - at,
5. San - cto si - mul Pa - rá - cli - to,

rall   *After last verse*

1. Ab al - to Je - sus pró - mi - eat.
2. Ut tol - lat o - mne nóx - i - um.
3. Pre - cé - mur in - dul - gén - ti - am.
4. Sed nos pi - us tunc pró - te - gat.
5. In sæ - cu - ló - rum sæ - cu - la.   A - men.

Jesu Redemptor Omnium

Vatican Antiphonale

1. Je-su Red-ém-ptor ó - mni - um, Quem lu-cis
2. Tu lu - men et splen-dor Pa - tris, Tu spes per-
3. Me-mén-to re - rum Cón- di - tor, No-stri quod
4. Te-stá- tur hoc præ-sens di - es, Cur-rens per
5. Hunc a - stra, tel - lus, áé - quo - ra, Hunc o - mne
6. Et nos, be - á - ta quos sa -cri Ri - gá - vit
7. Je-su, ti - bi sit gló - ri - a, Qui na - tus

1. an-te o - rí - gi - nem, Pa-rem pa-tér-nae gló-
2. én - nis ó - mni - um: In-tén- de quas fun-dunt
3. o - lim cór - po - ris, Sa-cráta ab al-vo Vír-
4. an - ni cír - cu - lum, Quod so - lus e si - nu
5. quod cœ - lo sub-est, Sa - lú - tis au-ctó-rem
6. un - da sán - gui-nis, Na - tá - lis ob di - em
7. es de Vír - gi - ne, Cum Pa-tre et al -mo Spi-

rall

1. ri - æ, Pa-ter su-pré-mis é - di-dit. *After last*
2. preces Tu- i per or - bem sér-vu-li. *verse*
3. gi-nis Nascén-do, for-mam súmpse-ris.
4. Pa-tris Mun-di sa-lus ad vé - ne-ris.
5. no-væ No-vo sa-lú - tat cán-ti - co.
6. tu- i, Hymni tri-bú-tum sól-vi-mus.
7. ri - tu, In sem-pi-tér-na sáe-cu- la. A - men.

155 b
Jesu Redemptor Omnium

Alternate setting by Taler
Dominican Monk
(May be sung in alter-
nate fashion with 155a)
Monastery of Strasbourg 1361
Arr. by N. A. M.

1. Je - su   Red - ém - ptor   ó - mni -
2. Tu   lu - men   et splen - dor   Pa -

um, Quem lu - cis an - te o - rí - gi - nem,
tris, Tu spes per - én - nis ó - mni - um:

Pa - rem pa - tér - nae   gló - ri - æ,
In - tén - de   quas   fun - dunt pre - ces

Pa - ter su - pré - mis é - di - dit.
Tu - i   per or - bem sér - vu - li.

A - men.

Resonet in Laudibus

Christmas Song of the XIV Century

1. Ré - so - net in láu - di - bus Cum ju - cún - dus
2. Si - on lau - da Dó - mi - num Sal - va - tó - rem
3. Pú - e - ri con - cúr - ri - te Na - to Re - gi
4. Na - tus est Em - má - nu - el Quem prae - dí - xit
5. Ju - da cum can - tó - ri - bus Grá - de - re de
6. Qui ré - gnat in aé - the - re, Ve - nit o - vem

1. pláu - si - bus, Si - on cum fi - dé - li - bus.
2. ó - mni - um Vir - go pa - rit Fí - li - um.
3. psál - li - te Vo - ce pi - a dí - ci - te.
4. Gá - bri - el Tes - tis est E - zé - chi - el.
5. fó - ri - bus Et dic cum pa - stó - ri - bus.
6. quaé - re - re, No - lens e - am pér - de - re.

1-6. Ap - pá - ru - it quem gé - nu - it Ma - rí - a.

Gau - dé - te, gau - dé - te, Chrístus ná - tus hó - di - e!

Gau - dé - te, gau - dé - te, ex Ma - rí - a Vír - gi - ne.

157
Ecce Nomen Domini Emmanuel

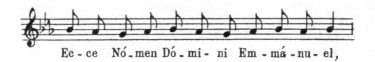

Ec - ce Nó - men Dó - mi - ni Em - má - nu - el,

Quod an-nun -ti - á -tum est per Gá - bri - el,

ho - di - e ap-pá - ru - it in Is - ra - el:

per Ma - rí - am Vír - gi - nem est na - tus Rex.

E - ia! Vir - go Dé - um gé - nu - it,

ut di-ví-na vó-lu-it cle-mén-ti-a.

In Béth - le - hem na - tus est,

Et in Jé-ru-sa-lem ví-sus est,

ét in ó-mnem ter-ram ho-no-

ri-fi-cá-tus est, Rex Is-ra-el!

158

Adeste Fideles

Andante   Traditional Melody

2 -(Optional)—

1. Ad - é - ste, fi - dé - les, lae - ti tri - um -
2. En gre - ge re - lí - cto, hu - mi - les ad
3. Ae - tér - ni Pa - rén - tis splen - dó - rem ae -
4. Pro no - bis e - gé - num et foe - no cu -

De - um, de De, - o, lu, - men de

3 -(Optional)— Cán - tet nunc I - o Cho - rus an - ge -

1. phán - tes; Ve - ní - te, ve - ní - te in
2. cu - nas Vo - ca - ti pa - stó - res ap -
3. tér - num Ve - lá - tum sub car - ne vi -
4. bán - tem Pi-is fo - ve - á - mus am -

(2) lu-mi - ne, Ges, - tant pu - él, - lae

(3) lo - rum, Cán - tet nunc au - la coe -

mf 2d time f

1. Béth - le - hem: Na - tum vi - dé - te
2. pró - pe - rant: Et nos o - ván - ti
3. dé - bi - mus: De - um in - fán - tem,
4. plé - xi - bus: Sic nos a - mán - tem

(2) vi - sce - ra. De - um ve - rum

(3) le - sti - um. Gló - ri - a, gló - ri - a

244

159   **Puer Nobis Nascitur**

David Scheidemann
1570-1625

Moderato

1. Pú - er nó - bis ná - sci - tur Re - ctor
2. In prae - sé - pe pó - ni - tur sub foe - no
3. Hinc He - ró - des tí - mu - it Ma - gna
4. Qui na - tus ex Ma - ri - a Di - e
5. Án - ge - li lae - tá - ti sunt Ét - i -
6. Nos de ta - li gáu - di - o Con - ci -
7. Laus et ju - bi - lá - ti - o No - stro

1. an - ge - ló - rum In hoc mun - do
2. ju - men - tó - rum Co - gnó - vit bos et
3. cum tre - mó - re In - fán - tes et
4. ho - di - ér - na Per - dú - cat nos cum
5. am de De - o Can - ta - vé - runt:
6. ná - mus cho - ro, In chor - dis et
7. sit in o - re, Et sem - per an -

1. pá - sci - tur Dó - mi - nus Do - mi - nó - rum.
2. á - si - nus Chri - stum re - gem coe - ló - rum.
3. pú - e - ros Oc - ci - det prae do - ló - re.
4. grá - ti - a Ad gáu - di - a su - pér - na.
5. gló - ri - a Sit in ex - cél - sis De - o.
6. ór - ga - no Be - ne - di - cá - mus Dó - mi - no.
7. gé - li - cas De - o di - cá - mus grá - ti - as.

Tollite Hostias

Motet for two-or four-part chorus

C. St. Saens
Arr. by N.A.M.

1. Tol-li - te ho-sti-as, et in-tro-í - te
2. Ád - o - ra - te, ad - o - ra - te

in a-tri-a e - jus.
Do-mi-num in a-tri-o San-cto e - jus.

3. 4. 6. Lae - tén-tur cóe-li et éx-súl-tet ter-ra

An-te fá - ci-em Dó-mi-ni quó-ni-am ve - nit.

Fine

nit. 5.Al - le - lú - ia, al - le -lú - ia, al - le-lú -
al - le-lú - ia,

ia, al-le-lú-ia, al-le-lú - ia, al-le-lú - ia, al-le-lú -

ia, al - le -lú - ia, al - le - lú - ia

247

Repeat from 𝄋 to 𝄐
Fine

161 a THE HOLY NAME
Jesu Dulcis Memoria
Motet for four part chorus
St. Bernard

T. L. da Vittoria
Arr. by N. A. M.

Je-su dul-cis me-mó-ri-a, Dans ve-ra,

ve-ra cor-dis gaú-di-a, gaú-

-di-a,— Sed su-per mel et o-

-mni-a, su-per mel et ó-mni-a e-

jus dul-cis prae-sen-ti-a,

-jus dul-cis prae-sén-ti-a, dulcis praesen-ti-a.

Jesu Dulcis Memoria 161 b

For unison or two part chorus

Cornelius Schmuck
(abridged)

Moderato
p

1. Je - su dul-cis me - mó - ri - a,
2. Nil cá-ni - tur su - á - vi - us,
3. Je - su, spes pæ - ni - tén - ti - bus,
4. Nec lin-gua va - let dí - ce - re,
5. Sis Je-su, no - strum gáu - di - um,

1. Dans ve - ra cor - dis gaú - di - a:
2. Nil aú - di - tur ju - cun - di - us,
3. Quam pi - us es pe - tén - ti - bus!
4. Nec lít - te - ra ex - prí - me - re,
5. Qui es fu - tú - rus præ - mi - um:

1. Sed su - per mel et o - mni - a,
2. Nil co - gi - tá - tur dul - ci - us,
3. Quam bo - nus te quæ - rén - ti - bus!
4. Ex - pér - tus po - test cré - de - re,
5. Sit no - stra in te gló - ri - a,

After last
verse

1. E - jus dul-cis præ-sen - ti - a.
2. Quam Je-sus De - i Fi - li - us.
3. Sed quid in - ve - ni - én - ti bus.
4. Quid sit Je-sum di - lí - ge - re.
5. Per cun-cta sem - per sǽ - cu - la. A - men.

161 c   Jesu Dulcis Memoria

Vatican Antiphonale

1. Je - su dul - cis me - mó - ri - a,
2. Nil cá - ni - tur su - á - vi - us,
3. Je - su, spes pæ - ni - tén - ti - bus,
4. Nec lin - gua va - let dí - ce - re,
5. Sis Je - su, no - strum gáu - di - um,

1. Dans ve - ra cor - dis gáu - di - a:
2. Nil aú - di - tur ju - cún - di - us,
3. Quam pi - us es pe - tén - ti - bus!
4. Nec lít - te - ra ex - prí - me - re:
5. Qui es fú - tu - rus præ - mi - um:

1. Sed su - per mel et ó - mni - a,
2. Nil co - gi - tá - tur dúl - ci - us,
3. Quam bo - nus te quæ - rén - ti - bus!
4. Ex - pér - tus po - test cré - de - re,
5. Sit no - stra in te gló - ri - a,

1. E - jus dul - cis præ - sén - ti - a. *After last*
2. Quam Je - sus De - i Fi - li - us. *verse*
3. Sed quid in - ve - ni - én - ti - bus.
4. Quid sit Je - sum di - lí - ge - re.
5. Per cun - cta sem - per sæ - cu - la. A - men.

Stabat Mater (1)
Sequentia

Jacopone da Todi (d. 1306)   Traditional Melody from the
Maintzesch Gesangbuch (1661)

1. Sta - bat Ma - ter do - lo - ró - sa
2. Cu - jus á - ni - mam ge - mén - tem,
3. O quam tri - stis et af - fli - cta
4. Quæ moe - ré - bat et do - le - bat,
5. Quis est ho - mo, qui non fle - ret,
6. Quis non pos - set con - tri - stá - ri,
7. Pro pec - cá - tis su - æ gen - tis
8. Vi - dit su - um dul - cem Na - tum

1. Ju - xta cru - cem la - cry - mó - sa,
2. Con - tri - stá - tam et do - lén - tem,
3. Fu - it il - la be - ne - dí - cta
4. Pi - a Ma - ter, dum vi - dé - bat
5. Ma - trem Chri - sti si vi - de - ret
6. Chri - sti Ma - trem con - tem - plá - ri
7. Vi - dit. Je - sum in tor - mén - tis,
8. Mo - ri - én - do de - so - lá - tum,

1. Dum pen - dé - bat Fí - li - us.   *After last*
2. Per - tran - sí - vit glá - di - us.   *verse*
3. Ma - ter U - ni - gé - ni - ti!
4. Na - ti poe - nas in - cly - ti.
5. In tan - to sup - plí - ci - o?
6. Do - lén - tem cum Fí - li - o?
7. Et fla - gél - lis súb - di - tum.
8. Dum e - mí - sit spí - ri - tum.   A - men.

9. Eia Mater, fons amóris,
Me sentíre vim dolóris
    Fac, ut tecum lúgeam.

10. Fac ut árdeat cor meum
In amándo Christum Deum,
    Ut sibi compláceam.

11. Sancta Mater, istud agas,
Crucifíxi fige plagas
    Cordi meo válide.

12. Tui nati vulneráti,
Tam dignáti pro me pati,
    Pœnas mecum dívide.

13. Fac me tecum pie flere,
Crucifíxo condolére,
    Donec ego víxero.

14. Juxta crucem tecum stare,
Et me tibi sociáre
    In planctu desídero.

15. Virgo vírginum præclára,
Mihi jam non sis amára:
    Fac me tecum plángere;

16. Fac ut portem Christi mortem,
Passiónis fac consórtem,
    Et plagas recólere.

17. Fac me plagis vulnerári,
Fac me cruce inebriári,
    Et cruóre Fílii;

18. Flammis ne urar succénsus,
Per te Virgo, sim defénsus
    In die judícii.

19. Christe, cum sit hinc exíre,
Da per Matrem me veníre
    Ad palmam victóriæ;

20. Quando corpus moriétur,
Fac ut ánimæ donétur
Paradísi glória. Amen.

Stabat Mater (2)   162 b

G. M. Nanini (1540-1607)
Arr. by N. A. M.

Sta - bat Ma-ter do-lo - ró-sa ʼJu-xta cru - cem

la-cri -mó - sa, Dum pendé - bat Fi - li - us .

Stabat Mater (3)   162 c

Giuseppe Tartini (1692-1770)

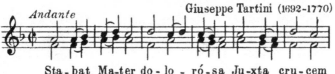

Sta - bat Ma-ter do - lo - ró-sa Ju-xta cru - cem

la - cri - mó-sa, Dum pen-dé - bat Fi - li - us .

163 PALM SUNDAY MUSIC
by Franz Schubert
Edited and revised by N. A. Montani

After the sprinkling of Holy Water, the Palms are blessed
and the Choir sings the following Antiphon:

Hosanna Filio David

Ho - san - na Fi - li - o Da - vid: be - ne -

di - - - ctus qui ve - nit in

no - mi - ne Do - mi - ni. Rex Is - ra -

el: Ho - san - na in ex - cel - sis.

In Monte Oliveti 164

After the singing of the Lesson the following Responsory is sung:

Adagio

1 In mon-te O-li-ve-ti o-ra-vit ad
2 Vi-gi-la-te, et o-ra-te, o-

Pa-trem: Pa-ter, si fi-e-ri pot-est, trans
ra-te, ut non in-tre-tis, in-tre-tis in

- e-at a me ca-lix i - ste.
ten-ta-ti-o - nem.

Piu Vivo

Spi-ri-tus qui-dem prom-ptus est, ca-ro au-tem in-

fir-ma: fi-at vo-lun-tas tu - - a.

After the Preface (with responses in ferial form, as at Requiems see No. 259 (8)) the choir sings the *Sanctus* and *Benedictus*.

165 Sanctus and Benedictus

Fr. Schubert

Adagio

San - ctus, San - - ctus, San - ctus

Do - mi - nus De - us Sa - ba - oth.

Allegro Moderato

Ple - ni sunt cœ - li et ter - ra glo - ri - a

tu - a. Ho - san - na in ex - cel - sis.

Slower

Be - ne - di - ctus qui ve - nit in no - mi - ne

Faster

Do - mi - ni. Ho - san - na in ex - cel - sis.

Pueri Hebraeorum 166

After a number of prayers and responses, at the distribution of Palms, the choir sings the following Antiphon.

Fr. Schubert

Pu - e - ri He - brae - o - rum, por - tan - tes ra - mos

o - li - va - rum, ob - vi - a - ve - runt

Do - mi - no, cla - man - tes, et di - cen -

tes: Ho - san - na in ex - cel - sis.

167   Cum Angelis et Pueris

Just before the Procession takes place the Deacon sings;
"Procedamus in pace" the choir answers: "In nomine Christi.
Amen." The following is then sung:

Fr. Schubert

When the procession has reached the portal of the Church
two or four chanters enter and, facing the door begin the
"Gloria Laus"; the clergy and singers outside repeat the
verse. Chanters sing each new stanza while the singers
outside repeat the "Gloria Laus". At the end of the last
stanza the procession enters the church the music be-
ing changed to "Ingrediente".

258

Gloria, Laus et Honor 168

O. Ravanello
(abridged)

Moderato

1. Glo-ri-a, laus, et ho-nor, ti-bi sit Rex Chri-

2. Is - - ra-el es tu Rex, Da - vi - dis et
3. Coe - tus in ex-cel-sis te lau - dat
4. Plebs He-bræ-a ti-bi cum pal - mis
5. Hi ti-bi˚pas-sú-ro sol - ve - bant
6. Hi pla-cu-e-re ti-bi, pla - ce - at de-

1. ste Re - dem - ptor: Cui pu-e - ri - le de-

2. in-cly-ta pro-les: No-mi-ne qui in Do-mi-
3. Cóe-li-cus o-mnis Et mor - ta-lis ho-
4. ób-vi-a ve-nit: Cum pre-ce, vo-to, hy-
5. mú-ni-a lau-dis: Nos ti-bi re - gnán-
6. vo-ti-o no-stra; Rex bo-ne, Rex cle-

1. cus prom-psit Ho-san - na pi - um.

2. ni, Rex be-ne-di - cte, ve - nis.
3. mo, et cun-cta cre - a-ta si - mul.
4. mnis, ad - - - su-mus ec-ce ti - bi.
5. ti, pan - - gi-mus ec-ce me - los.
6. mens, cui bo-na cun - cta pla - cent.

Ingrediente

Andante

Fr. Schubert

1. In - gre - di - en - te Do - mi - no in
2. Cum - que au - dis - set po - po - lus quod

san - ctam ci - vi - ta - tem, He - bræ - o - rum
Je - sus ve - ni - ret, Je - ro -

pu - e - ri, re - sur - rec - ti - o - nem
so - ly - mam, ex - i - e - runt

vi - tae pro - nun - ti - an - tes. 1-2. Cum
ob - vi - am e - i.

ra - mis pal - marum Ho-sanna cla-mabunt in ex-cel - sis.

In Monte Oliveti

For two or four part chorus

Michael Haydn (1778)
Edited and revised by N.A.M.

In mon-te O-li-ve-ti o-ra-vit ad

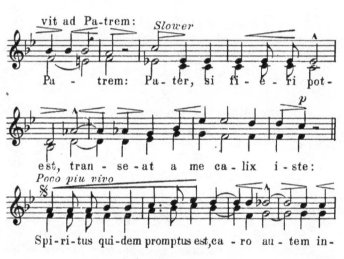

vit ad Pa-trem:

Pa - trem: Pa-ter, si fi-e-ri pot-

est, tran - se-at a me ca-lix i-ste:

Spi-ri-tus qui-dem promptus est, ca - ro au-tem in-

fir - ma: fi-at vo-lun-tas tu - a.

(over)

cresc. molto accel

allarg.

Vi - gi - la - te, et o - ra - te, ut

Repeat from 𝄋 to Fine

non in - tre - tis in ten - ta - ti - o - nem.

171 Tristis est anima mea

M. Haydn
Revised by N. A.M.

Largo con espressione

Tri - stis est a - ni - ma me - a us - que ad

mor - tem; sus - ti - ne - te hic, et vi - gi - la - te

me - cum; nunc vi - de - bi - tis tur - bam, quae

cir - cum - da - bit me. Vos fu - gam ca - pi -

et - tis, et e - go va - dam im - mo - la - ri pro

vo - bis: Ec - ce ap - pro - pin - quat

ho - ra, et Fi - li - us ho - mi - nis tra -

de - tur in ma - nus pec - ca - to - rum.

172

Una hora non potuistis vigilare

M. Haydn
Revised by N. A. M.

U - na ho - ra non pot - u - i - stis

vi-gi-la-re me-cum, qui ex-hor-ta-ba-mi-ni mo-ri pro me? Vel Ju-dam non vi-de-tis, quo mo-do non dor-mit, sed fe-sti-nat tra-de-re me Ju-dae - is? Quid dor-mi-tis? Sur-gi-te, et o-ra-te, ne in-tre-tis in ten-ta-ti-o-nem.

Tanquam ad latronem existis

M. Haydn
Arr. by N. A. M.

Tan-quam ad la - tro - nem ex - i - stis cum

gla - di - is et fu - sti-bus com-pre-hen-de - re me:

Quo - ti - di - e a - pud vos e - ram in tem-plo do -

cens, et non me te - nu - i - stis, et ec-ce flagel-la-tum

du - ci-tis ad cru - ci - fi - gen — — dum.

Cum-que in-je-cis-sent ma-nus in Je-sum,

et te-nu-is-sent e-um, di-xit ad e-os.

174
Velum templi scissum est

M. Haydn
Edited by N. A. M.

Ve-lum tem-pli scis-sum est, Et o-mnis

ter-ra tre-mu-it; la-tro de cru-ce cla-

ma - bat, di - cens: **pp** *Largo con espressione*

cla - ma - bat, di - cens: Me - men - to me - i,

rall. *Fine*

Do - mi - ne, dum ve - ne - ris in re - gnum tu - um.

Piu Vivo

Pe - trae scis - sae sunt, et mo - nu - men - ta a -

per - ta sunt, et mul - ta cor - po - ra san -

allarg. *Repeat from ℅ to Fine*

cto - rum, qui dor - mi - e - rant, sur - re - xe - runt.

175
Tenebrae factae sunt

Michael Haydn
Edited by N. A.M.

Te -ne-brae fa -ctæ sunt,dum cru-ci-fix - is - sent

Je-sum Ju - dae - i, et cir -ca ho - ram

no - nam, ex-cla-ma-vit Je-sus vo - ce

ma-gna: De - us me - us, ut quid me

de - re-li - qui - sti? Et in - cli-

na - to ca - pi - te, (*Piu lento*)

na - to ca - pi - te, e -

Fine

e - mi - sit spi - ri - tum.

mi - sit spi - ri-tum, spi - ri - tum.

Piu Vivo

ff

a -

Ex - cla - mans Je - sus vo - ce ma - gna a -

Largo

it: Pa - ter, in ma - nus tu - as

pp

- it: Pa - ter, in ma - nus

Repeat from ℈ to Fine

commendo spi - ri-tum me - um.

p

tu - as com-men-do spi - ri-tum me - um.

269

176
Ecce, Quomodo moritur justus

Michael Haydn
Edited and revised by N. A. M.

Ec - ce, quo-mo-do mo-ri-tur ju-stus, et
ne-mo per-ci-pit cor-de; et vi - ri ju-sti tol-
lun_tur, et ne_mo con-si - de - rat. A
fa-ci_e i-ni-qui-ta-tis sub-la-tus est ju -
atus: Et e - rit in pa-ce me - mo-ri -

a e - - - jus. Tanquam a _ gnus

co-ram ton-den_te se ob-mu-tu-it, et non a-

pe-ru-it os su-um; de an-gu-sti-a, et

de ju-di-ci-o sub-la-tus est. Et e-rit in

pa-ce me-mo-ri-a e - - - jus.

177
Unus ex discipulis meis

Michael Haydn
Revised by N. A. M.

U - nus ex dis - ci - pu -lis me -is tra-det me

ho - di - e: Vae il - li per quem tra-dar

e - go; Me - li -us il - li e - rat, si

na -tus non fu - is -set. Qui in - tin -git

me - cum ma - num in pa - rop - si - de, hic me

tra - di - tu - rus est in ma - nus pec - ca - to -

rum. Me - li - us il - us il - li e - rat, si

Repeat from beginning to 𝄋 then skip to ⊕

na - tus non fu - is - set. Me - li - us il - li

e - rat si na - tus non fu - is - - set.

178 Recessit Pastor noster

Michael Haydn
Edited by N. A.M.

Re-ces-sit pa-stor no-ster,fons a-quae vi-vae,

ad cu-jus tran-si-tum sol ob-scu-ra-tus est;

Nam et il-le cap-tus est, qui cap-ti-vum te-

ne-bat pri-mum ho-mi-nem: ho-di-e por-tas

mor-tis et se-ras pa-ri-ter Sal-va-tor no-ster

dis-ru-pit. De-struxit qui-dem claustra in-fer-ni,

et sub-ver-tit po-ten-ti-as di-a-bo-li.

274

Omnes amici mei dereliquerunt me

Michael Haydn
Edited by N. A. Montani

180 Ecce vidimus eum

Michael Haydn
Arr. by N. A. M.

Ec _ ce vi - di - mus e - um non ha - ben - tem spe - ci - em, ne - que de - co - rem: a - spe - ctus e - jus in e - o non est: hic pec - ca - ta no - stra por - ta - vit, et pro no - bis do - let; ip - se au - tem vul - ne - ra - tus est

276

rall (2d time to 𝄋) *Piu Vivo*

pro-pter i-ni-qui-ta-tes no - stras, Cu-jus li-

vo - re sa-na-ti su-mus. Ve - re lan-

guo-res no-stros i-pse tu-lit, et do-lo-res

no-stros i-pse por-ta - vit. Cu-jus li-

𝄋 *Lento*

vo - re sa-na-ti su-mus.★ Cu-jus le-

★ *Repeat from beginning to "nostras"* 𝄋
then skip to corresponding sign 𝄋

vo - re sa-na-ti su - - mus.

181

Caligaverunt oculi mei

Michael Haydn
Edited and revised by N. A.M.

Ca - li -ga - ve - runt o - cu - li me - i a

fle - - tu me - o; qui- a e - lon-

ga -tus est a me, qui con-so -la-ba - tur

me. Vi - de -te o -mnes po - pu - li: Si est

do - lor   si - mi - lis sic - ut   do - lor

me -   - us.   O vos   o - mnes,

qui tran-si-tis per vi - am,   at - ten - di - te

et vi - de - te!   si est do - lor   si - mi -

lis sic - ut   do - lor me -   - us.

182 a

Vexilla Regis Prodeunt (1)

Vatican Graduale

1. Vex-íl - la Re - gís pród-e - unt: Fúl-get Cru-
2. Quo vul-ne - rá - tus ín - su-per Mu-cró- ne
3. Im-plé-ta sunt quae cón-ci - nit, Da -vid fi -
4. Ar-bor de-có - rá et fúl-gi-da, Or - ná - ta
5. Be - á - ta, cu - jus brá-chi- is, Sæ-cli pe-
6. O Crux, a -ve, spes ú - ni - ca; Hoc Pas- si -
7. Te sum-ma De - us Trí - ni-tas, Col -láu-det

1. cis my-sté-ri - um, Quo car-ne car-nis Cón-di-
2. di - ro lán-ce - æ, Ut nos la-vá-ret crí - mi-
3. dé - li cár-mi - ne; Di-cens:in na-ti - ó - ni -
4. Re-gis púr-pu - ra, E - lé-cta di-gno stí - pi -
5. pén-dit pré-ti - um; Sta-té-ra fa-cta cór-po -
6. ó-nis tem-po - re, Au-ge pi-is ju-stí - ti -
7. o-mnis spí - ri-tus, Quos per Cru-cis mysté - ri -

1. tor Sus-pén _ sus est pa-tí-bu - lo . *After last*
2. ne, Ma - ná - vit, un-dá et san-gui-ne. *stanza*
3. bus' Re - gná - vit a li - gno De - us.
4. te, Tam san - cta membra tán-ge-re.
5. ris Præ-dám-que tu-lit tár-ta-ri.
6. am, Re - ís - que do-na vé-ni-am.
7. um, Sal - vas, re-ge per sáe-cu-la. A - men.

280

Vexilla Regis Prodeunt (2)

The entire hymn may be sung to the melody given at 182 a
r if preferred may be sung alternately with this melody (182 b)

N. A. Montani

1. Vex - íl - la   Re - gis   pród - e   - unt:
2. Quo vul - ne - rá - tus   ín - su - per

Fúl - get   cru - cis   my - sté - ri - um,
Mu - cró - ne   di - ro   lán - ce - æ,

Quo car - ne   car - nis   Cón - di - tor
Ut   nos la - vá - ret   crí - mi - ne,

Sus - pén - sus   est   pa - ti - bu - lo.
Ma - ná - vit   un - da et   san - gui - ne.

182 c
Vexilla Regis Prodeunt (3)

Traditional Melody (1699)

Andante (♩ = 92)

1. Ve - xil - la Re - gis pród - e - unt: Fúl - get cru -
2. Quo vul - ne - rá - tus ín - su - per Mu - cró - ne
3. Im - plé - ta sunt quæ cón - ci - nit, Da - vid fi -
4. Ar - bor de - có - ra et fúl - gi - da, Or - ná - ta
5. Be - á - ta, cu - jus brá - chi - is, Sæ - cli pe -
6. O Crux, a - ve, spes ú - ni - ca; Hoc Pas - si -
7. Te sum - ma De - us Trí - ni - tas, Col - láu - det

1. cis my - sté - ri - um, Quo car - ne car - nis Cón - di -
2. di - ro lán - ce - æ, Ut nos la - vá - ret crí - mi -
3. dé - li cár - mi - ne; Di - cens: in na - ti - ó - ni -
4. Re - gis púr - pu - ra, E - lé - cta di - gno stí - pi -
5. pén - dit pré - ti - um; Sta - té - ra fa - cta cór - po -
6. ó - nis tem - po - re, Au - ge pi - is jus - ti - ti -
7. ó - mnis spí - ri - tus, Quos per Cru - cis my - sté - ri -

1. tor Sus - pén - sus est pa - tí - bu - lo.
2. ne, Ma - ná - vit un - da et sán - gui - ne.
3. bus Re - gná - vit a li - gno De - us.
4. te, Tam san - cta membra tán - ge - re.
5. ris Prae - dám - que tu - lit tár - ta - ri.
6. am, Re - ís - que do - na vé - ni - am.
7. um, Sal - vas, re - ge per sæe - cu - la. A - men.

Music for the Three Hours' Agony

Note: These short pieces may be sung before the principal discourse on each word and a Haydn Passion Motet or an appropriate Lenten Hymn, either in English or Latin may be given at the close

First Word: "Pater, dimitte illis"

Ch. Gounod
Abridged and revised by N.A.M.

Pa-ter, di-mit-te il - - - lis,

non e-nim sci-unt, quid fa-ci-unt,

non e-nim sci-unt quid fa-ci-unt.

Second Word: 184
"Amen dico tibi, hodie mecum eris in Paradiso"

Ch. Gounod

A - - - men di - co ti - bi,

Ho - di - e, Ho - di - e me - cum e - ris

in Pa - ra - di - - - so.

185

Third Word:
"Mulier, ecce filius tuus! Ecce mater tua!"

Ch. Gounod

Mu - - li - er, Mu -
(Bass)
Mu - - li - er, Mu - -

- li - er, ec - ce fi - li - us

Ec - ce ma - ter
tu - - us. Ec - ce

tu - a, Ec - ce ma - ter,

ma - ter tu - a, Ec - ce ma - ter,

ma - ter tu - a.

rall

ma - ter tu - a.

Fourth Word: 186

"Deus meus, ut quid dereliquisti me?"

Lento con espressione   Ch. Gounod

De - us me-us, De - us me -us,

Ut quid de - re - li - qui - sti me?

ut quid de - re-li - qui - sti me?

187

Fifth Word: "Sitio"

Th. Dubois
Revised and adapted by N.A.M.

Adagio (unison or Solo)

Si - ti - o,____ Si - ti -

o,____ Si - ti - o,____

Si - - ti - o. ____

188

Sixth Word: "Consummatum est"

Th. Dubois
Adapted by N.A.M.

Andante

"Con - sum - ma - tum est" (Et in - cli -

na - to ca - pi - te,   tra - di - dit

spi - ri - tum). "Con - sum - ma - tum est."

189

Seventh Word: "Pater, in manus tuas"

Th. Dubois
(adapted)

Pa-ter, in ma-nus tu - as com - men - do spi-ri-tum

me - um,   Pa - ter in   ma - nus tu - as com -

men - do spi - ri - tum   me - - um.

190 a   Adoramus te Christe (1)

Th. Dubois

Adóramus te (2)
Motet for four-part Chorus

G. P. da Palestrina
Edited by N. A. M.

Ad - o - ra - mus te Chri - ste: et

be - ne - di - ci - mus ti - bi; qui - a per

san - ctam cru - cem tu - am red - e - mi - sti mun -

dum; qui pas - sus es pro no - bis; Do - mi -

ne, Do - mi - ne, mi - se - re - re no - bis.

ANTIPHON FOR GOOD FRIDAY
Ecce lignum Crucis
At the uncovering of the Cross

Celebrant — From the Vatican Graduale

Ec - ce li - gnum Crú - cis,

in quo sá - lus mún - di

Chorus

pe - pen - dit. Ve - ni -

te ad - o - re - mus.

Sung three times, in successively higher keys.

The following *Improperia* is sung during the adoration of the
cross
Popule meus

Vittoria
Full text added by N.A.M.

Adagio
pp

1. Po - pu - le me - us, quid fe - ci
2. Qui - a e - du - xi te de ter - ra Ae -

ti - bi? aut in quo con-tri-sta-vi te? re-
gy - pti: pa-ra-sti cru-cem Sal-va-to-ri

spon-de mi - hi. 3. A - gi-os o Thé-os.
tu - - - o.

4. San - ctus De - us. 5. A - gi-os i - schy - ros.

6. San - ctus for - tis. 7. A - gi - os a -

tha - na - tos, e - lé - i - son i - mas.

8. San - ctus im - mor - tá - - lis,

- se - ré - re no - - - bis.
mi - se - ré - re no - bis.

291

193   Christus factus est

Pietro A. Yon
(written expressly for the St. Gregory Hymnal)

Chrí - stus fá - ctus est pro no - bis o -

-- bé - di - ens

bé - di - ens us - que ad mor - tem,

(1ª nocte)
o - bé - di - ens usque ad mor - tem.
(2ª nocte additur)
mór - tem au - tem cru - - cis.

(Tertia nocte additur)
ex - al - ta - vit
Pro-pter quod et De - us, ex - al - tá - vit

il - lum,
il - lum, et de-dit il - li no - men,

allarg.
quod est su-per o - mne no - - men

After the blessing of the Font the following order is observed: (A) The Litany of the Saints is sung. (B) The
Kyrie follows (Chant or figured music without organ) then
the "Gloria" is intoned (C) the choir beginning with "Et in
terra pax" (with organ accompaniment).   The Epistle is
sung after which the "Alleluia" (D) is intoned.   This is
sung three times in successively higher keys by the celebrant, unaccompanied, and each time is repeated by the
choir in the same key as taken by the celebrant (with accompaniment, if preferred).

Al - le - - lú - ia .

Con - fi - té - mi - ni Do - mi - no, quó - ni - am bo - nus :

quó - ni - am in saé - cu - lum mi - se - ri - cór - di - a   e - jus.

Lau - dá - te Dó - mi - num   ó - mnes gen - tes :

293

ét col-lau-dá-te e-um ó-mnes po-pu-li.

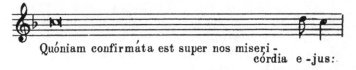

Quóniam confirmáta est super nos miseri -
córdia e -jus:

Et véritas Dómini manet in æ - tér-num.

The *Gospel response* is then sung; see No. 259 (4) *Cre-do* and *Offertory* are omitted.

Ⓖ *Preface* follows with usual responses (see 259-5) after which the *Sanctus* and *Benedictus* are sung. The "Agnus Dei" is not sung, but after the Communion the choir proceeds with the following Antiphon and Psalm.

Ⓗ Sixth Tone

Al - le - lú - ia, Al - le - lú - ia, Al - le - lú - ia.

1. Lau - dá - te Dó - mi - num ó - mnes gen-tes ;

1. lau - dá - te e - um ó - mnes pó - pu - li.

2. Quóniam confirmáta est super nos
misericórdi - a e - jus:
3. Glória Pátri et Fí-li-o ;
4. Sicut erat in princípio, et nunc et sem - per;

2. et véritas Dómini manet in ae - tér-num.
3. et Spirí - - - - tu - i San-cto.
4. et in saécula saecu - - - ló-rum. A - men.

Alleluia (H) is repeated; then choir proceeds immediately
with the Antiphon "Vespere." (I)

Ⓘ Cel. Choir

Vé-spe-re au - tem sáb - ba-ti * quae lu-cé-scit

in pri-ma-sab-ba-ti, Vé-nit Ma-rí-a

Mag-da-lé-ne, et ál-te-ra Ma-rí-a,

vi-dé-re se-púl-crum, al-le-lú-ia.

(or 276-f)

To Magnificat No. 216. After the Magnificat the Antiphon "Vespere" (I) is repeated, the celebrant then sings "Dominus Vobiscum" with proper choir response, then after a short oration and another "Dominus" the deacon sings the Paschal "Ite Missa Est" (J) the choir responding in the manner indicated. (K)

I-te missa est, al-le-lú-ia, al-le - lú-ia.

℟. De-o grá-ti-as, al-le-lú-ia, al-le - lú-ia.

296

O filii et filiae

Jean Tisserand (d. 1494)   Traditional Melody

Chorus: Al-le-lú-ia, al - le - lú - ia, al -le-lú-ia.

Chanters

1. O fí - li - i et fí - li - æ
2. Et ma - ne pri - ma sab - ba - ti,
3. Et Ma - rí - a Mag-da - lé - ne,
4. In ál - bis sé - dens An - ge - lus
5. Et Jo - án - nes A - pó - sto - lus
6. Di - scí - pu - lis as - tán - ti - bus,

1. Rex cœ - lés - tis, Rex glo - ri - æ
2. Ad ó - sti - um mo - nu - mén - ti
3. Et Ja - có - bi, et Sa - ló - me
4. Præ - dí - xit mu - li - é - ri - bus
5. Cu - cúr - rit Pé - tro cí - ti - us,
6. In mé - di - o stét - it Chrí - stus,

1. Mor-te sur-réx - it ho - di - e.
2. Ac-ces-sé-runt di - scí - pu - li.
3. Ve - né-runt cor-pus un - ge - re. } Al-le-lú - ia
4. In Gal-li - æ-a est Dó - mi-nus.
5. Mo - nu-mén-to vé - nit pri - us.
6. Dí - cens: Pax vó-bis ó - mni-bus.

7. Allelúia, Allelúia, Allelúia.
Ut intelléxit Didymus
Quia surréxerat Jesus,
Remánsit fide dúbius. Allelúia.

8. Allelúia, Allelúia, Allelúia.
Víde Thóma, víde látus
Víde pédes, víde mánus,
Nóli ésse incrédulus. Alleluia.

9. Allelúia, Allelúia, Allelúia.
Quando Thómas Christi látus,
Pédes vídit atque mánus,
Díxit: Tu es Déus méus. Alleluia.

10. Allelúia, Allelúia, Allelúia.
Beáti qui non vidérunt,
Et fírmiter credidérunt,
Vítam ætérnám habébunt. Alleluia.

11. Allelúia, Allelúia, Allelúia.
In hoc fésto sanctíssimo
Sit laus et jubilátio,
Benedicámus Dómino. Alleluia.

12. Allelúia, Allelúia, Allelúia.
De quíbus nos humíllimas
Devótas atque débitas
Deo dicámus Grátias. Allelúia.

298

Victimae Paschali laudes

Sequence for Easter

Vatican Graduale

First mode transposed

1. Víc - ti -mae Pa-schá- li láu-des im - mó - lent

Chri-sti - á - ni. 2. Á-gnus re-dé- mit ó -ves:
3. Mors et vi -ta du - él - lo

Chri-stus ín - no-cens Pá-tri re - con - cil - i - á -
con -fli -xé- re mi -rán -do: dux vi-tæ mór-tu -

vit pec -ca- tó -res. 4. Dic no -bis Ma - rí - a,
us re-gnat vi-vus. 6. An-gé - li -cos te -stes,

quid vi - dí - sti in vi - a? 5. Se-púl - crum Chri-
su - dá - ri - um, et ve - stes. 7. Sur - ré - xit Chri-

sti vi - vén - tis, et gló - ri - am vi - di re - sur - gén - tis.
stus spes me - a: prae - cé - det su - os in Ga - li - laé - am.

8. Scí - mus Chrí - stum sur - re - xís - se

a mór - tu - is ve - re: tu no - bis ví - ctor Rex,

mi - se - ré - re. A - men. Al - le - lú - ia.

Concordi Laetitia

Sixth mode

1. Con-cór-di lae-tí-ti-a, Pro-púl-sa mae-
2. Quae fe-lí-ci gáu-di-o, Re-sur-gén-te
3. Quam con-cén-tu pá-ri-li Cho-ri láu-dant
4. O Re-gí-na Vír-gi-num, Vo-tis fa-ve
5. Glo-ri-o-sa Tri-ni-tas, In-di-ví-sa

1. stí-ti-a, Ma-rí-ae prae-có-ni-a
2. Dó-mi-no, Fló-ri-ut et lí-li-um:
3. cóe-li-ci, Et nos cum coe-lés-ti-bus,
4. súp-pli-cum, Et post mor-tis stá-di-um,
5. U-ni-tas, Ob Ma-rí-ae me-ri-ta,

1. Ré-co-lat Ec-clé-si-a: Vir-go Ma-rí-a.
2. Vi-vum cer-nens Fi-li-um: Vir-go Ma-rí-a.
3. No-vum me-los pán-gi-mus; Vir-go Ma-rí-a.
4. Vi-tae cón-fer práe-mi-um: Vir-go Ma-rí-a.
5. Nos sál-va per saé-cu-la: Vir-go Ma-rí-a.

198

Veni Sancte Spiritus
Sequence for Pentecost

S. Webbe (1740-1816)

Moderato

1. Ve - ni Sanc - te Spi - ri - tus, Et e - mit - te
2. Con - so - la - tor o - pti - me, Dul - cis hos - pes
3. O lux be - a - tis - si - ma, Re - ple cor - dis
4. La - va quod est sor - di - um, Ri - ga quod est
5. Da tu - is fi - de - li - bus, In te con - fi -

1. coe - li - tus Lu - cis tu - ae ra - di - um. Ve - ni pa - ter
2. a - ni - mae, Dul - ce re - fri - ge - ri - um. In la - bo - re
3. in - ti - ma Tu - o - rum fi - de - li - um. Si - ne tu - o
4. a - ri - dum, Sa - na quod est sau - ci - um. Fle - cte quod est
5. den - ti - bus; Sa - crum sep - te - na - ri - um. Da vir - tu - tis

1. pau - pe - rum, Ve - ni, da - tor mu - ne - rum, Ve - ni lu - men
2. re - qui - es, In ae - stu tem - pe - ri - es, In fle - tu so -
3. nu - mi - ne, Ni - hil est in ho - mi - ne, Ni - hil est in
4. ri - gi - dum, Fo - ve quod est fri - gi - dum, Re - ge quod est
5. me - ri - tum, Da sa - lu - tis ex - i - um, Da pe - ren - ne

After last verse

1. cor - di - um.
2. la - ti - um.
3. no - xi - um.
4. de - vi - um.
5. gau - di - um.

A - men. Al - le - lu - ia.

Veni Creator Spiritus 199 a

Invocation to the Holy Ghost

Nicola A. Montani

Moderato

1. Ve - ni Cre - á - tor Spí - ri - tus, Men - tes tu -
2. Qui dí - ce - ris Pa - rá - cli - tus, Al - tís - si -
3. Tu sep - ti - fór - mis mú - ne - re, Digi - tus Pa -
4. Ac - cén - de lu - men sén - si - bus, In - fún - de a -
5. Ho - stem re - pél - las lón - gi - us, Pa - cém - que
6. Per te sci - á - mus da Pa - trem, No - scá - mus
7. De - o Pa - tri sit gló - ri - a, Et Fí - li -

1. ó - rum ví - si - ta: Im - ple su - pér - na grá - ti -
2. mi dó - num Dé - i, Fons vi - vus, i - gnis, cá - ri -
3. tér - nae déx - te - rae, Tu ri - te pro - mís - sum Pa -
4. mó - rem cór - di - bus, In - fír - ma no - stri cór - po -
5. do - nes pró - ti - nus: Du - ctó - re sic te præ - vi -
6. at - que Fí - li - um, Te - que u - tri - ús - que Spí - ri -
7. o qui a mór - tu - is Sur - ré - xit, ac Pa - rá - cli -

After last verse

1. a, Quæ tu cre - á - sti, pe - cto - ra.
2. tas, Et spi - ri - tá - lis ún - cti - o.
3. tris, Ser - mó - ne di - tans gút - tu - ra.
4. ris Vir - tú - te firmans pér - pe - ti.
5. o, Vi - té - mus o - mne nó - xi - um.
6. tum Cre - dá - mus o - mni tém - po - re.
7. to, In sæ - cu - ló - rum sǽ - cu - la. A - men.

199ᵇ Veni Creator Spiritus

Secundum usum recentiorem

Eighth Mode   Vatican Graduale

1. Ve - ni Cre - á - tor Spí - ri - tus,
2. Qui dí - ce - ris Pa - rá - cli - tus,
3. Tu sep - ti - fór - mis mú - ne - re,
4. Ac - cén - de lu - men sén - si - bus,
5. Ho - stem re - pél - las lón - gi - us,
6. Per te sci - á - mus da Pa - trem,
7. De - o Pa - tri sit gló - ri - a,

1. Men - tes tu - ó - rum ví - si - ta:
2. Al - tis - si - mi dó - num Dé - i,
3. Dí - gi - tus Pa - tér - næ déx - te - ræ,
4. In - fún - de a mó - rem cór - di - bus,
5. Pa - cém - que do - nes pró - ti - nus:
6. No - scá - mus at - que Fí - li - um,
7. Et Fí - li - o qui a mór - tu - is

1. Im - ple su - pér - na grá - ti - a,
2. Fons vi - vus, i - gnis, cá - ri - tas,
3. Tu ri - te pro - mis - sum Pa - tris,
4. In - fir - ma no - stri cór - po - ris
5. Du - ctó - re sic te præ - vi - o,
6. Te - que u - tri - ús - que Spí - ri - tum
7. Sur - ré - xit, ac Pa - rá - cli - to,

1. Quæ tu cre - á - sti, pé - cto - ra.
2. Et spi - ri - tá - lis un - cti - o.
3. Ser - mó - ne di - tans gút - tu - ra.
4. Vir - tú - te fir - mans pér - pe - ti.
5. Vi - té - mus o - mne nó - xi - um.
6. Cre - dá - mus o - mni tém - po - re.
7. In sæ - cu - ló - rum sǽ - cu - la.   A - men.

304

Ave Maria

200 a

First Mode (transposed)

Salutatio Angelica
Gregorian

A - ve Ma - rí - a, ✱ grá - ti - a plé - na;

Dó - mi - nus té - cum; be - ne - dí - cta tu

in mu - li - é - ri - bus, et be - ne -

dí - ctus frú - ctus vén - tris tu - i, Jé - sus.

Sán - cta Ma - rí - a, Má - ter De - i,

✱NOTE: Two versions of this phrase are given in the Official Books. This is
taken from the Vatican Antiphonale.

o - ra pro no - bis pec - ca - tó - ri - bus,

rall *pp*

nunc et in ho - ra mor-tis no-stræ. A-men.

200 b   Ave Maria
For unison, two or four part chorus

Jacques Arcadelt
Revised and full text added by N.A.M.

Andante
pp

A - ve Ma - ri - a, gra - ti - a   ple - na,

Do - mi - nus   te - cum, Do - mi - nus   te - cum;

f   *mf*

Be - ne - di - cta tu, be - ne - di - cta

tu in mu - li - e - ri - bus, et be - ne -

di - ctus fru - ctus ven - tris tu - i, Je - sus.

San - cta Ma - ri - a, Ma - ter De -

- i, o - ra pro no - bis pec - ca - to -

Slower

- ri - bus, nunc et in ho - ra

pp

mor - - tis no - stræ. A - men.

Ave Maria 200 c

César Franck
Rearranged for unison or
two part chorus by N.A.M.

Lento
pp sotto voce

A - ve Ma - ri - a, gra - ti - a ple - na,

Do-mi-nus te-cum, be-ne - di-cta tu in mu-li-e-ri--bus; et be-ne-di-ctus, et be-ne-di-ctus fru-ctus ven-tris tu-i, Je--sus. San-cta Ma-ri-a, Ma-ter De-i, o-ra pro no-bis pec-ca-to-ri-bus, nunc et in ho-ra mor-tis no-stræ. A-men. A-men.

Ave Maris Stella

201 a

First Mode (transposed)
optional keys *pp*
Vatican Antiphonale

1. A - ve má - ris stél - la, ____
2. Sú - mens íl - lud A - ve ____
3. Sól - ve vín - cla ré - is, ____
4. Món - stra te es - se má - trem, ____
5. Vír - go sin - gu - lá - ris, ____
6. Ví - tam præ - sta pu - ram, ____
7. Sit laus Dé - o Pá - tri, ____

1. Dé - i Má - ter al - ma At - que sem - per Vir -
2. Ga - bri - é - lis o - re, Fún - da nos in pa -
3. Pró - fer lú - men cǽ - cis, Má - la nó - stra pél -
4. Sú - mat per te pré - ces, Qui pro no - bis na -
5. In - ter ó - mnes mi - tis, Nos cúl - pis so - lú -
6. I - ter pa - ra tu - tum: Ut vi - dén - tes Je -
7. Sum - mo Chrí - sto de - cus, Spi - rí - tu - i San -

1. go ____ Fe - lix cœ - li por - ta. *After last*
2. ce, ____ Mú - tans Hévæ nó - men. *stanza*
3. le, ____ Bó - na cún - cta pó - sce.
4. tus, ____ Tú - lit és - se tú - us.
5. tos, ____ Mí - tes fac et ca - stos.
6. sum, ____ Sém - per col - læ - té - mur.
7. cto, ____ Tri - bus ho - nor u - nus. A - men.

Response: Da mihi virtútem cóntra hóstes túos. (T. P. Alleluia.) *(See preceding page)*.

201 b

Ave Maris Stella

For unison chorus

Andante religioso   Balthasar Florence

A - ve ma-ris stel - - la, De - i

Ma - ter al - ma, At - que sem - per Vir -

After last verse

go, Fe - lix coe - li por - ta. A - men.

201 c

Ave Maris Stella

Con moto   J. Mohr

A - ve ma-ris stel - la, De - i Ma - ter

al - ma, At-que sem-per Vir - go,

rall   *After last verse*

Fe - lix coe-li por - ta. A - - men.

For additional stanzas see 201 a

Ave Maris Stella

Edv. Grieg
Adapted for two part chorus by N.A.M.

1. A - ve Ma - ris stel - la, De - i Ma - ter al - ma, At - que sem - per Vir - go, Fe - lix coe - li por - ta.

2. Su - mens il - lud A - ve Ga - bri - e - lis o - re, Fun - da nos in pa - ce, Mu - - tans He - vae no - - men.

The last stanza is begun at the sign 𝄋

After last stanza

A - men.

311

202 Alma Redemptoris Mater

Antiphon sung from the Saturday before the first Sunday in Advent to the Second Vespers Feast of the Purification inclusive.

Ch. Gounod
Arr. for two or
four part chorus by N. A. M.

Al - ma Re - dem - ptó - ris Ma - ter, quae pér-vi-a coe-li por-ta ma-nes. Et stel - la ma-ris, suc-cúr-re ca-dén-ti súr-ge-re qui cu-rat po-pu-lo, suc-cúr-re, suc-cúr-re ca-den-ti súr-ge-re qui cu-rat pó-pu-lo;

Tu quae ge - nu - i - sti, na - tu - ra mi - rán - te, tu - um san - ctum Ge - ni - tó - rem: Vir - go pri - us ac po - sté - ri - us, Ga - bri - e - lis ab o - re su - mens il - lud A - ve, pec - ca - tó - rum mi - se - re - re, pec - ca - tó - rum mi - se - re - re.

Celebrant:- Angelus Dómini nuntiávit María
Choir Response:- Et concépit de Spíritu Sancto

    After Advent
Cel. :- Post Partum Virgo inviolàta permansísti
Choir:- Dei Génitrix intercéde pro nobis

203   Ave, Regina Coelorum

For Unison or Two-part Chorus of Equal Voices
(From February Second until Holy Thursday)

Nicola A. Montani

Andante con moto

A - ve, Re - gi - na coe - lo - rum, A - ve

Do - mi - na An - ge - lo - rum: Sal - ve ra - dix,

sal - ve por - ta, Ex qua mun - do lux est

or - ta: Gau - de Vi - go glo - ri - o - sa,

Su - per o - mnes spe - ci - o - sa: Va - le, o val - de

de - co - ra, Et pro no - bis Christum ex - o - ra.

Cel. :- Dignáre me laudáre te Virgo sacráta.
Choir :- Da mihi virtútem cóntra hóstes tuos.

Regina Coeli 204

From Compline, Holy Saturday, to None, Saturday, within
the octave of Pentecost.

Antonio Lotti (1667-1740)
Revised and edited for two or
four part chorus by N. A. M.

Re - gi - na coe - li læ - ta - re, al - le - lu - ia, læ -

ta - re al - le - lu - ia: Qui - a quem me - ru - i -sti por -

ta - re, al - le - lu - ia, al - le - lu - ia, Re-sur-rex-it

si - cut di - xit. Al - le - lu - ia, al - le - lu - ia.

O - ra pro no - bis, pro no - bis De - um.

Al - le - lu - ia, al - le - lu - ia, al - le - lu - ia.

℣. Gaude et laetáre Virgo Maria, allelúia.
℟. Quia surréxit Dóminus vere, allelúia.

205   Salve Regina

Fr. Schubert
Revised and edited by N.A.M.

Sal - ve, Re - gi - na, Ma - ter mi - se - ri - cor - di - ae:

Vi - ta, dul - ce - do, et spes no - stra, sal - ve,

et spes no - stra sal - ve. Ad te cla - ma - mus,

ex - su - les, fi - li - i He - vae. Ad

te' sus - pi - ra - mus, ge - men - tes et flen - tes in

hac la - cri - má - rum val - le. E - ia er - go

℣. Ora pro nobis sancta Dei Génitrix.
℟. Ut digni efficiámur promissiónibus Christi.
Copyright 1920 by N.A.M.

206 O Sanctissima, O piissima

Traditional Melody
Sicilian

Moderato

1. O San-ctis-si-ma, O pi-is-si-ma,
2. Tu so-la-ti-um Et re-fu-gi-um,
3. Ec-ce de-bi-les, Per-quam fle-bi-les,
4. Vir-go re-spi-ce, Ma-ter, ad-spi-ce,

1. Dul-cis Vir-go Ma-ri - a!
2. Vir-go Ma-ter Ma-ri - a!
3. Sal-va nos, Ma - ri - a!
4. Au-di nos, Ma - ri - a!

1. Ma-ter a-ma-ta, In-te-me-ra-ta,
2. Quid-quid o-pta-mus, Per te spe-ra-mus;
3. Tolle lan-gu-o-res, Sa-na do-lo-res;
4. Tu me-di-ci-nam, Por-tas di-vi-nam;

1. O - ra, O - ra pro no - bis.
2. O - ra, O - ra pro no - bis.
3. O - ra, O - ra pro no - bis.
4. O - ra, O - ra pro no - bis.

Regina coeli, Jubila

Traditional Melody 1584

1. Re-gi-na coe-li, ju-bi-la, Gau-de, Ma-ri -
2. Quam di-gna ter-ris gi-gne-re, Gau-de, Ma-ri -
3. Sunt fra-cta mor-tis spi-cu-la, Gau-de, Ma-ri -
4. A-cer-bi-tas so-la-ti-um, Gau-de, Ma-ri -
5. Tur-ba-ta spu-tis lu-mi-na, Gau-de, Ma-ri -
6. Ma-num pe-dum-que vul-ne-ra, Gau-de, Ma-ri -

1. a! Jam pul-sa ce-dunt nu-bi-la.
2. a! Vi-vis re-sur-get fu-ne-re.
3. a! Je-su ja-cet mors sub-di-ta.
4. a! Lu-ctus re-do-nat gau-di-um. 1-10. Al -
5. a! Phoe-be-a vin-cunt ful-gu-ra.
6. a! Sunt gra-ti-a-rum flu-mi-na.

le-lu-ia! Lae-ta-re, O Ma-ri-a!

7. Transversa ligni robora
    Gaude Maria!
Sunt sceptra regni fulgida.
    Alleluia!
Lætare, O Maria!

8. Lucet arundo purpura,
    Gaude Maria!
Ut fulva terræ viscera.
    Alleluia!
Lætare, O Maria!

9. Catena, clavi, lancea,
    Gaude Maria!
Triumphi sunt insignia.
    Alleluia!
Lætare, O Maria!

10. Ergo, Maria plaudito,
    Gaude Maria!
Clientibus succurrito.
    Alleluia!
Lætare, O Maria!

Inviolata
Antiphon B.V.M.

Ch. Gounod
Arranged for two part
chorus by N. A. M.

al - ma Chri - sti ca - ris - si - ma: Sus - ci - pe,

sus - ci - pe pi - a lau-dum prae-co - ni - a. Te nunc fla-gi-

tant de - vo - ta cor-da et o - ra: No-stra ut

pu - ra pe-cto-ra sint et cor-po-ra Tu-a per pre-

ca - ta dul-ci - so - na. Tu- a per pre-

ca - ta, pre - ca - ta dul - ci - so - na. No - bis con -

ce - das ve - ni - am per sæ - cu - la___ O be -

ni - gna!_____ O Re - gi - na!_

_____ O Ma - ri - a!_____ Quae

so - la in - vi - o - la - ta per - man - si - sti.

209
Salve Mater Misericordiæ

Fifth Mode   Gregorian

Sál - ve má - ter mi - se - ri - cór - di - æ,

Má - ter Dé - i, et má - ter vé - ni - æ,

Má - ter spé - i, et má - ter grá - ti - æ,

Má - ter plé - na san-ctæ læ-tí - ti - æ; O Ma-ri - a!

1. Sal - ve dé - cus hu - má - ni gé - ne - ris,
2. Sal - ve fe - lix Vir-go pu - ér - pe - ra:
3. Te cre - á - vit Pa - ter in - gé - ni - tus,
4. Te cre - á - vit De - us mi - rá - bi - lem,
5. Te be - á - tam lau - dá - re cú - pi - unt
6. E - sto, Ma - ter, no - strum so - lá - ti - um;

324

1. Sal - ve Vir - go di - gni - or cé - te - ris,
2. Nam qui se - det in Pa - tris déx - te - ra,
3. Ob - um - brá - vit te U - ni - gé - ni - tus,
4. Te re - spé - xit an - cíl - lam, hú - mi - lem,
5. O - mnes ju - sti, sed non suf - fí - ci - unt;
6. No - strum e - sto, tu Vir - go gau - di - um;

1. Quæ vir - gi - nes o - mnes trans - gré - de - ris,
2. Cœ - lum re - gens, ter - ram et æ - the - ra,
3. Fe - cun - dá - vit te San - ctus Spí - ri - tus,
4. Te quae - sí - vit spón - sam a - má - bi - lem,
5. Mul - tas lau - des de te con - cí - pi - unt,
6. Et nos tan - dem post hoc ex - sí - li - um,

Repeat "Salve Mater" after each stanza

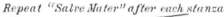

rall.

1. Et ál - ti - us se - des in sú - pe - ris, O Ma - rí - a!
2. In - tra tu - a se clau - sit vis - ce - ra, O Ma - rí - a!
3. Tu es fa - cta to - ta di - ví - ni - tus, O Ma - rí - a!
4. Ti - bi nun - quam fe - cit con - sí - mi - lem, O Ma - rí - a!
5. Sed in il - lis pror - sus de - fí - ci - unt, O Ma - rí - a!
6. Lae - tos jun - ge cho - ris coe - lé - sti - um, O Ma - rí - a!

325

210 a O Gloriosa Virginum (No. 1)

Unison Chorus

Melody from the "Harfe David"
Arr. by P. J. Van Damme

Moderato

1. O glo - ri - o - sa Vir - gi - num, Sub -
2. Quod He - va tri - stis áb - stu - lit, Tu
3. Tu re - gis al - ti já - nu - a, Et
4. Jé - su ti - bi sit gló - ri - a Qui

1. lí - mis in - ter sí - de - ra, Qui
2. réd - dis al - mo ger - mi - ne: In -
3. au - la lu - cis fúl - gi - da: Vi -
4. ná - tus es de Vír - gi - ne Cum

1. te cre - á - vit pár - vu - lum La - ctén - te
2. trent ut as - tra flé - bi - les, Coe - li re -
3. tam dá - tam per Vír - gi - nem Gén - tes re -
4. Pa - tre et al - mo Spí - ri - tu, In sem - pi -

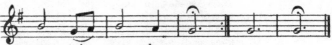

1. nu - tris u - be - re.
2. clu - dis car - di - nes.
3. dém - ptae pláu - di - te.
4. tér - na sáe - eu - la. A - men.

326

O Gloriosa Virginum (No. 2)

Unison or two-part chorus

F. de La Tombelle
Arr. by N. A. M.

Andante réligioso

1. O glo - ri - o - sa Vir - gi - num, Su-
2. Quod He - va tri - stis ab - stu - lit, Tu

1. O glo - ri - o - sa Vir - gi -
2. Quod He - va tri - stis ab - stu -

bli - mis in - ter si - de - ra,
red - dis al - mo ger - mi - ne:

num, Su - bli - mis in - ter si - de - ra,
lit, Tu red - dis al - mo ger - mi - ne:

Piu Vivo

Qui te cre - a - vit par - vu - lum
In - trent ut as - tra fle - bi - les,

rall

La - cten - te nu - tris u - be - re.
Coe - li re - clu - dis car - di - nes.

After last verse

rall

A - men, A - men, A - men.

211 Salve Regina Coelitum

Unison, two or three part chorus, equal voices
or four part unequal

Traditional Melody
Arr. by P. J. Van Damme

1. Sal - ve Re - gi - na coe - li - tum,
2. Ma - ter mi - se - ri - cor - di - ae,
3. Tu vi - tae lux fons gra - ti - æ,
4. Spes no - stra, sal - ve, Do - mi - na,

1. O Ma - ri - a! Sors u - ni - ca ter -
2. O Ma - ri - a! Dul - cis pa - rens cle -
3. O Ma - ri - a! Cau - sa no - strae læ -
4. O Ma - ri - a! Ex - stin - gue no - stra

1. ri - ge - num, O Ma - ri - a!
2. men - ti - ae, O Ma - ri - a!
3. ti - ti - æ, O Ma - ri - a!
4. cri - mi - na! O Ma - ri - a!

1-8. Ju - bi - la - te, Che - ru - bim, Ex - sul - ta - te,

Se - ra -phim! Con-so-nan-te per-pe-tim: Sal - ve,

Sal - ve, Sal - ve Re - gi - na.

5. Ad te clamámus éxsules,
    O Maria!
    Te nos rogámus súpplices,
    O Maria!
    Jubiláte, etc.

6. Audi nos Evæ filios,
    O Maria!
    In te sperántes míseros.
    O Maria!
    Jubilate, etc.

7. Eia ergo nos réspice;
    O Maria!
    Servos tuos ne déspice.
    O Maria!
    Jubilate, etc.

8. Convérte tuos óculos,
    O Maria!
    Ad nos in hoc exílio.
    O Maria!
    Jubilate, etc.

212 ## Tota Pulchra Es, Maria

Motet for unison or two-part chorus

Balthasar-Florence
Liturgically arranged by N.A.M.

To - ta pul - chra es, Ma - ri - a, et ma - cu - la o - ri - gi - na - lis non est in te. Tu glo - ri - a Je - ru - sa - lem. Tu lae - ti - ti - a Is - ra - el. Tu ho - no - ri - fi - cen - ti - a po - pu - li no - stri: tu ad - vo - ca - ta

330

213 a
Sub Tuum Præsidium (No.1)
Motet for two part chorus

M. Haller

Sub tu - um prae-si-di-um con - fu - gi - mus,

san-cta De - i Ge-ni-trix, no-stras de-pre-ca-ti-

o - nes ne de - spi-ci-as in ne-ces-si-

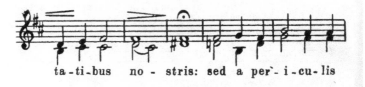

ta -ti-bus no - stris: sed a per - i - cu-lis

cun-ctis li-be-ra nos, li-be-ra nos, sem-

per, Vir-go glo-ri-o-sa, et be-ne-di-cta,

Do-mi-na no-stra, Me-di-a-trix no-stra,

ad-vo-ca-ta no-stra, tu-o Fi-li-

o nos re-con-ci-li-a, tu-o Fi-li-

o nos com - men - da, tu - o

Fi - li - o nos re - præ - sen - ta.

213 b
Sub tuum Præsidium (No. 2)
Antiphon

Usually sung before the Litany of the Blessed Virgin and before the "Nunc Dimittis."

Seventh Mode   Gregorian

Sub tú-um prae-sí - di -um con - fú - gi - mus,*

Sán-cta De-i Gé-ni-trix: nó-stras de-pre-ca-ti-ó - nes

ne de-spí-ci-as in ne-ces-si-tá-ti-bus:

sed a per-í-cu-lis cun-ctis

lí-be-ra nos sem-per, _____

Vir-go glo-ri-o-sa ___

Eastertide, add.

et be-ne-dí-cta. Al-le-lú-ia.

214 Litany of the Blessed Virgin

Litaniæ Lauretanæ
Unison or two part chorus

Nicola A. Montani

Moderately fast

Ký-ri-e e-lé-i-son. Chríste e-lé-i-son. Ký-ri-e e-lé- i-son.→

Chanters

1. Pa - - ter de cóe - lis De - us,→
2. Fi - li Re-dém - ptor mun-di De - us,→
3. Spi - - ri - tus San - cte De - us,→
4. San-cta Tri - ni -tas u - nus De - us,→

Piu Vivo (alla breve)
Chanters   Chorus

5. San - - cta Ma-ri - a, o - ra pro no-bis.→
7. San-cta Vir -go Vir-gi-num, o - ra pro no-bis.→
9. Ma-ter di-ví -næ grá-ti-æ, o - ra pro no-bis.→
11. Ma - - ter ca-stís-si-ma, o - ra pro no-bis.→
13. Ma-ter in-te-me-rá - ta, o - ra pro no-bis.→
15. Ma-ter ad-mi - rá-bi-lis, o - ra pro no-bis.→
17. Ma-ter Cre-a - tó - ris, o - ra pro no-bis.→

ⓓ Chri-ste au-di-nos. ⓔ Chri-ste ex-áu-di-nos.

Chorus

1. mi - se - ré - re no - bis.
2. mi - se - ré - re no - bis.
3. mi - se - ré - re no - bis.
4. mi - se - ré - re no - bis.

Chanters   Chorus

6. San-cta De - i Gé-ni-trix, o - ra pro no-bis.
8. Ma - ter Chri - sti, o - ra pro no-bis.
10. Ma - ter pu - rís-si-ma, o - ra pro no-bis.
12. Ma-ter in-vi - o - lá - ta, o - ra pro nó-bis.
14. Ma - ter a - má-bi-lis, o - ra pro no-bis.
16. Ma - ter bo-ni con-sí-li-i, o - ra pro no-bis.
18. Ma - ter Sal-va - tó - ris, o - ra pro no-bis.

337

19. Vir-go pru-den - tís-si-ma,   o - ra pro no - bis.→

21. Vir-go prae-di - cán - da,   o - ra pro no - bis.→

23. Vir - go   clé - mens,   o - ra pro no - bis.→

25. Spé-cu-lum jus - tí - ti - ae,   o - ra pro no - bis.→

27. Cau-sa no-strae lae-tí - ti - ae,   o - ra pro no - bis.→

29. Vas   ho-no - rá-bi-le,   o - ra pro no - bis.→

31. Ro - sa   mý-sti-ca,   o - ra pro no - bis.→

33. Tur - ris e - búr-ne-a,   o - ra pro no - bis.→

35. Fóe - de-ris   ar - ca,   o - ra pro no - bis.→

37. Stel-la ma-tu - tí - na,   o - ra pro no - bis.→

39. Re - fú-gi-um pec-ca - tó-rum,   o - ra pro no-bis.→

41. Au - xí - li-um Christi-a - nó-rum,   o - ra pro no-bis.→

43. Re-gí-na   Pa-tri-ar-chá-rum,   o - ra pro no-bis.→

45. Re-gí-na A-po-sto - ló-rum,   o - ra pro no-bis.→

47. Re-gí-na   Con-fes - só-rum,   o - ra pro no-bis.→

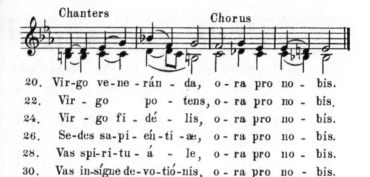

20. Vir-go ve-ne-rán-da, o-ra pro no-bis.
22. Vir-go po-tens, o-ra pro no-bis.
24. Vir-go fi-dé-lis, o-ra pro no-bis.
26. Se-des sa-pi-én-ti-æ, o-ra pro no-bis.
28. Vas spi-ri-tu-á-le, o-ra pro no-bis.
30. Vas in-sígne de-vo-tió-nis, o-ra pro no-bis.
32. Tur-ris Da-ví-di-ca, o-ra pro no-bis.
34. Do-mus áu-re-a, o-ra pro no-bis.
36. Já-nu-a coe-li, o-ra pro no-bis.
38. Sa-lus in-fir-mó-rum, o-ra pro no-bis.

40. Con-so-lá-trix af-fli-ctó-rum, o-ra pro no-bis.
42. Re-gí-na An-ge-ló-rum, o-ra pro no-bis.
44. Re-gí-na Pro-phe-tá-rum, o-ra pro no-bis.
46. Re-gí-na Már-ty-rum, o-ra pro no-bis.
48. Re-gí-na Vír-gi-num, o-ra pro no-bis.

339

49. Re-gí - na Sanctó - rum ó - mni-um,   ora pro nobis.
50. Re-gí-na sine labe origi-náli concépta,   ora pro nobis.
51. Re-gí-na Sacratíssimi Ro-sá - ri - i,   ora pro nobis.
52. Re-gí - na   Pa - cis,   ora pro nobis.

53. A-gnus De-i,qui tollis peccáta mundi;Parce nobis Dómine.
54. A-gnus De-i,qui tollis peccáta mundi;Ex-aúdinos Dómine.

55. A - gnus   De - i qui tol-lis peccá-ta   mun - di

mi - se - ré - re   no - bis.

℣. Ora pro nobis Sancta Dei Génitrix.
℞. Ut digni efficiámur promissiónibus Christi.

Veni Sponsa Christi
for two-part chorus

Nicola A. Montani

Ve - ni spon - sa Chri - sti,

Ve - ni spon - sa Chri - sti

ac - ci - pe co - ro - nam,

quam ti -bi Do-mi-nus præ-pa-ra - vit,

præ - pa - ra -vit in æ - ter - num.

Magnificat

Eighth Psalm Tone (Solemnis)

Gregorian

1. Ma-gní-fi - cat ∗
2. Et ex-sul-távit   spí-ri-tus mé - us: ∗→
3. Qui-a re _ spéxit humilitátem an-cíl-læ su - æ: ∗

4. Qui-a fe -cit mihi   ma-gna qui pót-ens est: ∗
5. Et mi-se - ricórdia ejus a
       progéni - e in pro-gé - ni-es. ∗
6. Fe-cit po - téntiam in   brá-chi-o sú - o: ∗
7. De-pó-su - it po - - - tén-tes de sé - de, ∗
8. E - su -ri - éntes   im-plé-vit bo - nis ∗
9. Sus-cé-pit Ísrael   pú - e -rum sú - um: ∗
10. Sic-ut lo - cútus est   ad pa-tres no - stros: ∗
11. Gló-ri - a   Pá-tri et Fí - li - o, ∗
12. Sic-ut e - rat in princípio,   et nunc, et sem - per, ∗

For the alternate verses the following falso bordone arrangement by Ciro Grassi may be used. (For two part chórus (or three part) equal voices.)

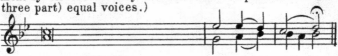

2. Et exsultávit   spí - ri-tus me - us: ∗→
4. Quia fecit mihi magna   qui pot - ens est: ∗
6. Fecit poténtiam in   brá- chi-o su - o: ∗
8. Esuriéntes   im- plé-vit bo - nis, ∗
10. Sicut locútus est ad   pa - tres no - stros, ∗
12. Sicut erat in princípio,   et nunc, et sem - per, ∗

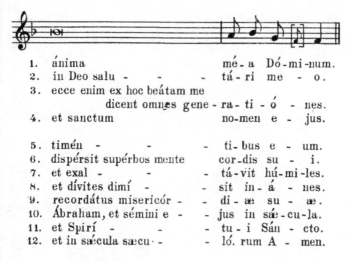

1. ánima   mé- a   Dó-mi-num.
2. in Deo salu -   -   -   tá- ri   me - o.
3. ecce enim ex hoc beátam me
         dicent omnes gene - ra- ti - ó - nes.
4. et sanctum   no-men e - jus.

5. timén -   -   -   ti- bus e - um.
6. dispérsit supérbos mente   cor-dis su - i.
7. et exal -   -   -   tá-vit hú-mi-les.
8. et dívites dimí -   -   sit in- á - nes.
9. recordátus misericór -   - di - æ su - æ.
10. Ábraham, et sémini e -   - jus in sǽ-cu-la.
11. et Spirí -   -   -   tu- i Sán - cto.
12. et in sǽcula sæcu -   - ló. rum A - men.

2. in Deo salu -   - tá- ri   me - o.
4. et sanctum   no-men   e - jus.
6. dispérsit supérbos mente cor-dis   su - i.
8. et divites dimísit in - á -   -   nes.
10. Abraham, et sémini   e - jus in sǽ-cu-la.
12. et in sǽcula sæcu - ló-rum.   A - men.

343

CEREMONY MUSIC
Motets for Reception, Profession etc.

Regnum Mundi

for two part chorus

Nicola A. Montani

Re - gnum mun - di, Re - gnum mun - di
et o-mnem or - na-tam sae - cu - li,
con-tem-psi pro-pter a - mo - rem Do-mi-ni
no - stri, Je - su Chri - sti.
Quem vi - di quem a - ma - vi,
in quem cre-di -di quem di - le - xi.

Repeat from ℀ "Quem vidi" to Ps. then to ✠ "Elegi"

(Ps. 44.) E-ructá-vit cor meum vérbum bónum: dico ego ópera mea Regi.

E - le-gi ab-jé-cta es - se, in do-mo Do-mi-no

Repeat "Quem vidi" to Ps. then to "Gloria"

me - i, Je - su Chri - sti!

Repeat "Quem vidi" to Fine

Gló-ri-a Patri et Fi-li-o Et Spi-rí-tu-i San-cto.

RESPONSES

℣. Kyrie eléison. ℟. Christi eléison. ℣. Pater noster.

℣. Etne nos indúcas in tentatiónem.

℟. Sed líbera nos a malo.

℣. Manda Deus etc.

℟. Confírma hoc Deus quod operátus es in eis.

℣. Salvas fac etc. ℟. Deus meus sperántes in te.

℣. Esto nobis etc. ℟. A facie inimíci.

℣. Nihil proficiat etc.

℣. Et Filius iniquitátis non appónat nocére nobis.

℣. Ora pro nobis etc.

℟. Ut dignae efficiántur promissiónibus Christi.

℣. Domine exaudi etc. ℟. Et clamor meus ad te véniat.

℣. Dominus etc. ℟. Et cum Spiritu tuo.

℣. Domine Deus virtutem, converte nos.

℟. Et osténde fáciem tuam et salvi erimus.

Suscipe Domine
(St. Ignatius)
for two part chorus

Nicola A. Montani

Sus - ci - pe Do - mi - ne, u - ni -
ver - sam li - ber - ta - tem me - am,
Ac - ci - pe me - mo - ri - am in - tel -
le - ctum at - que vo - lun - ta - tem
o - - mnem. Quid quid ha - be - o
vel pos - si - de - o mi - hi lar - gi - tus

id ti - bi to - tum re - sti - tu - o, ac

es id ti - bi to - tum re -

tu - ae pror - sus

sti - tu - o, ac tu - ae pror - sus vo - lun - ta - te

rall

tra - do gu - ber - nan - dum.

Moderato

p

A - mo - rem tu - i so - lum cum

gra - ti - a tu - a mi - hi

do - nes et di - ves sum sa - tis nec

a - li - ud quid quam ul - tra po - sco.

347

219

Conserva me Domine

Third Tone   Psalm 15

in - te: (†)
vi - tae: (+)

1. Con-sér - va me, Dómine, quoniam
   sperávi in te. (†)
      Dixi Dómino Deus | mé - us | es tu,

2.   Sanctis, qui sunt in | ter - ra | e - jus,

3.   Multiplicátae sunt in-
   firmi-| tá - tes e-ó-rum

4.   Non congregábo conven-
   tícula eórum | de san-guí - | ni-bus.

5.   Dóminus pars haeredi-
   tátis meae, et | cá-li-cis | me - i:

6.   Funes cecidérunt mihi | in´ prae-| clá-ris,

7.   Benedícam Dóminum,
   qui tribuit mihi | in - tel - | léc-tum:

8.   Providébam Dóminum in
   conspéctu | me - o | sem-per:

9.   Própter hoc laetátum est
   cor meum et exsultávit | lin - gua | me - a:

10. Quóniam non derelínques
    ánimam | me-am in in-| fér-no:

11. Notas mihi fecísti vias
    vitae†adimplébis
    me laetítia cum | vul - tu | tu - o:

12. Glória | Pa -tri et Fi - | li-o,

13. Sicut erat in princípio, et | nunc, et | sem-per,

348

1. quóniam bonórum meórum   non e - ges.

2. mirificávit ómnes voluntates meas   in e - is.

3. postea accelle -   -   - ra - vé - runt.

4. nec memor ero nóminum eórum
                per lábi - a me - a.

5. tu es, qui restítues hæreditátem
                     me - am mi - hi.

6. étenim hæréditas mea præclá - ra est mi - hi.

7. insuper et usque ad noctem
         increpuérunt me re - nes me - i.

8. quóniam a déxtris est mihi, ne   com - mó-ve-ar.

9. ínsuper et caro mea requié - - scet in spe.

10. nec dabis sánctum tuum videre
                 corru - pti - ó - nem.

11. delectationis in déxtera tua úsque in - fi - nem.

12. et Spirítu -   -   -   - i San - cto.

13. et in saécula saeculó - - rum. A - men.

220 MUSIC FOR RECEPTION, VOW DAY, ETC.
Ecce Quam Bonum
for two-part chorus
Psalm 132

Nicola A. Montani

quod de - scen - dit in bar - bam,
be - ne - di - cti - o - nem et vi - tam
et nunc, et sem - per, et in sae - cu -

allarg. *Repeat from "Ecce" to* ⌒

bar - bam Aa - - - ron.
us - que in sae - cu - - lum.
la sae - cu - lo - rum. A - men.

4. Quod de - scen - dit in o - ram ves - ti - men - ti
8. Glo - ri - a Pa - tri, et

e - jus: sic - ut ros Her - mon, qui de -
Fi - li - o, et Spi - ri - tu - i

Repeat "Ecce" to ⌒

scen - dit in mon - te Si - on.
San - - - - cto.

351

Quam dilecta tabernacula tua
Psalm 83

Seventh Tone

1. Quam di - lécta tabernácula tua,
   Dómi-ne vir - tú - tum!→

2. Cor meum et   ca-ro   me - a
3. Etenim passer invénit si - bi   do - num:
4. Altária tua, Dómi - ne vir - tú - tum:
5. Beati, qui hábitant in
        domo tu - a,   Do-mi-ne:
6. Beátus vir, cujus est
        au- xi - li - um abs te:

7. Étenim benedictiónem
   dabit legislátor,
   ibunt de virtúte   in vir - tú - tem:
8. Dómine, Deus virtútum
        exáudi orati - ó -nem   me - am:
9. Protéctor nóster,   á -spi-ce De - us:
10. Quia mélior est dies
         una in á -tri-is tu - is,
11. Elégi abjéctus esse
         in dómo De- i   me - i:

12. Quia misericórdiam,
    et veritátem dí-li -git De - us:
13. Non privábit bónis eos,
    qui ámbulant in in-no - cén-ti-a:

14. Gloria   Pa-tri et Fi-li - o,
15. Sicut erat in princí-
    pio, et nunc, et sem - per,

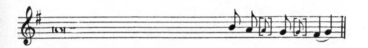

1. concupíscit, et déficit ánima
               mea in   á-tri-a Dó-mi-ni.
2. exsultavérunt in   De-um   vi - vum.
3. et turtur nidum sibi, ut ponat pul-los   su - os.
4. Rex meus, et   De - us   me - us.

5. in sáecula saecu -   - ló-rum lau-dá-bunt me.

6. ascensiónes in corde suo dispó-
     suit, in valle lacrimárum, in lo-co quem pó-su-it.

7. vidébitur Deus de - - - ó - rum in Si-on.

8. áuribus percipe,   Dé- us Já - cob.
9. et réspice fáciem   Chri-sti tu - i:

10. ——————————— sú-per mí-li - a.

11. magis quam habitáre in taber-
           náculis pec-ca - tó - rum

12. grátiam et glóriam   da - bit Dó-mi-nus.

13. Domine virtutum, beátus
         homo, qui spé-rat in   te.
14. et Spi - - - - rí-tu-i San - cto

15. et in sáecula saecu - - ló-rum A - men.

Quae est ista
Two part or unison chorus

Traditional Italian Chorale
Arr. by N. A. Montani

Moderato

Quae est is - ta, quae est is - ta,

quae a - scen - dit de de - ser - to; de -

li - ci - is af - flu - ens e - nix - a

su - per di - le - ctum su - um? To - ta pul - chra

es, a - mi - ca me - a, su - a - vis et de -

có - ra. Vé - ni de Li - ba - no

spon - sa me - a Ve - ni de

rall

Li - ba - no ve-ni co - ro - na-be-ris.

Tu gloria Jerusalem 223
Unison or four part chorus

(For additional Ceremony Music see Magnificat; Hymns in honor of the Blessed Virgin, Motets in honor of the Bl. Sacrament, Te Deum etc.)

César Franck
Andante religioso Adapted from the Motet "Quae est ista"

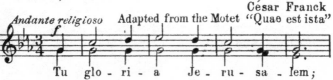

Tu glo - ri - a Je - ru - sa - lem;

tu lae - ti - ti - a Is - ra - el; tu ho - no -

ri - fi - cen - ti - a po - pu - li no - stri. Ma -

Slower

ri - a Do - mi - na - re no - stri tu et

Fi - li - us tu - us In - ter - ce - de ad

pp rall

Do - mi - num De - um no - strum, in - ter -

cresc

ce - de ad Do - mi - num De - um no - strum, ad De - um

ff *allarg.*

no - strum, ad Do - mi - num De - um no - strum.

MUSIC FOR FORTY HOURS' ADORATION
Musical Programme

AT THE EXPOSITION

1. MASS, after which the Blessed Sacrament is incensed.
2. ✷ *PROCESSION* during which the "Pange Lingua" is sung;
after the procession the
3. "TANTUM ERGO" is sung, and the Blessed Sacrament is
incensed. The "Panem de coelo, etc.", is omitted
4. THE LITANY OF THE SAINTS is chanted. 224
5. PSALM LXIX, "Deus in adjutorium etc.", is intoned, then
sung alternately by the clergy or choir, after which the celebrant, still kneeling, sings the versicles "Salvos fac, etc."
After the"Domine, exaudi orationem meam," the celebrant rises and sings the prescribed orations.

MISSA PRO PACE

On the second day of the Devotion the "Missa pro pace"
(mass for peace) is offered on a side altar, and the color of
the vestments is violet, unless a feast of higher rank occurs
prohibiting the use of this color.

AT THE REPOSITION

1. MASS, after which is sung the
2. LITANY with Psalm LXIX and the versicles "Salvos
fac,etc." down to "Dominus Vobiscum" (exclusive,) after
which the Blessed Sacrament is incensed.
3. ✷ *PROCESSION* during which the "Pange Lingua" is
sung. After the procession when the Blessed Sacrament
has been placed on the altar, the
4."TANTUM ERGO" is sung, and at the "Genitori" the
Blessed Sacrament is incensed. The "Panem de coelo"
is intoned and the celebrant rises and sings the
5. ORATIONS; Benediction follows.

✷ In case the Procession does not take place the "Pange
Lingua" cannot be omitted.

Pange Lingua; (see No. 241)

224 The Litany of the Saints
According to the Vatican Graduale

Sung on Holy Saturday, The Rogation Days, Forty Hours'
Adoration.

Chanters

Ký - ri - e   e - lé - i - son. Chrí -ste e - lé - i - son.

Ký - ri - e e - lé - i -son. Chrí-ste au-di -nos. Chri-ste ex-áu-di-nos.

(♮)

Pá - ter de cǽ - lis   De - us,   mi - se - ré - re nó - bis.
Fíli Redémptor múndi De - us,   mi - se - ré - re nó - bis.
Spí - ri - tus Sán-cte   De - us,   mi - se - ré - re nó - bis.
Sáncta Trínitas únus De - us,   mi - se - ré - re nó - bis.

Sán - cta Ma - rí - a,   ó - ra pro nó - bis.

Sán - cta Dé - i Gé - ni - trix, ó - ra pro nó - bis.
Sán - cta Vír - go vír - gi - num, ó - ra pro nó - bis.
Sán - cte Mí - cha - el,   ó - ra pro nó - bis.
Sán - cte Gá - bri - el,   ó - ra pro nó - bis.
Sán - cte Rá - pha - el,   ó - ra pro nó - bis.

1. O-mnes sán-cti An-gé-li et Ar-chán-ge-li,
2. O-mnes sán-cti beató-rum Spíritum ór-di-nes,

1. o - rá - te pro nó - bis.
2. o - rá - te pro nó - bis.

Sán-cte Jo-án-nes Bap-tí-sta, ó-ra pro nó-bis.

Sán-cte Jó-seph, ó-ra pro nó-bis.

O-mnes sán-cti Pa-tri-ár-chæ et Pro-phé-tæ,

ó-ra-te pro nó-bis. Sán-cte Pé-tre, ó-ra pro nó-bis.

Sáncte Páule,
Sáncte Andréa,
Note ✶ Sáncte Jacóbe,
Sáncte Joánnes,
✶ Sáncte Thóma,
✶ Sáncte Jacóbe,
✶ Sáncte Philíppe,
✶ Sáncte Bartholomǽe, ⎬ óra pro nóbis.
✶ Sáncte Mathǽe,
✶ Sáncte Símon,
✶ Sáncte Thaddǽe,
✶ Sáncte Mathía,
✶ Sáncte Bárnaba,
✶ Sáncte Lúca,
✶ Sáncte Márce,

Omnes sáncti Apóstoli et Evangelístæ,
Omnes sáncti Discípuli Dómini, ⎬ oráte pro nóbis.
✶ Omnes sáncti Innocéntes,

Sáncte Stéphane,
Sáncte Laurénti, ⎬ óra pro nóbis.
Sáncte Vincénti,

✶ Sáncti Fabiáne et Sebastiáne,
✶ Sáncti Joánnes et Páule,
✶ Sáncti Cósma et Damiáne, ⎬ oráte pro nóbis.
✶ Sáncti Gervási et Protási,
Omnes sancti Mártyres,

✶ Note: Omitted on Holy Saturday.
360

Sáncte Silvéster,　┐
Sáncte Gregóri,
✶ Sáncte Ambrósi,
Sáncte Augustíne,　⎬ óra pro nóbis.
✶ Sáncte Hierónyme,
✶ Sáncte Martíne,
✶ Sáncte Nicoláe,　┘

Omnes sáncti Pontífices et Confessóres, oráte pro nóbis.

Omnes sáncti Doctóres, oráte pro nóbis.

Sáncte Antóni,　┐
Sáncte Benedícte,
✶ Sáncte Bernárde,　⎬ ora pro nobis.
Sáncte Domínice,
Sáncte Francísce,　┘

Omnes sáncti Sacerdótes et Levítæ, oráte pro nóbis.

Omnes sáncti Mónachi et Eremítæ, oráte pro nóbis.

✶✶
(a) Sáncta María Magdaléna,　┐　✶✶ *See note below.*
(d) Sáncta Agatha,
✶ Sáncta Lúcia,
(b) Sáncta Agnes,　⎬ óra pro nóbis.
(c) Sáncta Cæcília,
✶ Sáncta Catharína,
(e) Sáncta Anastásia,　┘

Omnes sánctæ Virgines et Víduæ, oráte pro nóbis.

Omnes Sáncti et Sánctæ Déi, intercédite pro nóbis.

✶✶ *Note: On Holy Saturday the order is according to the letters a, b, c, d, e.*

✶ *Omitted on Holy Saturday*

Pro - pí - ti - us é - sto, pár-ce nó-bis Dó - mi - ne
Pro - pí - ti - us é - sto, ex-áu-di nos Dó - mi - ne
Ab o - mni ma - lo, lí - be - ra nos Dó - mi - ne

Ab ómni peccáto,
★ Ab íra túa,
  Ab imminéntibus pericalis (1) ◄————
★ A subitánea et improvísa mórte,
★ Ab insídiis diáboli ;
★ Ab íra, et ódio, et ómni mála volun-
    táte,
★ A spíritu fornicatiónis ,
★ A fúlgure et tempestáte ,
★ A flagéllo terræmótus,
★ A péste, fáme, et béllo,
A mórte perpétua ,
Per mystérium sánctæ incarnati-
    ónis túæ,
Per advéntum túum ,
Per nativitátem túam,
Per baptísmum et sánctum jejúni-
    um túum,
Per crúcem et passiónem túam,
Per mortem et sepulturam tuam ,
Per sánctam resurrectiónem túam,
Per admirabilem ascensionem tuam,
Per advéntum Spíritus Sáncti Pa-
    rácliti ,
In díe judícii ,

1 - ** *See note below.*	
2 - *A flagéllo terraemótus*	
3 - *A péste, fame, et béllo*	
4 - *Ab subitanea et impro -*	
visa mórte	
5 - *Ab insídiis diáboli*	
6 - *Ab íra, et ódio, et ómni*	
mála voluntáte	
7 - *A spírita fornicatiónis*	
8 - *A fúlgure et tempestáte*	
9 - *A mórte perpétua etc.*	

líbera nos Domine.

★ ★ (1) *Included only for Forty Hours' Adoration* (1-to 9-) *and remainder as indicated.*
★ *Omitted on Holy Saturday*

362

Pec - ca - tó - res, te ro - gá - mus aú - di - nos.

Ut nóbis párcas ,
★ Ut nóbis indúlgeas ,
★ Ut ad véram pæniténtiam nos perdúcere
  dignéris,
 Ut Ecclésiam túam sánctam†régere et conserváre dignéris,
 Ut Dómnum Apostólicum/et ómnes eccle- ⁽²⁾
  siásticos órdines'†in sáncta religióne
  conserváre dignéris ,
 Ut inimícos sánctæ Ecclésiæ†humiláre
  dignéris,
 Ut régibus et princípibus christiánis'†pá-
  cem et véram concórdiam donáre dignéris ,
★ Ut cúncto pópulo christiáno' pácem et
  unitátem largíri dignéris ,(See note below) ⁽¹⁾
 Ut nosmetípsos in tuo sáncto servítio'†
  confortáre et conserváre dignéris ,
★ Ut méntes nóstras ad coeléstia desidé-
  ria érigas,
 Ut ómnibus benefactóribus nóstris†sem-
  pitérna bóna retríbuas ,
★ Ut ánimas nostras', frátrum, propin-
  quórum et benefactórum nostrórum'
  ab ætérna damnatióne erípias,
 Ut frúctus térræ dáre et conserváre
  dignéris,
 Ut ómnibus fidélibus defúnctis†réquiem
  ætérnam donáre dignéris,
 Ut nos exaudíre dignéris,
★ Fíli Déi,

te rogamus
audi nos

(1) NOTE: After this invocation sing the following;
"*Ut ómnes errántes ad unitàtem Ecclésiae revocáre, et infidéles univérsos ad
Evangélii lumen perdùcere dignéris*" (*Te rogámus* etc.)
(2) *Séde Vacante* the words *Domnum Apostolicum et* are omitted and the petition
reads "Ut ómnes " etc.

A - gnus Dé - i, qui tól - lis pec - cá - ta mún - di,

pár - ce nó - bis Dó - mi - ne. A - gnus Dé - i,

qui tól - lis pec - cá - ta mún - di,

ex - aú - di nos Dó - mi - ne. A - gnus Dé - i,

qui tol - lis pec - cá - ta mún - di, mi - se - ré - re nó - bis.

Chri - ste au - di - nos. Chri - ste ex - aú - di - nos.

On Holy Saturday the "Kyrie" of the Mass is begun at this point.

Forty Hours etc. chanters proceed.

Ky-ri - e   e - lé - i - son.   Chri-ste e - lé - i - son.

Ky-ri - e   e - lé - i - son.   Pa-ter No-ster.   secreto.

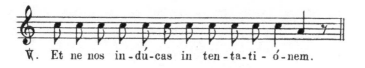

℣. Et ne nos in - dú - cas in ten - ta - ti - ó - nem.

℟. Sed lí - be - ra nos   a   ma - lo.

365

225 Deus in adjutorium

Psalm 69

1. Deus in adjutórium   mé - um in - tén - de: →

2. Confundántur et   re - ve - re - an - tur,

3. Avertántur retrósum,   et e - ru - be - scant,

4. Avertántur státim   e - ru - be-scen - tes,

5. Exsúltent et laeténtur

       in te ó-mnes qui qúe-runt te:

6. Ego vero e - - - gé-nus et páu-per sum:

7. Adjútor meus et liberá - tor me-us es   tu:

8. Glória   Pa-tri et Fí - li - o,

9. Sicut erat in princípio,   et nunc, et sém - per,

(small notes ending for No. 6.)

ad-ju-va me.

1. Dómine ad adjuván-
    dum me fe - stí - na.

2. qui quaerunt ánimam mé - am.

3. qui vólunt mihi ma _ la.

4. qui dicunt mihi: Éuge, é - u - ge.

5. et dicant sémper: Ma-
    gnificétur Dóminus:
    qui díligunt salutáre tu - um.

6. Deus _____ (★ see above ád-ju-va me.)

7. Dómine ne mo - - ré _ ris.

8. et Spirítui Sán - cto.

9. et in saécula saecu-
    lórum. A - men.

RESPONSES

Cel.

1. Sal-vos fac ser-vos tu-os, De-us me-us spe-rán-tes in te.

All other responses end in the
following manner except No. 9

tú-di-nis.

2. ℣ Esto nóbis Dómine túrris fortitúdinis.
   ℟ A fácie inimíci.
3. ℣ Níhil profíciat inimícus in nóbis,
   ℟ Et fílius iniquitátis non appónat nocére nóbis.
4. ℣ Dómine non secúndum peccáta nóstra fácias nóbis.
   ℟ Neque secúndum iniquitátes nóstras retríbuas nóbis.
5. ℣ Orémus pro Pontifice nóstro N.
   ℟ Dóminus consérvet éum, et vivíficet éum,† et beátum
   fáciat éum in térra, ✶ et non trádat éum in ánimam ini-
   micórum éjus. *Sede Vacante*, This ℣ and ℟ (5) are omitted.
6. ℣ Orémus pro benefactóribus nóstris.
   ℟ Retribúere dignáre Dómine,† ómnibus nóbis bóna faci-
   éntibus, própter nómen túum,✶ vítam ætérnam. Amen.
7. ℣ Orémus pro fidélibus defúnctis.
   ℟ Réquiem ætérnam dóna éis Dómine,✶ et lux perpétua
   lúceat éis.
8. ℣ Requiéscant in páce. ℟. Amen.
9. ℣ Pro frátribus nóstris abséntibus.
   ℟ Sálvos fac sérvos túos,✶ Déus méus, sperántes in te.
   (See No.1)
10. ℣ Mítte éis Dómine auxílium de sáncto.
    ℟ Et de Síon tuére éos.
11. ℣ Dómine exáudi oratiónem méam. ┌At the Reposition during
    ℟ Et clámor méus ad te véniat. ◄──Forty Hours' the procession
12. ℣ Dóminus vobíscum. ℟. Et cum spíritu tuo.│takes place
                                                 │here.

13. ℣ Per ómnia saécula saeculórum. ℟. Amen.
14. ℣ Dóminus vobíscum. ℟. Et cum spíritu túo.(See Note)
15. ℣ Exáudiat nos omnípotens et miséricors Dóminus.
    ℟ ✶(Et custódiat nos semper.) ✶Amen. ✶ (Forty Hours' only)
16. ℣ Fidélium ánimae etc. ℟. Amen.
*Note: At the closing of the Forty Hours' after the "Tantum Ergo" and "Genitori" with the Versicle
and response have been sung the celebrant sings the versicle "Domine exaudi" etc., the choir an-
swering: "Et clamor meus ad te veniat," then "Exaudiat nos," etc., with its proper response: "Et
custodiat nos semper," followed by "Fidelium animae" etc., closing with "Amen."*

O Salutaris Hostia (No. 1)
(Verbum Supernum Prodiens)

S. Webbe (1740-1816)

O sa - lu - tá - ris hó - sti - a, Quae
U - ni tri - nó - que Dó - mi - no Sit

cœ - li pan - dis ó - sti - um: Bél -
sem - pi - tér - na gló - ri - a, Qui

la pré - munt ho - sti - li - a, Da
ví - tam si - ne tér - mi - no No -

ró - bur, fer au - xí - li - um.
bis do - net in pá - tri - a.

A - men.

226 b
O Salutaris Hostia (No. 2)

Duguet (1780)

Moderato

O sa - lu - tá - ris hó - sti - a, Quæ
U - ni tri - nó - que Dó - mi - no Sit

cœ - li pan - dis ó - sti - um: Bél -
sem - pi - tér - na gló - ri - a, Qui

la pré - munt ho - stí - li - a, Da
ví - tam si - ne tér - mi - no No -

ró - bur, fer au - xí - li - um.
bis do - net in pá - tri - a. A - men.

O Salutaris Hostia (No. 3)

(Verbum Supernum Prodiens)

Gregorian

O sa - - lu - tá - ris hó - sti - a,
U - ni tri - nó - que Dó - mi - no

Quæ coe - li pan - dis ó - sti - um:
Sit sem - pi - tér - na gló - ri - a,

Bél - la pré - munt ho - stí - li - a,
Qui ví - tam si - ne tér - mi - no

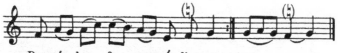

Da ró - bur, fer au - xí - li - um.
No - bis do - net in pá - tri - a. A - men.

226 d
O Salutaris Hostia (No. 4)
Unison Chorus

J. Rheinberger
Abridged and arr. by N.A.M.

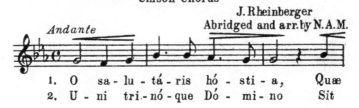

1. O sa - lu - tá - ris hó - sti - a,   Quæ
2. U - ni tri - nó - que Dó - mi - no   Sit

cœ - li pan - dis ó - sti - um: Bél - la
sem - pi - tér - na gló - ri - a,   Qui ví - tam

pré - munt ho - stí - li - a, Da ró - bur, fer au -
si - ne

xi - li - um. 2. tér - mi - no No - bis do -

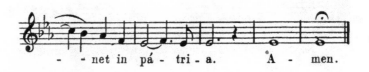

- net in pá - tri - a.   A - men.

O Salutaris Hostia (No. 5) 226 e

For three-part chorus (S.S.A. or T. T. B.)

Balthasar Florence
Arr. by N. A. M.

Andante religioso

O sa - lu - ta - ris ho - sti - a,
U - ni tri - no - que Do - mi - no

Quæ cœ - li pan - dis o - sti - um:
Sit sem - pi - ter - na glo - ri - a,

Bel - la pre - munt ho - sti - li - a,
Qui vi - tam si - ne ter - mi - no

cresc. e rit.

Da ro - bur, fer au - xi - li - um.
No - bis do - net in pa - tri - a. A - men.

* Small notes to be utilized in 3-part chorus.

226 f
O Salutaris Hostia (No. 6)

Nicola A. Montani

O sa-lu-ta-ris ho-sti-a, Quæ
U-ni tri-no-que Do-mi-no Sit

cœ-li pan-dis o-sti-um: Bel-la pre-
sem-pi-ter-na glo-ri-a, Qui vi-tam

munt ho-sti-li-a, Da ro-bur, fer au-
si-ne ter-mi-no No-bis do-net in

xi-li-um.
pa-tri-a. A-men.

O Salutaris Hostia (No. 7)

A. Werner

O sa - lu - ta - ris ho - sti - a,
U - ni tri - no - que Do - mi - no

Quae cœ - li pan - dis o - sti - um:
Sit sem - pi - ter - na glo - ri - a,

Bel - la pre - munt ho - sti - li - a,
Qui vi - tam si - ne ter - mi - no

Da ro - bur, fer au - xi - li - um.
No - bis do - net in pa - tri - a. A - men.

227 a
Adoro te devote (No. 1)

St Thomas Aquinas 1227-1274
Fifth Mode

Gregorian

1. A - dó - ro te de - vó - - te, la - tens Dé - i - tas, Quæ sub his fi - gú - ris ve - re la - ti - tas:
2. Vi - sus ta - ctus gú - stus in te fál - li - tur, Sed au - dí - tu so - lo tu - to cré - di - tur:
3. In crú - ce la - té - bat só - la Dé - i - tas, At hic lá - tet si - mul et hu - má - ni - tas:
4. Plá - gas, sic - ut Thó - mas, non in - tú - e - or, Dé - um ta - men mé - um te con - fí - te - or:
5. O me - mo - ri - á - le mór - tis Dó - mi - ni, Pá - nis ví - vus, ví - tam præ - stans hó - mi - ni:
6. Pí - e Pel - li - cá - ne, Jé - su Dó - mi - ne, Me im - mún - dum mún - da tú - o sán - gui - ne,
7. Jé - su, quem ve - lá - tum nunc ad - spí - ci - o, O - ro fí - at íl - lud quod tam sí - ti - o:

376

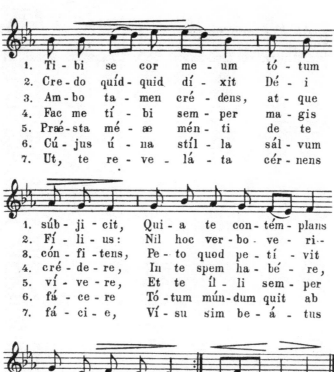

1. Ti - bi se cor me - um tó - tum
2. Cre - do quíd - quid dí - xit Dé - i
3. Am - bo ta - men cré - dens, at - que
4. Fac me tí - bi sem - per ma - gis
5. Praé - sta mé - æ mén - ti de te
6. Cú - jus ú - na stíl - la sál - vum
7. Ut, te re - ve - lá - ta cér - nens

1. súb - ji - cit, Qui - a te con - tém - plans
2. Fí - li - us: Nil hoc ver - bo ve - ri -
3. cón - fi - tens, Pe - to quod pe - tí - vit
4. cré - de - re, In te spem ha - bé - re,
5. ví - ve - re, Et te íl - li sem - per
6. fá - ce - re Tó - tum mún - dum quit ab
7. fá - ci - e, Ví - su sim be - á - tus

1. to - tum dé - fi - cit.
2. ta - tis vé - ri - us.
3. la - tro pæ - ni - tens.
4. te di - lí - ge - re.
5. dúl - ce sá - pe - re.
6. ó - mni scé - le - re.
7. tú - æ gló - ri - æ.   A - men.

377

227 b   Adoro te devote (No. 2)

Ch. Gounod
Arr. by N.A.M.

Lento

A - dó - ro te de - vo - te, la - tens
Vi - sus, ta - ctus, gus - tus in te

De - i - tas, Quae sub his fi -
fal - li - tur, Sed au - di - tu

gu - ris ve - re la - ti - tas:
so - lo tu - to cre - di - tur:

Ti - bi se cor me - um to - tum sub - ji -
Cre - do quid - quid di - xit De - i Fi - li -

cit; Qui - a te con - tem - plans to - tum
us: Nil hoc Ver - bo ve - ri - ta - tis

de - fi - cit.
ve - ri - us.   A - men.

Additional stanzas given on preceding page.

O Esca Viatorum (No.1)

Heinrich Isaak (1493 1531)
Arr. by J.S. Bach

228 a

1. O e - sca vi - a - to - rum, O
2. O lym - pha, fons a - mo - ris, Qui
3. O Je - su, tu - um vul - tum, Quem

1. pa - nis An - ge - lo - rum, O
2. pu - ro Sal - va - to - ris, E
3. co - li - mus oc - cul - tum Sub

1. man - na coe - li - tum: E - su - ri - en - tes
2. cor - de pro - flu - is; Te si - ti - en - tes
3. pa - nis spe - ci - e: Fac ut, re - mo - to

1. ci - ba, Dul - ce - di - ne non
2. po - ta, Haec so - la no - stra
3. ve - lo, Post, li - be - ra in

1. pri - va, Cor - da quae - ren - ti - um.
2. vo - ta, His u - na suf - fi - cis.
3. coe - lo, Cer - na - mus a - ci - e.

379

228 b O Esca Viatorum (No. 2)

For Unison or Two-Part Chorus

Traditional Melody
Arr. by P. J. Van Damme

Moderato

1. O e - sca vi - a - to - rum,
2. O lym - pha, fons a - mo - ris, Qui
3. O Je - su, tu - um vul - tum, Quem

1. pa - nis An - ge - lo - rum, O man - na coe - li -
2. pu - ro Sal - va - to - ris E cor - de pro - flu -
3. co - li - mus oc - cul - tum Sub pa - nis spe - ci -

1. tum: E - su - ri - en - tes ci - ba, Dul -
2. is; Te si - ti - en - tes po - ta, Hæc
3. e: Fac ut, re - mo - to ve - lo, Post,

1. ce - di - ne non pri - va, Cor - da quæ - ren - ti -
2. so - la no - stra vo - ta, His u - na suf - fi -
3. li - be - ra in cœ - lo, Cer - na - mus a - ci -

1. um, Cor - da quæ - ren - ti - um.
2. cis, His u - na suf - fi - cis.
3. e, Cer - na - mus a - ci - e. A - men.

Panis Angelicus (No. 1)
Sacris Solemniis

P. Meurers

Pa - nis an - ge - li - cus fit pa - nis
Te tri - na De - i - tas u - na - que

ho - mi - num; Dat pa - nis coe - li - cus fi -
po - sci - mus, Sic nos tu vi - si - ta, sic -

gu - ris ter - mi - num: O res mi -
ut te co - li - mus; Per tu - as

ra - bi - lis! mán - du - cat Do - mi - num
se - mi - tas duc nos quo ten - di - mus,

Pau - per, ser - vus, et hu - mi - lis.
Ad lu - cem quam in - ha - bi - tas. A - men.

229 b

Panis Angelicus (No. 2)

Unison, Two or Four-part chorus

Fr. Lambilotte

Andante religioso

Pa - nis an - ge - li - cus fit pa - nis
Te tri - na De - i - tas u - na - que

ho - mi - num; Dat pa - nis coe - li - cus fi - gu - ris
po - sci - mus, Sic nos tu vi - si - ta, sic - ut te

ter - mi - num: O res mi - ra - bi - lis!
co - li - mus; Per tu - as se - mi - tas

man - du - cat Do - mi - num Pau - per,
duc nos quo ten - di - mus, Ad lu - -

After last verse

ser - vus, et hu - mi - lis.
cem quam in - ha - bi - tas. A - men.

Sacris Solemniis
(Panis Angelicus)
For Unison Chorus

J. Mohr

Andante devota

1. Sa - cris so - lé - mni - is   jun - cta   sint
2. No - ctis   re - co - li - tur   coe - na   no -

gau - di - a,   Et   ex   præ - cor - di - is
vis - si - ma,   Qua Chri - stus   cre - di - tur

so - nent præ - co - ni - a;   Re - cé - dant ve - te - ra,
a - gnum et a - zy - ma   De - dís - se   fra - tri - bus,

no - va   sint   o - mni - a,   Cor - da,
jux - ta   le - gi - ti - ma   Pri - scis

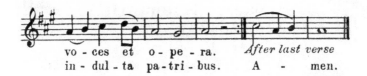

vo - ces et o - pe - ra. *After last verse*

in - dul - ta pa - tri - bus. A - men.

3. Post ágnum týpicum, explétis épulis,
   Corpus Domínicum datum discípulis,
   Sic totum ómnibus, quod totum síngulis,
   Ejus fatémur mánibus.

4. Dedit fragílibus córporis férculum,
   Dedit et trístibus sánguinis póculum,
   Dicens: Accípite, quod trado vásculum,
   Omnes ex eo bíbite.

5. Sic sacrifícium istud instítuit,
   Cujus offícium commítti vóluit
   Solís presbýteris, quibus sic cóngruit,
   Ut sumant, et dent céteris.

6. Panis Angélicus fit panis hóminum;
   Dat panis coelicus figúris términum;
   O res mirábilis! mandúcat Dóminum
   Pauper, servus, et húmilis.

7. Te trina Déitas unáque póscimus,
   Sic nos tu vísita, sicut te cólimus:
   Per tuas sémitas duc nos quo téndimus
   Ad lucem quam inhábitas. Amen.

384

Ecce Panis Angelorum (No.1)
Lauda Sion

Portuguese Melody

Andante religioso

1. Ec - ce pa - nis An - ge - lo - rum,
2. In fi - gu - ris prae - si - gna - tur,

Fa - ctus ci - bus vi - a - to - rum:
Cum I - sa - ac im - mo - la - tur,

Ve - re pa - nis fi - li - o - rum,
A - gnus Pa - schæ de - pu - ta - tur,

Non mit - ten - dus ca - ni - bus.
Da - tur man - na pa - tri - bus.

231 b
Ecce Panis Angelorum (No. 2)
Lauda Sion

Vatican Graduale

1. Ec - ce pá - nis An - ge - ló - rum,
2. In fi - gú - ris præ - si - gná - tur,

Fá - ctus ci - bus vi - a - tó - rum:
Cum I - sa - ac im - mo - lá - tur.

Vé - re pá - nis fi - li - ó - rum,
A - gnus Pa - schæ de - pu - tá - tur,

Non mit - tén - dus cá - ni - bus.
Da - tur mán - na pá - tri - bus.

Bone Pastor

3. Bo - ne pa - stor, pa - nis ve - re,
4. Tu qui cún - cta scis et vá - les,

Je - su, nó - stri mi - se - ré - re: Tu nos pá -
Qui nos pa - scis hic mor - tá - les: Tu - os i -

sce, nos tu - é - re, Tu nos bó - na fac vi - dé - re
bi com - men - sá - les, Co - hae - ré - des et so - dá - les

In ter - ra vi - vén - ti - um.
Fac san - ctórum cí - vi - um. A - men. Al - le - lu - ia.

232

Adoramus te, panem coelitum

For unison or two part chorus

Traditional Melody
Harmonized by P. J. Van Damme

Ad - o - ra - mus te, pa - nem coe - li -
tum, Ci - bum vi - tae de - sur - sum prae - sti -
tum. A - ve, a - ve, a -
ve, coe - li pa - nis vi - ve. Lau - de - tur in æ -
ter - num san - ctis - si - mum Sa - cra - men - tum.

Ave Verum Corpus (No. 1)

Unison, two or four part chorus

Ch. Gounod
Liturgically arranged by N. A.M.

A - ve, a - ve ve - rum Cor - pus

na - tum de Ma - ri - a Vir - gi - ne: Ve - re

pas - sum, im - mo - la - tum, im - mo - la - tum in

cru - ce pro ho - mi - ne, in cru - ce pro ho - mi - ne:

Cu - jus la - tus per - fo - ra - tum

flu - xit a - qua et san - gui - ne:

E - sto no - bis prae - gu - sta - tum mor - tis

in ex - a - mi - ne. O Je - su dul - cis!

O Je - su pi - e! O Je - su fi - li Ma - ri - -

æ, O Je - su fi - li Ma - ri - æ!

Ave Verum Corpus (No. 2)

Unison, two or four part chorus

C. St. Saens

Liturgically arranged by N: A.M.

233 c
Ave Verum Corpus (No. 3)

W. A. Mozart
Arr. for unison, two or
four part chorus by N. A. M.

A - ve, a - ve ve - rum

Cor - pus na - tum de Ma - ri - a Vir - gi - ne:

Ve - re pas - sum, im - mo - la - tum in

cru - ce, pro ho - mi - ne:

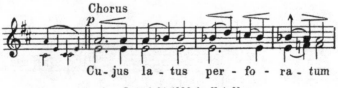

Cu - jus la - tus per - fo - ra - tum

flu - xit a - qua et san - gui - ne:

E - sto no - bis prae - gu - sta - tum

mor - tis in ex - a - mi - ne,

mor - tis, mor - tis in

ex - a - mi - ne.

233 d
Ave Verum Corpus (No. 4)

Alex. Guilmant
Adapted and arranged for unison, two
or four part chorus by N. A. M.

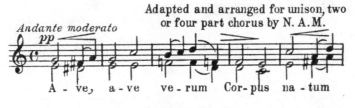

A - ve, a - ve ve - rum Cor- pus na - tum

de Ma - ri - a Vir - gi - ne: Ve - re pas - sum,

im - mo - la - tum in cru - ce pro ho - mi -

ne: Cu - jus la - tus

per - fo - ra - tum flu - xit a - qua et san - gui-

ne: E - sto no - bis prae - gu - sta - tum

mor - tis in ex - a - mi - ne:

Tempo I
Chorus

O Je-su dul - cis! O Je-su pi - e! O Je-su

dul - cis! Je-su pi - e! O Je - su fi - li Ma-

ri - ae, fi - li Ma - ri - ae!

233 e
Ave Verum Corpus (No. 5)
Prosa antiqua usu recepta

Sixth Mode   Gregorian

1. A - ve vé - rum Cór - pus ná - tum
2. Ve - re pás-sum, im - mo - lá - tum

de Ma - rí - a Vír - gi - ne:__
in crú - ce pro hó - mi - ne:__

3. Cu-jus la-tus per - fo - rá - tum flú - xit á -
4. E -sto no-bis præ-gu-stá - tum mór - tis

qua et sán-gui-ne. 5. O   Je-su dul - cis!
in ex-á -mi -ne: 6. O   Je-su pi - e!

7. O   Je - su fi - li Ma - ri - æ.__

396

O quam suavis est

Antiphon. (according to the Vatican Edition of the Antiphonale.)
Sixth Mode

O - - quam su- a - vis est, Dó - -

- - mi-ne, spí - ri-tus tú - us!

qui, ut dul-cé-di - nem tu - am

in fi - li - os de - mon - strá - res,

pa - ne   su - a - vís - si - mo _____

de _____ cœ - lo præ - stí - to,

e - su - ri - én - tes   re - ples   bó - nis,

fa - sti - di - ó - sos   dí - vi _ tes

di - mít - tens   in - - - á - nes.

O Sacrum Convivium 235

Motet   R. Remondi

Arr. for unison, two or four part chorus by N.A.M.

Adagio (con espressione)

O sa - crum con - vi - vi - um! in quo Chri - stus

su - mi - tur: re - co - li - tur me - mo - ri - a pas - si -

o - nis e - jus, pas - si - o - nis e - jus:

Mens im - ple - tur gra - ti - a, mens im - ple - tur gra - ti - a: et fu -

tu - ræ glo - ri - æ no - bis pi - gnus da - tur, Al - le -

lu - ia, al - le - lu - ia, al - le - lu - ia.

THE SACRED HEART

O Cor Jesu
Two part chorus

Don Lorenzo Perosi

O cor Je - su fla-grans a - mo - re
no - stri,— O cor Je - su fla-grans a -
mo - re no - - stri, in - flam-ma cor
no-strum a - mo-re tu - i, in - flam-ma cor
no-strum a - mo - re tu - i.

Cor Jesu, salus in te sperantium

Unison or two part chorus

W. Schultes (1815-1879)
Abridged and arr. by N.A.M.

Andante sostenuto

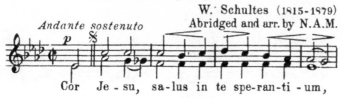

Cor Je - su, sa - lus in te spe - ran - ti - um,

mi - se - re - re no - bis, Cor Je - su,

spes in te mo - ri - en - ti - um, mi - se - re - re

no - bis. Cor Je - su de - lí - ci - æ san - ctó - rum

o - mni - um, mi - se - re - re, mi - se - re - re no - bis. Cor

238 a
INVOCATION TO THE SACRED HEART *

Cor Jesu Sacratissimum (No. 1)

First Mode   Gregorian

1. Cor Jesu	Sa-cra-tíssimum, miseré-re no-bis.
2. Cor Maríæ im -	ma-cu-lá-tum, o - ra pro no-bis.
3. Sanctæ Joseph	
patrónæ noster	di-lec-tís-si-me, o - ra pro no-bis.

238 b
Cor Jesu Sacratissimum (No. 2)*

Fourth Mode   Gregorian

Cor Je- su. Sa-cra-tís-si -mum, mi-se-ré-re no-bis.

* Note: These Invocations can be sung before each verse of the "Laudate Dominum" (First and Fourth Tones) in place of the "Adoremus". (No. 243 a - d)

239   PLEA FOR GOD'S MERCY
Usually sung before the 50th Psalm: Miserere mei Deus

Parce Domine
Gregorian

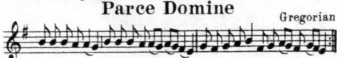

Parce Domine, parce populo tu-o· ne in ætérnum irascáris nobis
Sung three times

Ss. Cordis Jesu

Cor, arca legem continens

15th Century Melody
"Alta Trinita"

1. Cor, ar-ca le-gem con-ti-nens Non ser-vi-
2. Cor san-ctu-a-ri-um no - vi In - te-me-
3. Te vul-ne-ra-tum ca - ri - tas I - ctu pa-
4. Hoc sub a - mo-ris sym-bo - lo Pas-sus cru-
5. Quis non a-man-tem re - da - met? Quis non re-
6. De-cus Pa-ren-ti, et Fi - li - o San-cto-que

1. tu - tis ve-te - ris, Sed gra-ti-æ, Sed ve-ni-
2. ra-tum foe-de-ris, Tem-plum ve-tu-sto san-cti -
3. ten-ti vo-lu-it, A - mo-ris in-vi - si-bi -
4. en-ta et my-sti-ca, Ut-rum-que sa-cri-fi - ci -
5. dem-ptus di-li-gat, Et Cor-de in i-sto se-li -
6. sit Spi - ri-tu - i, Qui-bus po-tes-tas, glo-ri -

1. æ, Sed et mi-se-ri-cor-di - æ.
2. us, Ve-lum-que scis-so u-ti - li - us.
3. lis Ut ve-he-re-mur vul-ne - ra.
4. um Chri-stus sa-cer-dos ob - tu - lit.
5. gat Æ - ter-na ta-ber-na-cu - la?
6. a, Regnumque in omne est sae-cu-lum. A - men.

PROCESSIONS, BENEDICTION, 40 HOURS'

Pange Lingua (No.1)
(Tantum Ergo)

Third Mode

Gregorian
Vatican Graduale

1. Pan - ge lín - gua glo - ri - ó - si, *
2. No - bis da - tus, no - bis na - tus
3. In su - pré - mæ no - cte coe - nae,
4. Ver - bum ca - ro, pa - nem ve - rum
5. *Tan - tum er - go Sa - cra - mén - tum*
6. *Ge - ni - tó - ri, Ge - ni - tó - que*

1. Cór - po - ris my - sté - ri - um _____
2. Ex in - tá - cta Vír - gi - ne, _____
3. Ré - cum - bens cum frá - tri - bus, _____
4. Ver - bo car - nem éf - fi - cit: _____
5. *Ve - ne - ré - mur cér - nu - i: _____*
6. *Laus et ju - bi - lá - ti - o, _____*

1. San - gui - nís - que pre - ti - ó - si,
2. Et in mún - do con - ver - sá - tus,
3. Ob - ser - vá - ta le - ge ple - ne
4. Fit - que san - guis Chri - sti me - rum,
5. *Et an - tí - quum do - cu - mén - tum*
6. *Sa - lus, ho - nor, vir - tus quo - que*

1. Quem in mún - di pré - ti - um
2. Spar - so vér - bi sé - mi - ne,
3. Ci - bis in le - gá - li - bus,
4. Et si sen - sus dé - fi - cit,
5. *No - vo ce - dat rí - tu - i;*
6. *Sit et be - ne - dí - cti - o:*

1. Fru - ctus ven - tris ge - ne - ró - si
2. Su - i mo - ras in - co - lá - tus
3. Ci - bum tur - bae du - o - dé - nae
4. Ad fir - mán - dum cor sin - cé - rum
5. *Prœ - stet fi - des sup - ple - mén - tum*
6. *Pro - ce - dén - ti ab u - tró - que*

1. Rex ef - fu - dit gen - ti - um.
2. Mi - ro clau - sit or - di - ne.
3. Se dat su - is ma - ni - bus.
4. So - la fi - des suf - fi - cit.
5. *Sen - su - um de - fe - ctu - i.*
6. *Com - par sit lau - da - ti - o.* A - men.

After last verse

Pange Lingua (No. 2)
(Tantum Ergo)

Gregorian
(Apud Italos usitatum)

First Mode

1. Pan - ge lín - gua glo - ri - ó - si, *
2. No - bis da - tus, no - bis na - tus
3. In su - pré - mae no - cte coe - nae,
4. Ver - bum ca - ro, pa - nem ve - rum
5. Tan - tum er - go Sa - cra - mén - tum
6. Ge - ni - tó - ri, Ge - ni - tó - que

1. Cór - po - ris my - sté - ri - um, —
2. Ex in - tá - cta Vír - gi - ne, —
3. Ré - cum - bens cum frá - tri - bus, —
4. Ver - bo car - nem éf - fi - cit: —
5. Ve - ne - ré - mur cér - nu - i: —
6. Laus et ju - bi - lá - ti - o, —

1. San - gui - nís - que pre - ti - ó - si,
2. Et in mún - do con - ver - sá - tus,
3. Ob - ser - vá - ta le - ge ple - ne
4. Fit - que san - guis Chri - sti me - rum,
5. Et an - tí - quum do - cu - mén - tum
6. Sa - lus, ho - nor, vir - tus quo - que

406

1. Quem in mún-di pré-ti-um ____
2. Spar-so ver-bi sé-mi-ne, ____
3. Ci-bis in le-gá-li-bus, ____
4. Et si sen-sus dé-fi-cit, ____
5. *No-vo ce-dat rí-tu-i;* ____
6. *Sit et be-ne-dí-cti-o:* ____

1. Fru-ctus ven-tris ge-ne-ró-si
2. Su-i mo-ras in-co-lá-tus
3. Ci-bum tur-bæ du-o-dé-næ
4. Ad fir-mán-dum cor sin-cé-rum
5. *Præ-stet fi-des sup-ple-mén-tum*
6. *Pro-ce-dén-ti ab u-tró-que*

1. Rex ef-fú-dit gén-ti-um
2. Mi-ro clau-sit ór-di-ne
3. Se dat su-is má-ni-bus
4. So-la fi-des súf-fi-cit
5. *Sén-su-um de-fé-ctu-i*
6. *Com-par sit lau-dá-ti-o*

After last verse

A - men.

407

242 a   Tantum Ergo (No. 1)

(The "Pange Lingua" may be sung to this and any of the melodies of the Tantum Ergo.)

Jos. H. Beltjens
Abridged and arranged by N. A.M.

Tan-tum er - go Sa - cra - men - tum Ve - ne -
Ge - ni - to - ri, Ge - ni - to - que Laus et

re - mur cer - nu - i: Et an - ti - quum
ju - bi - la - ti - o, Sa - lus, ho - nor,

do - cu - men - tum No - vo ce - dat ri - tu -
vir - tus quo - que Sit et be - ne - di - cti -

i: Præ - stet fi - des sup - ple - men - tum
o: Pro - ce - den - ti ab u - tro - que

Sen - su - um de - fe - ctu - i.
Com - par sit lau - da - ti - o.

After last verse

A - men.

Tantum Ergo (No. 2) 242 b

Arr. by N. A. M.

Traditional Melody from Ms.
dated 1751 Stonyhurst
Also Epitome Rit. Trevir.

Tan - tum er - go Sa - cra - men - tum
Ge - ni - to - ri, Ge - ni - to - que

Ve - ne - re - mur cer - nu - i: Et an - ti - quum
Laus et ju - bi - la - ti - o, Sa - lus, ho - nor,

do - cu - men - tum No - vo ce - dat
vir - tus quo - que Sit et be - ne -

ri - tu - i: Prae - stet fi - des sup - ple - men - tum
di - cti - o: Pro - ce - den - ti ab u - tro - que

Sen - su - um de - fe - ctu - i.
Com - par sit lau - da - ti - o. A - men.

Response: Omne delectaméntum in se habéntem.(T. P. Alleluia).

409

242 c Tantum Ergo (No. 3)

For unison chorus or chorus in 2 or 4 parts
(Also 3-pt.chorus*)

Balthasar Florence
Arr. by N.A.M.

Moderato

Tan-tum er - go Sa - cra - men-tum Ve - ne -
Ge - ni - to - ri, Ge - ni - to - que Laus et

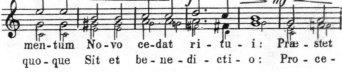

re-mur cer-nu - i: Et an - ti-quum do - cu -
ju - bi - la - ti - o, Sa - lus, ho-nor, vir -tus

mentum No-vo ce-dat ri - tu - i: Prae - stet
quo - que Sit et be - ne - di - cti - o: Pro - ce -

fi - des sup - ple-men - tum Sen-su - um de -
den- ti ab u - tro-que Com - par sit lau -

fe - ctu - i.
da - ti - o.   A -   - men.

Small notes to be utilized in 3-part chorus.

Tantum Ergo (No. 4)
Choral

Moderato

O. Ravanello

Tan-tum er-go Sa-cra-men-tum,
Ge-ni-to-ri, Ge-ni-to-que

Ve-ne-re-mur cer-nu-i: Et an-
Laus et ju-bi-la-ti-o, Sa-lus,

ti-quum do-cu-men-tum, No-vo ce-dat
ho-nor, vir-tus quo-que, Sit et be-ne-

ri-tu-i: Præ-stet fi-des sup-ple-men-tum
di-cti-o: Pro-ce-den-ti ab u-tro-que

Sen-su-um de-fe-ctu-i.
Com-par sit lau-da-ti-o.   A-men.

Response: Omne delectaméntum in se habentem. (T.P. Alleluia.)

242 e **Tantum Ergo** (No. 5)

Unison or two part chorus

Andante religioso   W. A. Smit

Tan - tum er - go Sa - cra - men - tum
Ge - ni - to - ri, Ge - ni - to - que

Ve - ne - re - mur cer - nu - i: Et an -
Laus et ju - bi - la - ti - o, Sa - lus,

ti - quum do - cu - men - tum No - vo ce - dat
ho - nor, vir - tus quo - que Sit et be - ne -

ri - tu - i: Præ - stet fi - des sup - ple - men - tum
di - cti - o: Pro - ce - den - ti ab u - tro - que

Sen - su - um de - fe - ctu - i.
Com - par sit lau - da - ti - o. A - men.

Omne delectaméntum in se habéntem. (T. P. Alleluia).

Tantum Ergo (No. 6)

M. Haydn (1737-1806)

Tan - tum er - go Sa - cra - men - tum
Ge - ni - to - ri, Ge - ni - to - que

Ve - ne - re - mur cer - nu - i: Et an - ti - quum
Laus et ju - bi - la - ti - o, Sa - lus, ho - nor,

do - cu - men - tum No - vo ce - dat
vir - tus quo - que Sit et be - ne -

ri - tu - i: Prae - stet fi - des sup - ple - men - tum
di - cti - o: Pro - ce - den - ti ab u - tro - que

Sen - su - um de - fe - ctu - i
Com - par sit lau - da - ti - o A - men.

242 g

Tantum Ergo (No. 7)

Melody from a Slovak Hymnal
Adapted by N. A. M.

Moderately fast

Tan - tum er - go Sa - cra - men - tum
Ge - ni - to - ri, Ge - ni - to - que

Ve - ne - re - mur cer - nu - i: Et an -
Laus et ju - bi - la - ti - o, Sa - lus,

ti - quum do - cu - men - tum No - vo ce - dat
ho - nor, vir - tus quo - que Sit et be - ne -

ri - tu - i: Præ - stet fi - des sup - ple - men - tum
di - cti - o: Pro - ce - den - ti ab u - tro - que

Sen - su - um de - fe - ctu - i.
Com - par sit lau - da - ti - o. A - men.

Tantum Ergo (No. 8)

J. Mohr

Moderato
mf

Tan - tum er - go Sa - cra - men - tum
Ge - ni - to - ri, Ge - ni - to - que

Ve - ne - re - mur cer - nu - i: Et an - ti - quum
Laus et ju - bi - la - ti - o, Sa - lus, ho - nor,

do - cu - men - tum No - vo ce - dat
vir - tus quo - que Sit et be - ne -

ri - tu - i: Præ-stet fi - des sup - ple - men - tum
di - cti - o: Pro - ce - den - ti ab u - tro - que

rall

Sen - su - um de - fe - ctu - i.
Com-par sit lau - da - ti - o. A - men.

415

242 i   Tantum Ergo (No. 9)

Unison or two part chorus

Th. Dubois
Arr. by N. A. M.

Andante religioso.

Tan - tum er - go Sa - cra - men - tum
Ge - ni - to - ri, Ge - ni - to - que

Ve - ne - re - mur cer - nu - i: Et an -
Laus et ju - bi - la - ti - o, Sa - lus,

ti - quum do - cu - men - tum No - vo ce - dat
ho - nor, vir - tus quo - que Sit et be - ne -

ri - tu - i: Prae - stet fi - des sup - ple -
di - cti - o: Pro - ce - den - ti ab u -

men - tum Sen - su - um de - fe - ctu - i.
tro - que Com - par sit lau - da - ti - o. A - men.

Tantum Ergo (No. 10)

Unison Chorus

Nicola A. Montani

Not too slow

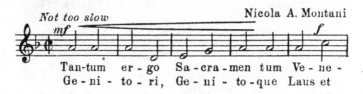

Tan-tum er-go Sa-cra-men tum Ve-ne-
Ge-ni-to-ri, Ge-ni-to-que Laus et

re-mur cer-nu-i, Et an-ti-quum
ju-bi-la-ti-o, Sa-lus, ho-nor,

do-cu-men-tum No-vo ce-dat ri-tu-
vir-tus quo-que Sit et be-ne-di-cti-

i: Præ-stet fi-des sup-ple-men-tum
o: Pro-ce-den-ti ab u-tro-que

Sen-su-um de-fe-ctu-i.
Com-par sit lau-da-ti-o.   A-men.

Adoremus: **Laudate Dominum** (No. 1)
Psalm Tones

Instead of the *Adoremus* the Invocation to the Sacred
Heart or to the Holy Family (No. 238 A-B) may be sung
before the *Laudate Dominum*.

First Psalm Tone   Gregorian
                                    Vatican Antiphonale

1. Lau-dá - te Dóminum   ó-mnes   gén - tes: *→

2. .... Quóniam confirmáta est

             súper nos miseri - cór- di - a   e   - jus: *→

3. .... Glória   Pá-tri, et Fí- li - o: *→

4. .... Sícut erat in princípio,

             et nunc, et   sem - per: *→

Sanctíssimum   Sa-cra-mén - tum.

1. laudáte éum   ó-mnes pó - pu - li.

2. et véritas Dómini mánet   in æ - tér - num.

3. et Spirí -   - - - tu - i Sán - cto.

4. et in sáecula sæcu -   - ló-rum. A - men.

Repeat "Adoremus"
or "Invocation"

243 b
Adoremus and Laudate (No. 2)

Second Psalm Tone

A - do - ré - mus in æ - - - - tér - num →

1. Lau dá te   Dóminum ómnes   gén - tes:*→
2. ....   Quóniam confirmáta est
                súper nos misericórdia   e - jus:*→
3. ....   Glória Pátri, et   Fí - li - o:*→
4. ....   Sícut erat in princípio,
                et nunc, et   sem - per:*→

243 c

Adoremus and Laudate (No. 3)

Third Psalm Tone

A - do - rémus   in   æ - tér-num →

1. Lau-dú - te Dóminum   ó - mnes gén - tes:*→
2. ....   Quóniam confirmáta
                est súper nos miseri-cór-di- a   e - jus:*→
3. ....   Glória   Pá-tri. et Fí-li - o:*→
4. ....   Sícut erat in prin-
                cípio, et nunc, et   sem-per:*→

Sanctíssimum Sa - - - cra - mén - tum.

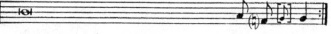

1. laudáte éum ó _ _ _ _ mnes pó-pu-li.

2. et véritas Dómini mánet in   æ - tér - num.
3. et Spirítu - - - - i Sán - cto.

4. et in saécula saeculó - - - rum. A - men.

Repeat "Adoremus"
or "Invocation"

Sanctíssimum   Sa - cra-mén - tum.

1. laudáte éum   ó - mnes pó-pu-li.

2. et véritas Dómini mánet   in æ - tér - num.
3. et Spirí - - - - tu - i Sán - cto.

4. et in saécula saecu - - - ló-rum. A - men.

Repeat "Adoremus"

243 d
Adoremus and Laudate (No.4)

Fourth Psalm Tone

A - do - rémus   in æ -tér - num →

1 Lau-dá - te Dóminum   ó-mnes gén - tes: ✳→
2. .... Quóniam confirmáta est
                 súper nos misericór - di - a e - jus: ✳→
3. .... Glória Pá - - - tri, et Fí-li - o: ✳→
4. .... Sícut erat in princípio,
                       et nunc, et sém _ per: ✳→

243 e
Adoremus and Laudate (No.5)

Fifth Psalm Tone

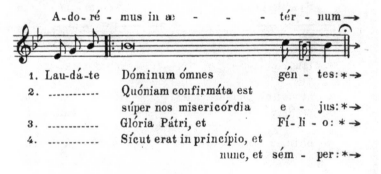

A - do - ré - mus in æ - - - tér - num →

1. Lau-dá-te   Dóminum ómnes   gén - tes: ✳→
2. .... Quóniam confirmáta est
                 súper nos misericórdia   e - jus: ✳→
3. .... Glória Pátri, et   Fí- li - o: ✳→
4. .... Sícut erat in princípio, et
                       nunc, et sém - per: ✳→

422

1. laudáte e - - - um o-mnes po-pu-li.

Sanctíssi - - - - mum Sa-cra-mén - tum.

1. laudáte é - - - um ó-mnes pó-pu-li.

2. et véritas Dómini má - - net in æ - - tér-num.

3. et Spi - - - - rí-tu-i San-cto.

4. et in sǽcula sae - - - cu-ló-rum. A - men.

Repeat "Adoremus"

Sanctíssimum Sa - cra - mén - tum.

1 laudáte éum ó - mnes pó-pu-li.

2. et véritas Dómini mánet in æ - tér - num.

3. et Spi - - - rí-tu-i Sán - cto.

4. et in sǽcula sǽcu - - ló-rum. A - men.

Repeat "Adoremus"

243 f
Adoremus and Laudate (No. 6)

Sixth Psalm Tone

243 g
Adoremus and Laudate (No. 7)

Seventh Psalm Tone

Sanctíssimum   Sa - cra - mén - tum.

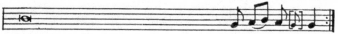

1. laudáte éum   ó - mnes pó-pu-li.

2. et véritas Dómini mánet   in æ - tér - num.
3. et Spirí -   -   -   - tu - i Sán - cto.

4. et in sǽcula sæcu -   -   - ló-rum. A - men.

Repeat "Adoremus"

Sanctíssimum   Sa - cra - mén - tum.

1. laudáte éum   ó - mnes pó - pu - li.

2. et véritas Dómini mánet   in æ - tér - num.
3. et Spi -   -   -   - rí - tu - i Sán - cto.

4. et in sǽcula sæcu -   -   - ló-rum. A - men.

Repeat "Adoremus"

425

243 h
Adoremus and Laudate (No. 8)

Eighth Psalm Tone

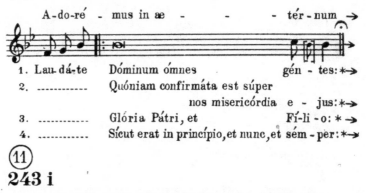

1. Lau-dá-te Dóminum ómnes   gén - tes: *→
2. .... Quóniam confirmáta est súper
            nos misericórdia e - jus: *→
3. .... Glória Pátri, et   Fí-li - o: * →
4. .... Sícut erat in princípio, et nunc, et sém - per: *→

(11)
243 i

Adoremus and Laudate (No. 9)

Moderato   Arr. by N. A. M.

(optional)

1. Lau-da-te Dóminum ómnes   gén - tes: *→
2. .... Quóniam confirmáta est súper
            nos misericórdia e - jus: *→
3. .... Glória Pátri, et   Fí-li - o: * →
4. .... Sícut erat in princípio, et nunc, et sém - per: *→

Sanctíssimum   Sa-cra-mén -tum.

1. laudáte éum   ó-mnes pó-pu-li.

2. et véritas Dómini mánet   in ae-tér - num.
3 et Spirí -   -   -   - tu- i Sán -cto.
4. et in saécula saecu -   -   - ló-rum.A - men.

Repeat "Adoremus"

San -ctís - si - mum Sa - cra - mén - - - tum.

Sanctíssimum   Sa - cra-mén - tum.

1. laudáte éum   ó- mnes pó-pu-li.

2. et véritas Dómini mánet   in ae - tér - num.
3. et Spirí -   -   -   - tu - i Sán - cto.
4. et in saécula saecu -   -   - ló-rum. A - men.

Repeat "Adoremus"

244 ## Sacerdos et Pontifex

Sung at the entrance of the Bishop, Archbishop or Cardinal
("Ecce Sacerdos" may be sung instead if preferred.)

Antiphon. First Mode   Gregorian

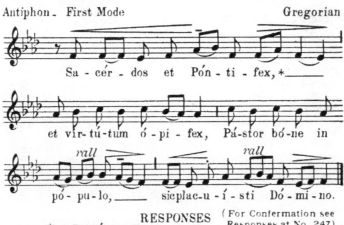

Sa - cér - dos   et   Pón - ti - fex, *
et vir - tú - tum ó - pi - fex,   Pá-stor bó-ne in
rall   *rall*
pó - pu - lo,   sicplac-u - í - sti Dó - mi - no.

RESPONSES   (For Confirmation see Responses at No. 247)

℣. Protéctor noster --- etc.
℟. Et réspice in fáciem Christi tui.
℣. Sálvum fac --- etc.
℟. Deus meus sperántem in te
℣. Mitte ei Dómine --- etc.
℟. Et de Sion tuére eum.
℣. Nihil Profíciat --- etc.
℟. Et fílius iniquitátis non oppónat nocére ei.
℣. Dómine exáudi --- etc.
℟. Et clámor meus ad te véniat.
℣. Dóminus vobíscum
℟. Et cum Spíritu tuo. (Orémus etc.) Amen.

Note: During the Confirmation, Choir may sing appropriate
Hymns: Veni Sancte Spiritus, Veni Creator, Magníficat, etc.
After the recitation of the Creed, "The Lord's Prayer" and "Hail
Mary" English Hymns may be sung.

245

Confirma hoc Deus

(Sung after Confirmation, at the washing of hands)

J. Rheinberger
Arr. by N. A. M.

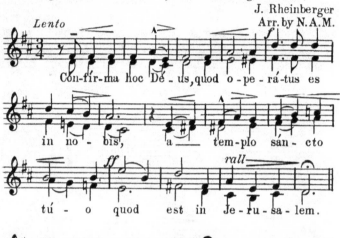

Con-fír-ma hoc Dé - us, quod o - pe - rá-tus es
in no - bis, a — tem-plo sán - cto
tú - o quod est in Je-rú-sa-lem.

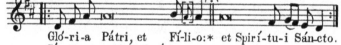

Gló-ri-a Pátri, et   Fí-li-o:✳ et Spirí-tu-i Sán-cto.
Sí-cut e - rat in princí-
pio, et nunc,
       et sémper:✳ et in sǽ-
        cula sæ -
         cu-ló-rum. A-men.
         Repeat "Confirma"

RESPONSES

℣. Osténde nobis, etc .   ℞. Et salutáre tuum da nobis.
℣. Dómine exáudi, etc .   ℞. Et clamor meus ad te véniat.
℣. Dóminus vobíscum   ℞. Et cum Spíritu tuo.

Ceremonies may terminate with singing of "Te Deum" (No. 264)
For the responses, at the Pontifical Blessing See No. 259-(11)

246

Ecce Sacerdos

Stadler
Arr. for unison or four
part chorus by N.A.M.

After the singing of "Ecce Sacérdos," *or the* "Sacerdos et Póntifex," *the Bishop sings :*

(*The Bishop*)—℣. Spíritus Sánctus supervéniat in vos, et virtus Altíssimi custódiat vos a peccátis.

(*The Choir*)—℟. Amen. (7-1)

℣. Adjutórium nóstrum in nomine Dómini.

℟. Qui fécit coelum et tér-rắm.

℣. Dómine exáudi oratiónem meắm.

℟. Et clámor méus ad te vé-ni-at.

℣. Dóminus vobiscum.

℟. Et cum spíritu tuo (*all on* "*Do*" *recto tono.*)

℣. Oremus, etc. *ending with* "coelis?"

℟. Amèn.

℣. Spíritum sapiéntiae, et intelléctus.

℟. Amèn.

℣. Spíritum consílii, et fortitúdinis.

℟. Amèn.

℣. Spíritum sciéntiae, et pietátis.

℟. Amèn.

℣. Oremus, etc., *ending with* "saeculórum."

℟. Amèn.

NOTE:— *During the Confirmation, choir may sing Motets and Hymns such as the* "Veni Sancte Spiritus," "Veni Creator," "Come Holy Ghost," *the Lord's Prayer,* "Hail Mary" *and like appropriate, devotional compositions (English or Latin). The* "Confirma hoc" *is sung at the close (at the washing of hands). Responses after the* "Confirma Hoc" *are given at No. 245.*

See No.310 for another arrangement of this text.

Christus Vincit, Christus Regnat

Ancient French Melody
Arr. by N.A.M.

Chri - stus vin - cit, Chri - stus re - gnat,

Chri - stus im - pe - rat.

Chri - stus im - pe - rat.

★ This melody dates from the year 1080. It was sung at the closing of the Council called by order of William the Conqueror. Gregory VII was Pope and Philip I King of France. To this day, in the Cathedral of Rouen it is customary to render this chant on all solemn Pontifical feasts.

Languentibus in Purgatorio

Sixth Mode

Solesmes chant

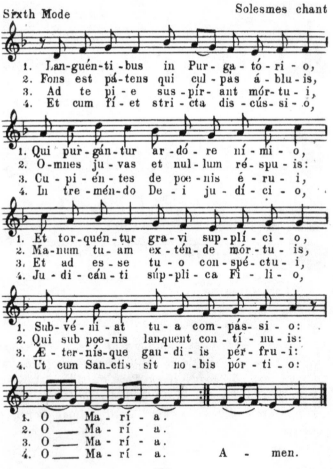

1. Lan-guén-ti-bus   in   Pur - ga - tó - ri - o,
2. Fons est pá-tens qui cul-pas á - blu - is,
3. Ad   te   pi - e   sus - pír- ant mór-tu - i,
4. Et   cum fí - et stri - cta dis - cús- si - o,

1. Qui pur-gán-tur ar - dó - re ní - mi - o,
2. O-mnes ju - vas et nul-lum ré-spu - is:
3. Cu - pi - én - tes de poe - nis é - ru - i,
4. In tre - mén-do De - i ju - dí - ci - o,

1. Et tor-quén-tur gra- vi sup-plí - ci - o,
2. Ma-num tu- am ex - tén - de mór-tu - is,
3. Et ad es - se tu - o con-spé-ctu - i,
4. Ju - di - cán - ti súp-pli - ca Fi - li - o,

1. Sub- vé - ni - at tu - a com- pás- si - o:
2. Qui sub poe-nis lan-quent con - tí - nu - is:
3. Æ - ter-nís-que gau - di - is pér- fru - i:
4. Ut cum San-ctis sit no - bis pór - ti - o:

1. O —— Ma - rí - a.
2. O —— Ma - rí - a.
3. O —— Ma - rí - a.
4. O —— Ma - rí - a.   A - men.

Beati Mortui

Motet for two or four part chorus

Ch. Gounod. Op. 1
Arr. by N. A. M.

Be - á - ti mór - tu - i in Do - mi -

no mo - ri - én - tes, Be - á - ti

mór - tu - i in Do - mi - no mo -

- ri - én - tes, Be - á - ti

mór - tu - i in Do - mi - no mo - ri -

én - tes de - ín - ceps. Di - cit e-nim

Di - cit e-nim Spi - ri - tus

Spi - ri - tus, Spi - ri-tus ut re - qui-

é - scant a la - bó - ri - bus

et ó - pe - ra il-

su - is et o - pe - ra il -

ló - rum,

lo - rum, et o - pe - ra il -

Repeat "Beati" to 𝄐 Fine ad lib.

ló - rum se - quun - tur il - los.

Ego Sum

See No. 270-k for the Canticle -"Benedictus"and Music for
the Absolution. (Page 520)

Antiphon   Vatican Antiphonale

Second Mode

Chanters: E -go sum* re-sur-ré-cti-o et vi _ ta:

qui cré-dit in me, é - ti-am si mór-tu-us

fú- e - rit, vi-vet: et o - mnis qui vi -vet et

cré-dit in me, non mo-ri-é -tur in æ-tér-num.

251*   Pie Jesu

3 or 4 part chorus equal voices a cappella S.S.A.(A),or T.T.B.(B).
or unison (or two-part) chorus S.A.or T.B. with Accompaniment.

Nicola A. Montani

Pi - e   Je - su, Dó-mi - ne,—   Pi - e

Je - su, Dó - mi - ne,—   Do - na   e - is
(e — i)

ré - qui - em,—   do-na   e - is   ré - qui-
(e — i)

*Note: In the earlier Editions of the St. Gregory Hymnal the Anti-
phon "Ego Sum" and the Canticle "Benedictus" were given at No. 251
These are now to be found in their proper place at No. 270 -K.
(Page 520)

em.___ Pi - e Je - su, Dó-mi - ne ___

Do - na e - is ré - qui - em, do - na
(e - i)

e - is ré - qui - em ___
(e - i)

252 Miserere mei Deus

First Mode

(First portion only, is sung)
(before the Psalm

(The entire antiphon is)
(sung at the end of Psalm)

Chanters

Ex-sul-tá-bunt Dó-mi-no os-sa hu-mi-li-á-ta.

Optional Intonation

1. Mi-se- re-re_____ mé-i Dé-us,*

1	Miserere	mé-i	Dé-us,	
2	Et secúndum multitúdinem	miserati-ó-num tu-á-rum,*		
3	Amplius láva me ab iniqui -	-tá-te	mé-a:*	
4	Quóniam iniquitátem méam __	é-go co-gnó-sco:*		
5	Tíbi sóli peccávi, et málum__	có-ram te fé-ci:*		
6	Ecce enim in iniquitáti -	-bus con -céptus sum:*		
7	Ecce enim veritátem _____	di-le-xí-sti:*		
8	Aspérges me hyssópo,_____	et mun-dá-bor:*		
9	Audítui méo dábis gáudium __	et læ-tí-ti-am:*		
10	Avérte fáciem túam a pec -	cá-tis	mé-is:*	
11	Cor múndum créa _____	in me	Dé-us:*	
12	Ne projícias me a _____	fá-ci-e	tú-a:*	
13	Rédde míhi lætítiam salu -	tá-ris	tú-i:*	
14	Docébo iníquos _____	ví-as	tú-as:*	
15	Líbera me de sanguínibus, Déus, Déus sa-lú-tis	mé-æ:*		
16	Dómine, lábia _____	mé-a a-pé-ri-es:*		
17	Quóniam si voluísses sacrifí-cium, de-dís-sem	ú-tı-que:*		
18	Sacrifícium Déo spíritus con -	tri-bu -	lá-tus:*	
19	Benígne fac Dómine in bóna voluntáte	tú-a	Sí-on:*	
20	Tunc acceptábis sacrifícium justítiæ, oblatiónes et	ho-lo-cáu-sta:*		
21	Réqui - - - -	em æ-tér-nam *		
22	Et	lux per-pé-tu-a *		

440

Vatican Antiphonale

THE HOLY SOULS
Officium Defunctorum
Lent and Holy Week, etc.

1 secúndum magnam misericór - -di - am tu - am.
2 dele iniqui - - - - - - tá - tem me - am.
3 et a peccáto _____ me - o mun-da me.
4 et peccátum méum contra _____ me est sem - per.
5 ut justificéris in sermónibus
                tuis, et vincas cum ju - di - cá - ris.
6 et in peccátis concépit me _____ ma-ter me - a.
7 incérta et occúlta sapiéntiæ
                tuæ manife - stá-sti mi - hi.
8 lavábis me, et super nivem _____ de - al - bá - bor.
9 et exsultábunt ossa hu - - - mi - li - á - ta.
10 et ómnes iniquitátes _____ mé - as dé - le.
11 et spíritum rectum ínnova in viscé - ri-bus me - is.
12 et spíritum sánctum tuum ne áu - fe-ras a me.
13 et spíritu principá - - - li con-fír -ma me.
14 et ímpii ad te _____ con-ver-tén - tur.

15 et exsultábit lingua mea justí - ti-am tu - am.
16 et os meum annuntiábit_____ lau-dem tu - am.

17 holocáustis non _____ de-le -ctá - be - ris.
18 cor contrítum et humiliátum Deus non de-spí - ci - es.

19 ut ædificéntur mú - - - ri Je-rú -sa -lem.

20 tunc impónent super altáre _____ tú-um ví - tu -los·
21 dona   e - is Dó- mi - ne.
                                   (e - i)
22 lú - - - - - - - ce-at e - is.
                                   (e - i).

441

THE HOLY SOULS
Pro Defunctis

Miserere Illi Deus

First Mode

Nicola A. Montani

Adagio

★ Mi - se - re - re, mi - se - re - re,

mi - se - re - re il - li De - us,

Tu Je - su Chri - ste Do - mi - ne

rall   *Fine*

Vé - ni - am e - i con - cé - de.

(Solesmes)

Con moto

1. Qui ré - gnas in per - pé - tu - um,
2. Tu ve - ra, sán - cta Trín - i - tas,
3. O pi - a De - i Gé - ni - trix,
4. Tu Mí - cha - el Arch - án - ge - le,
5. In - ter chó - rus cœ - lé - sti - um,

1. Tri - nus et u - nus Dó - mi - nus,
2. Et u - nus in sub - stán - ti - a,
3. Ma - rí - a má - ter vír - gi - num,
4. Con - ti - nu - á - tis pré - ci - bus
5. Iu - ter ca - tér - vas már - tyr - um,

1. De - fún - cti hu - jus á - ni - mam
2. De - fún - cti hu - jus á - ni - mam
3. In - ter - cé - de pi - ís - si - ma
4. Ad - e - sto nunc pro - pí - ti - us
5. Re - súr - gat hic in glo - ri - a

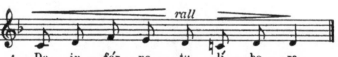

rall

1. De in - fér - no tu lí - be - ra.
2. Cum e - lé - ctis ag - gló - me - ra.
3. Pro hoc de - fún - cto fá - mu - lo.
4. Pro hoc de - fún - cto fá - mu - lo.
5. O - vans ad Chrí - sti déx - te - ram.

★ _Repeat "Miserere"_

Laudate Dominum

Unison, two or four part chorus

Fr. Schubert
Arr. by N. A. M.

Lau - da - te Do - mi - num, lau - da - te

Do - mi - num, o - mnes gen - tes: lau - da - te,

la - u - da - te e - um o - mnes

po - pu - li. Organ

Chorus

Quo - ni - am con - fir - ma - ta est

445

Fi - li - o, et Spi - ri - tu - i San - cto.

Sic _ ut e - rat in prin - -

ci - pi - o et___ nunc, et sem - per,

et nunc, et sem - per, et

in sae - - - cu - la

sae - cu - lo - rum. A - - men.

446

Jubilate Deo

Motet for two or four part chorus

W. A. Mozart
Edited and arr. by N.A.M.

Ju - bi - la - te De - o o - mnis ter -

ra, ser - vi - te, ser -

Ser - vi - te Do - mi - no in lae -

vi - te Do - mi - no, Do-mi - no in lae -

ti - ti - a, in lae - ti - ti - a.

O Bone Jesu!

Motet

G. P. da Palestrina

See Supplement for Gregorian Asperges

257   SUNDAY AT HIGH MASS

Asperges Me

For Unison, two or four part chorus

Sung each Sunday before High Mass from Trinity Sunday
to Palm Sunday inclusive.

Nicola A. Montani

A - spér - ges   me.   Do - mi - ne, hys -

só - po,   et   mun - dá - bor: la - vá - bis

me,   et su-per   ni-vem   de - al - bá - bor.

Ps. 50.   Mi - se - ré - re   me - i,   De - us,   se - cún - dum

ma - gnam mi - se - ri-cór - di - am tu - am.*

(★Note)

Faster

Gló - ri - a Pa - tri, et

Fí - li - o, et Spi-rí - tu-i San - cto.

Sic - ut e - rat in prin - cí - pi - o, et

nunc, et sem - per, et in sǽ - cu - la

★ Note: On Passion Sunday and Palm Sunday the "Gloria Patri" etc. is omitted and repetition is made from the beginning "Asperges" to Fine. ⌒

rall

sae - cu - ló - rum. A - - men.

a tempo

A - sper - ges me

Repeat from 𝄋 to Fine ⌒

RESPONSES

	After Aspergis	Eastertide After Vidi Aquam
Cel. 1. ℣. Osténde nobis Dómine misericórdiam	tú - am.	tú-am. Al-le-lú-ia.
2. ℣. Dómine exáudi oratiónem	mé - am.	
3. ℣. Dóminus vobíscum.		
Choir. 1. Et salutáre túum da	nó - bis.	nó-bis. Al-le-lú-ia.
2. Et clamor meus ad te	vé-ni-at.	
3. Et cum Spíritu tuo.		
4. Amen.		

See Supplement for Gregorian "Vidi Aquam"

SUNDAY AT HIGH MASS **258**

Vidi Aquam

For Unison, two part or four part chorus

Sung before High Mass on Sundays from Easter to Pentecost
inclusive.

Nicola A. Montani

di - cent, al - le - lú - ia, al - le - lú - -

ia, al - le - lú - - ia.

Ps. 117 Con - fi - té - mi - ni Dó - mi - -

no quó - ni - am bo - - nus:

quó - ni - am in sáe - cu - lum mi - se - ri -

cór - di - a   e -   - jus. Glo - ri - a   Pa - tri,

et   Fi - li - o,   et   Spi - rí - tu - i   San -

cto. Sic - ut   e - rat in prin - cí - pi - o,

et   nunc, et sem -   per, et in sáe - cu - la

sáe - cu - ló - rum. A -   -   - men.

Repeat from beginning "Vidi Aquam" to ⌢ Fine.

For responses see Page 452 (Eastertide)

259 HIGH MASS, REQUIEMS, BENEDICTION
VESPERS, PONTIFICAL BLESSING, ETC.

Responses

Note: It is not permissible (according to the decrees of the Congregation of Rites), to accompany the celebrant on the organ at the Orations, Preface, or Pater Noster etc. The laudable custom of not accompanying the Choir for the responses is also being generally observed.

The key of A flat here given, is suggested as being best suited to all voices.

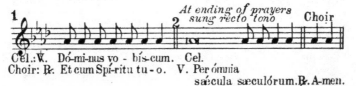

Cel.: V. Dó-mi-nus vo - bís-cum. Cel.
Choir: R. Et cum Spí-ritu tu - o. V. Per ómnia
saécula saeculórum. R. A-men.

When prayers are sung with the following ending choir responds with the "Amen" as indicated below.

Cel.: V. Per ómnia saécula saecu - - ló-rum.
Cel.: V. Per Chrístum Dóminum nó-strum. R. A-men.

Note: After the Epistle it has been (incorrectly) the custom in certain churches for the choir to sing "Deo Gratias". This response (as well as the "Laus tibi Christi" after the Gospel) is for the Ministers of the mass, or Acolytes only, and has never been included in the Graduale and the official books in the notation of the parts to be sung by the choir. See "Ecclesiastical Review", (Philadelphia, Pa., Nov., 1903, page 539.)

4 AT THE GOSPEL

Cel.: Dominus etc. as at No. 1. Choir : Et cum (No. 1)

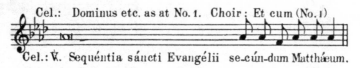

Cel.: ℣. Sequéntia sáncti Evangélii se-cún-dum Matthǽum.

Choir

℞. Glo - ri - a ti - bi Dó - mi - ne.

5 AT THE PREFACE. Solemn Tone. Sundays, Holydays, etc.

Choir

Cel.: Per ó-mni-a sǽ-cu-la sæ-cu-ló-rum. ℞. A -men.

Choir

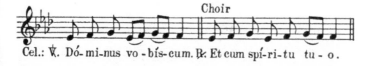

Cel.: ℣. Dó-mi-nus vo-bís-cum. ℞. Et cum spí-ri-tu tu - o.

Choir

Cel.: ℣. Sur-sum cor-da. Ha - bé -mus ad Do-mi-num.

Cel.: ℣. Grá-ti-as a-gá-mus Dó-mi-no De-o nó-stro.

℞. Di - gnum et ju - stum est.

6 AT THE PATER NOSTER

"Per omnia" etc. as at No. 5. At the conclusion of the "Pater Noster:"

Cel.: ℣. Et ne nos in-dú-cas in 'ten-ta-ti-ó - nem.

Sed lí - be - ra nos a má - lo.

7 BEFORE THE "AGNUS DEI." "Per omnia" etc. as at No. 5

Cel.: ℣. Pax † Dó - mi - ni sit † sem-per vo - bís -† cum.

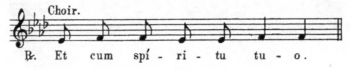

℞. Et cum spí - ri - tu tu - o.

458

8 FOR REQUIEMS etc. (Tonus ferialis) AT THE PREFACE

"Per omnia" etc. (No. 5)

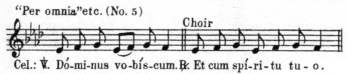

Cel.: ℣. Dó-mi-nus vo-bís-cum. ℟. Et cum spí-ri-tu tu - o.

Cel.: ℣. Sur-sum cor-da. ℟. Ha-bé-mus ad Dó-mi - num.

Cel.: ℣. Grá-ti-as a-gá-mus Dó-mi-no De-o nó-stro.

℟. Di - gnum et ju - stum - est.

9 AT THE END OF REQUIEM MASS

Re-qui - é-scant in pa - ce. ℟. A - men.

459

RESPONSES

10 AT THE ABSOLUTION: after the "Libera"

Ky - ri - e e - lé - i - son. Chri - ste e - lé - i - son.

Ky - ri - e e - lé - i - son. Cel.
Pater
Noster
(secreto)

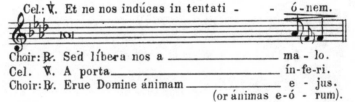

Cel.: ℣. Et ne nos indúcas in tentati - - ó - nem.

Choir: ℟. Sed líbera nos a _____ ma - lo.
Cel. ℣. A porta _____ ín - fe - ri.
Choir: ℟. Erue Domine ánimam _____ e - jus.
(or ánimas e - ó - rum).

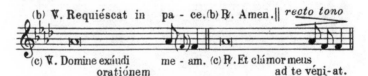

(b) ℣. Requiéscat in pa - ce. (b) ℟. Amen. ‖ *recto tono*

(c) ℣. Domine exáudi me - am. (c) ℟. Et clámor meus
oratiónem ad te véni - at.

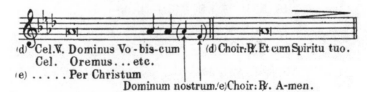

(d) Cel. ℣. Dominus Vo - bis - cum (d) Choir: ℟. Et cum Spiritu tuo.
Cel. Oremus... etc.
(e) ..... Per Christum
Dominum nostrum. (e) Choir: ℟. A - men.

PONTIFICAL CEREMONIES etc.

11 AT THE PONTIFICAL BLESSING

Cél. (a) ℣. Sit nomen Dómi-
ni bene-dí-ctum. ℞.(a) Ex hoc nunc et
usque in sǽculum.

(b) ℣. Adjutórium no-
strum in nómine Dómini. ℞.(b) Qui fécit cǽ-
lum et tér- ram.

(c) Be - ne -dí-cat vos o - mní- po-tens De-us: Pá -ter,

et Fí- li - us, et Spí-ri-tus Sán-ctus. ℞. A -men.

BENEDICTION

12 BENEDICTION OF THE BLESSED SACRAMENT

Chanters: ℣. Pánem de cóelo præ-
stitísti e - is. e - is. Al-le-lú-ia.
Choir. ℞. Omne delectamén-
tum in se ha-bén-tem. bén-tem. Al-le-lú-ia .

13 Responses at the end of Mass꞉ Toni "Ite Missa Est"

a) From Holy Saturday to Low Sunday (exclusive)
Eighth Mode

De-o grá-ti-as, al-le-lú- ia, al-le - lú - ia.

b) From Low Sunday to the Saturday after Pentecost (inclusive)
Seventh Mode

De - o ⸻ grá - ti- as.

c) For Solemn Feasts
Fifth Mode

rall

De-o ⸻ grá - ti-as.

d) For Doubles (No. 1)
First Mode   X.s.

rall

De-o ⸻ grá-ti - as.

e) (De Angelis) Doubles

Fifth Mode   XV. s.

De - o———————— grá -ti -as

f) Feasts of the Blessed Virgin Mary

First Mode   XII. s.

De - o———————— grá -ti - as.

g) For the Sundays of the Year (Orbis Factor)

First Mode   X. s.

De - o——— grá - - - ti - as.

h) Sundays in Advent and Lent

First Mode   X. s.

De - o——— grá - - - - ti -as.

i) Sundays in Advent or Lent (2nd form)(optional)   XIV. s.

Priest, V, Be-ne-di-cá-mus Dó - - - mi -no .
Choir, R, Dé - o grá - - - ti as .

463

260

Lucis Creator Optime

Nicolaus Decius
1480-1529

1. Lu-cis Cre-á-tor ó-pti-me, Lu-cem di-é-rum
2. Qui ma-ne junctum vé-spe-ri Di-em vo-cá-ri
3. Ne mens gra-vá-ta crí-mi-ne, Vi-tæ sit ex-sul
4. Coe-lé-ste pul-set ó.-sti-um: Vi-tá-le tol-lat
5. Præ-sta, Pa-ter pi-ís-si-me, Pa-trí-que compar

1. pró-fe-rens, Prim-ór-di-is lu-cis no-væ Mun-
2. præ-ci-pis: Il-lá-bi-tur te-trum cha-os, Au-
3. mú-ne-re, Dum nil per-´én-ne có-gi-tat, Se-
4. præ-mi-um: Vi-té mus o-mne nó-xi-um, Pur-
5. U-ni-ce, Cum Spí-ri-tu Pa-rá-cli-to, Re-

1. di pa-rans o-rí-gi-nem:
2. di pre-ces cum flé-ti-bus.
3. sé-que cul-pis íl-li-gat.
4. gé-mus o-mne pés-si-mum.
5. gnans per o-mne sǽ-cu-lum.

After last verse

A - men.

Te Lucis Ante Terminum
Ad Completorium

Moderately fast Severus Gastorius (d. 1678)

1. Te lu-cis an - te ter - mi - num, Re-rum Cre-
2. Pro-cul re - cé-dant só - mni - a , Et nó - cti -
3. Præ - sta, Pa-ter pi - is - si - me, Pa-trí- que

1. á - tor, po - sci - mus, Ut pro tu - a cle - men - ti -
2. um phan -tás - ma - ta; Ho - stém-que no-strum cóm-pri -
3. com - par U - ni - çe, Cum Spi - ri - tu Pa - ra - cli -

After last verse

1. a , Sis præ-sul et cu - sto - di - a.
2. me, Ne pol - lu - án - tur cór - po - ra.
3. to, Re-gnans per o - mne saé - cu - lum. A - men

(*Tempore Paschali, in*)
(*Dominicis et in Festis*)

3. Deo Patri sit glória,
  Et Filio, quia mórtuis
  Surréxit, ac Paraclito,
  In sempiterna saécula.
  Amen.

(*In festis Corporis Christi*)
(*et B. Mariæ Virginis*)

3. Jesu, tibi sit gloria,
  Qui natus es de Vírgine ,
  Cum Patre et almo Spíritu,
  In sempitérna sæcula.
  Amen.

Nunc Dimittis
Officium Parvum B.M.V.
CANTICUM SIMEONIS

Seventh Tone

1. Nunc di - míttis sérvum   tú - um Dó-mi-ne,*→

2. Qui - a   vidérunt   ó-cu-li me - i,*→

3. _____ Quod   pa - rá - sti,*→

4. Lú-men ad revelati -   - ó -nem gén-ti-um,*→

5. Gló-ri - a   Pá-tri et Fí-li-o,*→

6. Sic -ut   erat in princípio, et   nunc, et sém - per,*→

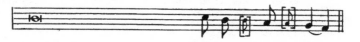

1. secúndum vérbum   tú-um in pa - ce.

2. salu -   -   -   - tá-re   tú - um.

3. ante fáciem omnium   po - pu - ló - rum.

4. et glóriam plébis   tu - æ   Is - ra- el.

5. et Spi -   -   -   - rí - tu -i San - cto.

6. et in saécula saecu -   - ló-rum .   A - men.

263

In Manus Tuas Domine
Responsorium breve

Per annum   Vatican - Antiphonale

In má-nus tu-as Dó-mi-ne,*Comméndo spí-ri-tum méum.

℣. Re-de-mí-sti nos Dó-mi-ne, Dé-us ve-ri-tá-tis.

℣. Gló-ri-a Pá-tri, et Fí-li-o, et Spi-rí-tu-i Sáncto.

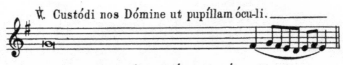

℣. Custódi nos Dómine ut pupíllam ócu-li. _____

Choir: ℟. Sùb umbra alárum tuárum protége nos. _____

Te Deum Laudamus

Juxta morem Romanum

Vatican Graduale
Harmonized by N. A. M.

Third Mode
Celebrant

Chorus

1. Te Déum laudá-mus:* Te Dó-mi-num con-fi-té-mur.

Chorus (in alternate sections)

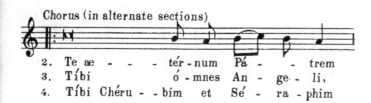

2. Te æ - - - tér - num Pá - - trem
3. Tíbi ó - mnes An - ge- li,
4. Tíbi Chéru - - bim et Sé - ra - phim

2. ó - mnis tér - - ra ve - ne - rá - tur.
3. tí - bi coéli et univér- sæ pot - es - tá - tes:
4. in - ces - sá - bili vó - ce pro - clá - mant:

5. Sán - - ctus: 7. Sánctus Dóminus Déus Sába-oth.
6. Sán - - ctus:

8. Pléni sunt coé-li et tér - ra ma-jes -
9. Te glo- ri- ó - sus
10. Te Pro- phe- tá, - rum
11. Te Mártyrum can- di- da - tus
12. Te per ór - bem ter- rá - rum sán - cta

8. tá - tis gló - ri - æ tú, - - æ.
9. A - po - sto - ló - rum chó - - rus:
10. lau - - dá - bi - lis nú - me - rus:
11. láu - dat ex - ér - ci - tus.
12. con - fi - té - tur Ec - clé - si - a.

13. Pá - - trem im - mén - sæ ma - je - stá - tis:

14. Ve- ne- rán- dum tú- um vé- - rum, et ú - ni- cum Fí-li- um:

15. Sán - - ctum quo- que Pa - rá- cli- tum Spí- ri- tum.

470

16.(a) Tu Rex gló - ri - æ, Chrí - ste.

Tutti

16.(b) Tu Pá-tris sem-pi-tér-nus es Fí-li-us.

17. Tu ad liberándum
        susce-ptú-rus hó-mi-nem, non hor-ru-
18. Tu devícto mór-tis a-cú-le-o   a-pe-ru-
19. Tu ad déxteram Dé-i sé-des

17. í - sti   Vír-gi-nis ú - te-rum.
18. í - sti cre-dén-ti-bus re-gna cœ-ló - rum.
19. in   glo-ri-a Pa - tris.

20. Jú - - dex cré-de-ris és-se ven-tú-rus.

All kneel here

21. Te er - go quǽe-su-mus, tú-is fá-mu-lis súb-ve-ni,

quos pre -ti - ó -so sán-gui -ne red - e - mí - sti.

22. Ae - tér - na fac cum sán-ctis

tú - is in gló - ri - a nu -me-rá - ri.

23. Sál- vum fac pó-pu-lum tú-um Dó-mi - ne,

et bé- ne-dic hæ - re - di - tá -ti tú - æ.

472

24. Et ré - ge é - os,   et ex - tól - le

íl - los   us - que   in   ae - tér - - - num.

25. Per sín-gu - los dí - es,   be -ne-dí -ci-mus te.

26. Et laudá- mus nómen   tú-um in saé-cu-lum,
27. Di - gná - re Dómi -   - ne dí- e í - - sto
28. Mi - se - ré - - - re nó-stri Dó-mi- ne,
29. Fí - at   misericórdia túa Dó-mi-ne su-per nos,

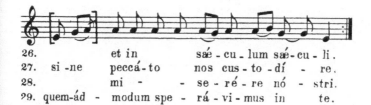

26.   et in   saé - cu - lum saé-cu - li.
27. si - ne   peccá- to   nos cus - to - dí - re.
28.   mi - - se - ré - re nó - stri.
29. quem-ád - modum spe - rá - vi- mus in   te.

30. In te Dó - mi - ne spe - rá - - vi:

non con - fún - dar in æ - tér - - num.

RESPONSES

(1)Cel. ℣. Benedíctus es Dómine Deus patrorum nostrórum.

Choir. ℟. Et laudábilis et gloriósus in saecula.

Cel. ℣. Benedicámus Pátrem et Fílium cum Sáncto Spíritu.

Choir. ℟. Laudémus et superexaltémus eum in saecula.

Cel. ℣. Benedíctus es Dómine, in firmaménto coeli.

Choir. ℟. Et laudábilis, et gloriósus, et superexaltá-tus in saecula.

Cel. ℣. Bénedic anima mea Dómino.
Choir. ℟. Et noli oblivísci omnes retributiónes Ejus.
Cel. ℣. Domine exaudi oratiónem méam.
Choir. ℟. Et clamor meus ad te véniat.

Cel. ℣. Dominus vobíscum.

Choir. ℟. Et cum Spíritu tuo.

(1) Responses in italics for occasional services and when the "Te Deum" is a part of a Thanksgiving Service.
474

Mass of the Blessed Virgin Mary

Cum jubilo
No. IX

Kyrie

First Mode (transposed)   XII Century
With devotion but also with animation   From the Vatican Graduale
Chanters   Harmonized by Nicola A. Montani

476

Seventh Mode (transposed)

XI Century Melody

Gló - ri - a in ex - cél - sis Dé - o.

Choir I

Et in ter - ra pax ho - mi - ni - bus

bó - nae vo - lun - tá - tis. Lau - dá - mus te.

Be - ne - - dí - ci - mus te.

Poco meno

Ad - o - - rá - mus te.

A - gnus De - i, Fí - li - us Pá - tris.

Qui tol - lis pec - cá - ta mún - di:

mi - se - ré - re nó - bis.

Qui tol - lis pec - cá - ta mún - di;

sús - ci-pe de-pre-ca-ti-ó - nem nó-stram.

Qui sédes ad déxteram Pátris, mi-se-ré-re no-bis.

II Quó - ni - am tu so - lus sán - ctus.

I Tu so - lus Dó - mi - nus.

II Tu so - lus Al - tís - si - mus, Je - su Chrí - ste.

poco piu vivo

Tutti Cum San - cto Spí - ri - tu, in gló - ri - a

De - i Pa - tris. A - - - men.

Responses to the Gospel. See 259-4

Credo
No. 4

First Mode   XV Century

Cre - do   in   u - num De - um.

Pá - trem o - mni - pot - én - tem,   fa - ctó - rem

cǿ - li et ter - ræ,   vi - si - bí - li - um

ó - mni - um, et in - vi - si - bí - li - um.

Et in u-num Dó-mi-num Je-sum Chri-stum,

Fí-li-um De-i u-ni-gé-ni-tum.

Et ex Pa-tre na-tum an-te ó-mni-a sǽ-cu-la.

De-um de De-o, lu-men de lú-mi-ne,

De-um ve-rum de De-o ve-ro.

483

II *a tempo*

Cru - ci - fí - xus e - ti - am pro no - bis:

pp   *rall*

sub Pón-ti -o Pi -lá - to pas-sus et se-pul-tus est.

Tutti
f a tempo   *p*

Et re-sur-ré -xit tér - ti - a di - e

I *f*

se-cún-dum Scriptú - ras. Et a-scén-dit in cǿe- lum:

se - det ad déx - te - ram Pa - tris.

484

Et í - te - rum ven - tú - rus est cum gló - ri - a,

ju - di - cá - re ví - vos et mór - tu - os: cu - jus

re - gni non e - rit fi - nis. Et in Spí - ri - tum

Sán - ctum, Dó - mi - num, et vi - vi - fi - cán - tem:

qui ex Pa - tre Fi - li - ó - que pro - cé - dit.

II

Qui cum Pa - tre et Fí - li - o

si _ mul a - do - rá - tur, et con glo - ri - fi -

cá - tur: qui lo - cú - tus est per Pro - phé - tas.

I

Et u - nam, sán - ctam ca - thó - li - cam

et a - po - stó - li - cam Ec - clé - si - am.

Con - fí - te - or u - num ba - ptís - ma

in re - mis - si - ó - nem pec - ca - tó - rum.

Et ex-spé-cto ré-sur-re-cti-ó-nem mor-tu-ó - rum.

Et ví - tam ven-tú - ri sáe - cu - li.

A - - - - - men.

268   Sanctus and Benedictus

Fifth Mode   XIV Century

Sán - ctus, Sán - ctus, Sán - ctus

Dó-mi-nus Dé - us Sá - - ba-oth.

Plé - ni sunt coe-li et ter - - ra

gló-ri-a tu-a. Ho-sán-na in ex-cél-sis.

Be - ne-dí-ctus qui vé - nit

in nó - mi-ne Dó - - mi-ni.

Ho - - sán-na in ex-cél - - sis.

Fifth Mode (X) XIII Century

For "Deo Gratias" see "Responses" No. 259 - 13 - f

PROGRAM FOR THE CHOIR AT REQUIEM MASS
THE GREGORIAN REQUIEM MASS

Note: According to the Ceremonial of Bishops, I.c.xxviii, n.13
S.R.C. 4156, the use of musical instruments is not permitted
in the Office of the dead; At the Mass and at the Absolutionaf-
ter Mass, the organ may be used to accompany the voices but
shall be silent when the chant ceases. (S.R.C. 3827, and 4265).
From this it will be understood that Funeral Marches before and
after the Mass are not permitted. For this reason it is suggested
that the Responsory *"Subvenite"* be sung as the Procession
enters the Church. In some places it is customary for the
Choir to lead the Funeral procession from the door of the
Church to the Altar, singing the *"Subvenite"* as given in the
proper Chant or in other approved forms.

"MISSA CANTATA" or SOLEMN HIGH MASS.

1.PROCESSION: "Subvenite" See page 493 or 495

2.INTROIT: "Requiem aeternam" (Begun when the Celebrant goes
toward the foot of the Altar for the first prayers.) To
be sung as given in full   Page 498

3.KYRIE: Follows the Introit without pause. (270-A)

4.PRAYERS AND EPISTLE: After the first prayer, if it be a
Solemn High Mass,the Choir will wait until the Epistle
is sung before beginning the Graduale; If a High Mass
the Choir will begin the Graduale etc.while the Priest
recites the Epistle.

5.GRADUALE: "Requiem Aeternam" (270-B) bb-or b,b,b.

6.TRACTUS: "Absolve Domine"   (270-C) cc-or c,c,c.

7.SEQUENCE: "Dies Irae"   (270-D)

The Graduale and Tractus may either be sung as indicated in the Graduale or may be recited "Recto Tono,"
or in "Falso Bordone" style. (270-bb-cc-)

The "Dies Irae" may not be omitted in a High Mass
of Requiem because everything that appertains to
the *Precatio Suffragii,* the supplication of the Suf-
frage, must be sung (S. R.C. 2959 ad 2), and the words
"Precatio Suffragii" include also the Sequence
"Dies Irae" (S.R.C. 3051 ad 1).

(Another Decree S.R.C. 4054 ad V. declares that the
"Dies Irae" must be sung entire.)

Note: The Complete Requiem Mass is published in separate form. V. Part & sep. Organ Acc.

8.RESPONSES, GOSPEL: (Note; The Choir does not sing the
"Laus tibi Christi" after the Gospel or the "Deo Gra-
tias" after the "Epistle;" these responses are for the
Acolytes only)

9.RESPONSE: To "Dominus Vobiscum;" "Et Cum Spiritu Tuo."
Celebrant sings "Oremus" and the Choir proceeds with
the "Domine Jesu Christe" which is sung in its entirety.

10.OFFERTORY: The interpolation of solos, "Ave Maria;" or other
songs is entirely uncalled for in Requiem Masses at
this point. (270 - E) or 270 - EE

11.RESPONSES: Preface responses are to be sung in Ferial tone
as indicated.

12.SANCTUS—is begun immediately after the last word of the Preface "dicentes" and the singers continue until the "Benedictus" (exclusive). (270 - F)

13.ELEVATION: (Complete silence during the Elevation.)

14.BENEDICTUS: Choir begins immediately after the Elevation
of the Chalice (after the last bell). (270 - G)
(A Decree of the Sacred Congregation of Rites dated
Jan. 14, 1921, clearly states that the "Benedictus" must
always be sung *after* the Elevation).
(If time permits, a motet may be sung after the *Benedictus* but according to a decree (3827) of the S.R.C.
the words must be taken from the Liturgy and must
have reference to the Blessed Sacrament.)

15.RESPONSES: "Amen" and after the "Pater Noster" which clos-
es with "et ne nos inducas in tentationem" the Choir
answers "Sed libera nos a malo" after which there
is complete silence until the Priest again sings "Per
omnia" etc. to which the Choir responds with "Amen"
and after the Celebrant's "Pax Domini sit semper vobiscum" the Choir responds; "Et cum spiritu tuo"
as indicated.

16.AGNUS DEI—is sung as indicated. (270 - H)

17.COMMUNION: "Lux Aeterna" is sung immediately after the Ab-
lutions. (270 - I)

18.RESPONSES: "Et cum spiritu tuo" and the proper "Amen."

THE ABSOLUTION

1.LIBERA: When the Celebrant reaches the bier
and recites or sings the *"Non Intres"* (to which the
Choir responds "Amen" if sung)*the Choir sings the
"Libera me" at the end of which the Chanter sings
"Kyrie Eleison" which is followed by the remainder of the Choir singing "Christe eleison" and all join-
ing in the final "Kyrie" after which the Celebrant
sings "Pater Noster" and continues the prayer in a
low voice. (270 - J)

2.RESPONSES: As indicated on (p. 519)
Note:- If the body is present (a) either the body is accompanied to the grave in procession or (b) it is tak-
en away without procession or other ceremony.

3.......In the first case the Choir will sing *"In Paradisum"*
(270-L) as they leave the Church. If the distance to the grave
is considerable, the *Miserere* may be added. (252)

4.......On arrival at the gate of the burial ground the Celebrant intones the words "Ego Sum". (270-k)

5.......Choir starts "Benedictus" at once.

6.......On conclusion of "Benedictus" Choir sings the whole
antiphon (*Ego sum _ _ in aeternum*). (P.522)

7.......Priest...Kyrie eleison.
Choir....Christe eleison
Choir....Kyrie eleison

8.......Choir sings responses to "Pater Noster" and versicles which follow. Page 522

9.......Choir returns to Church in procession.

10......In case (b) everything (except the "Miserere" which
would have been sung at the place of burial) is
sung here or round the catafalque or round the cof-
fin at the door of the Church.
Note:- In this case "In Paradisum" can be sung in
its usual place, if such is the custom.

* *Non Intres is said only when the body is present.*

492

Subvenite (1)

Vatican Graduale
Transcribed by Nicola A. Montani

493

A - bra-hae An-ge-li   de - dú - cant

te: ★ Sus - ci - pi - én-tes á-ni-nam é -

jus: Of - fe - rén-tes é - am   in con - spé -

ctu Al - tis - si - mi. V. Ré-qui - em

ae - tér-nam dó - na é - i

Dó-mi - ne: et lux per-pé-tu-a   lú -

ce - at   é - i.   † Of-fe - rén-tes é - am

in con-spé - ctu Al - tis-si - mi.

494

Subvenite (2)

Nicola A. Montani

Another Setting for Unison, Two or Three-Part Chorus
(S. S. A. or T. T. B.)

Sub-ve-ní-te Sáncti Dé-i, oc-cúr - -ri-te An-geli Dómi-ni: Su-scipiéntes su- sci-pi-én-tes á - ni-nam é - -jus: Of-fe-réntes é - am in con-spéctu Al-tís-si-mi.

2nd time skip to (✲) (Requiem)

495

et lux perpétua lúceat é - i.

Andante

Of - fe - rén - tes é - am in con-

marcato

spé - ctu Al - tís - si - mi.

497

270 The Requiem Mass
Missa Pro Defunctis

SIXTH MODE   Introit   Vatican Graduale
Transcribed by N. A. Montani

Ré - qui - em * ae - tér - nam dó - na é - is Dó - mi - ne: et lux per-pé-tu - a lú - ce - at e - - is. *Fine* Ps. Te dé - cet hýmnus Dé - us in Sí - on, et tí - bi red-dé - tur vó - tum in Je - rú - sa - lem: * ex - áu - di o - ra - ti - ó - nem mé - am, ad te óm - nis cá - ro vé - ni - et.

Repeat *"Requiem"* from beginning to the *Psalm* ♫ then proceed immediately to the *"Kyrie*.

Kyrie

270 - a

SIXTH MODE

Chanters — I. Tutti

Ký - ri - e ★ e - lé - i - son.

II — Tutti

Ký - ri - e e - lé - i - son. Ký - ri - e

I

e - lé - i - son. Chri - ste e - lé - i - son.

II — Tutti

Chri - ste e - lé - i - son. Chri - ste

I.

e - lé - i - son. Ký - ri - e e - lé - i - son.

II

Ký - ri - e e - lé - i - son.

Chanters — Tutti — rall.

Ký - ri - e ★ e - lé - i - son.

CHOIR

CEL.: V. Dómi-nus vo - bis-cum. CEL.

CHOIR: R. Et cum Spíri-tu tu - o. V. Per ómnia

saecula saeculórum. R. A-men.

499

270-b

Graduale ★ (1)

SECOND MODE

★ Arrangements of the Graduale and Tractus in "Recto Tono" form
may be utilized if desired. See 270 bb-cc also -b-b-b
c-c-c

- - - na e - - -

rit ju - - - - - stus:

ab au-di-ti-ó-ne má - - -la

non ti - mé -

bit. *rit.* *pp* (t)

Tractus (1)

270-c

EIGHTH MODE

Chanters Tutti

Ab-sól - ve★ Dó - mi-ne,

á - ni-mas ó-mni-um fi-dé - li-um de-fun-ctó -

501

- - rum   ab ó - mni vín - cu -lo

de - li - ctó - rum.

℣. Et grá - ti - a tu - a   il - lis suc - cu - rén- -

te,   me - re - án - tur e - vá - de - re

ju - di - ci - um ul - ti - ó - nis.

℣. Et lú - cis ae - tér - nae.   be - a - ti - tú -

- di - ne* pér - fru - i (ee)

502

Graduale (2)

Optional Setting of the *Graduale* and *Tractus*. (Unison or parts)
The following Chords can be used to accompany the recitation of the
Graduale and Tractus, should a shorter version be preferred.

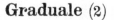

ORGAN Réquiem aetérnam, dona eis Dómine:

et lux perpétua lúceat eis. ℣. In memória aetérna erit jústus:

ab auditióne mala non ti - mé - bit.

Tractus (2)

Absólve, Dómine, ánimas ómnium fidélium defun -

ctó - rum ab ómni vínculo delictórum.

℣. Et grátia tua illis succurrénte, mereántur evádere

judicium ultiónis. ℣. Et lucis aetérnae beatitúdine per-fru -i.

503

270-b-b-b
        c-c-c

Graduale and Tractus

Optional
Setting(3)

(FALSO BORDONE)

Unison or Three-Part Chorus

Réquiem Mass
N. A. Montani

Graduale (1) Réquiem aetérnam, dona eis   Dó-mi-ne:

     (2) In memoria aetérna erit   jú - stus:

Tractus (3) Absólve, Dómine ánimas ómnium

                     fidélium defun-ctó - rum:

     (4) Et grátia tua illis succur -   - - rén - te:

     (5) Et lúcis ae '- - - - - tér - nae:

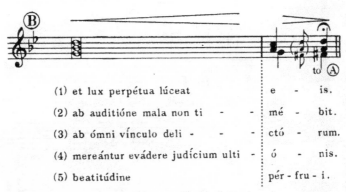

    (1) et lux perpétua lúceat   e - is.

    (2) ab auditióne mala non ti - - mé - bit.

    (3) ab ómni vínculo deli - - - ctó - rum.

    (4) mereántur evádere judícium ulti - ó - nis.

    (5) beatitúdine   pér - fru - i.

(Proceed to Dies Irae)

504

Sequence　　　270-d
Dies Irae

FIRST MODE　Verses should be sung alternately by different sections of the Choir.

1. Di - es i - rae, di - es il - la, Sol - vet sae - clum
2. Quan-tus tre-mor est fu-tú-rus, Quan-do ju - dex

in fa - víl - la: Te - ste Da-vid cum Si-býl - la.
est ven-tú - rus, Cun - cta stri-cte dis-cus-sú - rus!

3. Tu - ba mi - rum spar-gens so-num Per se-púl-cra
4. Mors stu-pé-bit et na-tú-ra, Cum re-súr-get

re - gi - o - num, Có - get ó - mnes an-te thro-num.
cre-a - tú - ra, Ju - di - cán - ti re-spon-sú - ra.

5. Li - ber scri - ptus pro-fe - ré - tur, In quo to-tum
6. Ju-dex er - go cum se-dé - bit, Quid-quid la-tet

con-ti - né - tur, Un-de mun-dus ju - di - cé - tur.
ap - pa-ré - bit: Nil in-úl-tum re-ma-né-bit.

7. Quid sum mi-ser tunc di-ctú-rus?Quem pa - tró - num
8. Rex tre-mén-dae ma-je-stá-tis, Qui sal-ván-dos

ro - ga-tú - rus? Cum vix ju - stus sit se-cú - rus.
sal-vas gra-tis, Sal - va me, fons pi - e - tá - tis.

505

a tempo

9. Re - cor - dá - re Je - su pi - e, Quod sum cau - sa
10. Quae-rens me, se - di - sti las-sus: Red - e - mí - sti

tu - ae vi - ae: Ne me per - das il - la di - e.
cru-cem pas-sus: Tan-tus la - bor non sit cas-sus.

p a tempo

11. Ju - ste ju - dex ul - ti - ó - nis, Do - num fac re-
12. In - ge - mí-sco, tam-quam re - us: Cul - pa ru - bet

mis - si - ó - nis; An - te di - em ra - ti - ó - nis.
vul - tus me - us: Sup - pli - can - ti par - ce De - us.

a tempo mf

13. Qui Ma - rí - am ab - sol - ví - sti, Et la - tró - nem
14. Pre - ces me - ae non sunt di - gnæ: Sed tu bo - nus

ex - au - di - sti, Mi - hi quo - que spem de - dí - sti.
fac be - ní - gne, Ne per - én - ni cre - mer i - gne.

a tempo

15. In - ter o - ves lo - cum práe-sta, Et ab hóe - dis
16. Con - fu - tá - tis ma - le - dí - ctis, Flammis á - cri-

me se - qué-stra, Stá - tu - ens in par - te dex - tra.
bus ad - dí - ctis: Vo - ca me cum be - ne - dí - ctis.

506

17 O - ro súp-plex et ac-clí-nis, Cor contrítum quasi ci-nis:

Ge-re curam me-i fi-nis. 18.Lacri-mó-sa di - es il - la,

Qua resúr-get ex _____ fa-víl-la. 19.Ju-di-cán-dus ho -

mo re - us: Hu-ic er-go par - ce De-us. 20.Pi-e Je-su

Dó-mi-ne, do-na e - is re-qui-em. A - men.

Responses at the Gospel

CELEBRANT V. Dóminus vobí-scum. CHOIR R. Et cum Spí-ri-tu tú-o.

CELEBRANT V. Seqúentia sán-cti E-van-gé-li - i se-cúndum Matthéum.

CHOIR R. ————————————→ Gló-ri-a ti - bi Do-mi-ne.

270-e

OFFERTORY

Domine Jesu Christe (1)

SECOND MODE

Dó - mi - ne Je - su Chri - ste,⋆_____ Rex_____ gló -

_ _ _ ri - ae,_____ lí - be - ra á - ni - mas

ó - mni - um fi - dé - li - um de - fun - ctó - rum

de poe - nis in - fér - ni et de pro - fún - do la - cu:

lí - be - ra e - as de o - re le - ó - nis,_____

ne ab-sór-be-at e-as tár-ta-rus,ne ca-dant in ob-scú-rum: sed sí-gni-fer san-ctus Mí-cha-el re-prae-sén-tet e--as in lu-cem san-ctam:

Tutti
★Quam ó-lim Á-bra-hae pro-mi-sí-sti, et sé-

509

mi - ni e - jus. ℣. Hó - sti - as

et pré - ces ti - bi Dó - mi - ne lau - dis

of - fé - ri - mus: tu súr - ci - pe

pro a - ni - má - bus il - lis, quá - rum hó - di - e

me - mó - ri - am fá - ci - mus: fac e - as, Dó -

mi - ne, de mor - te trans - í - re ad vi - tam.

Repeat from "*Quam olim*" to "*ejus*"

510

Domine Jesu Christe (2)

Optional Setting
(FALSO BORDONE)
Unison, 2, 3 or 4-part Chorus with Organ Acc.

N. A. Montani

Recited in a smooth, flowing manner

1) Dómine Jesu
      Christe,* Rex gló - ri - ae, libera ánimas
      ómnium fidélium
                  de-fun-ctó - rum

2) de poenis inférni et
      de profúndo la - cu: líbera éas de
                  ore le-ó - nis,

3) ne absórbeat eas tár - ta - rus, ne cádant in obscú - rum:

4) sed sígnifer sanctus Mí-cha-el repraeséntet
                  éas in lucem sán - ctam:

5) *Quam ólim Ábrahae
      prómi - sí - sti, et sémini e - jus.

6) V. Hóstias et préces
      tibi Dómine
      landis of-fé - ri-mus: tu súscipe
                  pro animábus il - lis,

7) quárum hódie
      memóriam fá-ci-mus: fac eas,
                  Dómine, de
                  morte trans-
                  íre ad vi - tam.

8) Quam ólim
      Ábrahae promi - sí - sti, et sémini e - jus.

Ferial Responses at the Preface

CEL.: Per ó-mni-a sáe-cu-la sae-cu-ló-rum. ℟. A-men.

CEL.: V. Dó-mi-nus vo-bís-cum. ℟. Et cum spí-ri-tu tu-o.

CEL.: V. Sur-sum cor-da. ℟. Ha-bé-mus ad Dó-mi-num.

CEL.: V. Grá-ti-as a-gá-mus Dó-mi-no De-o nó-stro.

℟. Dí-gnum et ju-stum est.

Preface follows: (unaccompanied) The *"Sanctus"* is begun immediately after the singing of *"dicentes."*

Sanctus
270-f

Chanters   Tutti   I

San - ctus,* San - ctus,   Sanctus Dómi-nus De-us Sá-ba-oth

II

Ple-ni·sunt coe-li et ter-ra gló-ri-a tu-a. Ho-sánna in ex-cél-sis.

(After the Elevation)
Benedictus
270-g

pp Chanters   Tutti

Be-nedíctus qui venit in nómine Dómini. Ho-sán-na in ex-cél-sis.

(* See **Program** regarding motet that may be sung after the "**Benedictus**."

Responses at the Pater Noster

CELEBRANT   CHOIR   pp

Per ó-mni-a sae-cu-la sae-cu-ló-rum. ℞ A-men.

CELEBRANT: Oremus etc. ending with:

℣ Et ne nos in-dú-cas in ten-ta-ti-ó-nem.

CHOIR   pp

℞ Sed li - be - ra nos a ma - lo.

Here there is a slight pause. (No singing or playing.)

Before the Agnus Dei

CELEBRANT: Per ómnia saeculórum. (as above.)
CHOIR: Amen. (as above.)   CHOIR   rall. pp

CEL.℣ Pax Dó-mi-ni sit semper vobís-cum. Et cum Spí-ri-tu tu-o.

Proceed immediately to the "*Agnus Dei.*"

513

270-h

Agnus Dei

A - gnus De - i,★ qui tol - lis pec - cá - ta mun - di:

do - na e - is ré - qui - em. A - gnus De - i,★

qui tol - lis pec - cá - ta mun - di: do - na e - is ré - qui - em

A - gnus De - i, qui tol - lis pec - cá - ta mun - di:

dó - na e - is ré - qui - em★★ sem - pi - tér - nam.

Communion

EIGHTH MODE

Chanters — Tutti

Lux ae - tér - na★ lú - ce - at e - is,

Dó - mi - ne: ★Cum Sanctis tu - is in ae - tér - num,

Chanters *(faster)*

qui - a pi - us es. V. Ré - qui - em ae - tér - nam do - na

e - is Dó - mi - ne, et lux per - pé - tu - a lú - ce - at e - is.

Tutti *(a tempo)* *rall.* *Fine.*

★Cum Sanctis tu - is in ae - tér - num, qui - a pi - us es.

CEL.: Dominus Vobiscum
CHOIR: Et cum Spiritu tuo

CHOIR

CEL.: V. Per ómnia sáecula saecu - ló - rum.
CEL.: V. Per Chrístum Dóminum nó - strum. R. A - men.

CHOIR

Deacon (or Cel.): V. Re - qui - é - scant in pa - ce. R. A - men.

515

270-j Libera me Domine ★

Responsorium

FIRST MODE

Lí - be - ra me, Dó - mi - ne,★ de mor -

te ae - tér - na in di - e il - la tre -

mén - da: ★Quan-do coe - li mo -

vén-di sunt et ter - ra: + Dum vé -

- - - - - ne - ris ju - di - cá -

★ The *"Libera"* is not sung until the priest has finished recit-
ing or singing the prayer *"Non intres."*
(*"Non Intres"* is said only when the body is present.)

re _____ saé - cu - lum per i -

rall. *Fine* I *a tempo* *mf*
- -gnem. V. Tremens fáctus sum e -go, et tí - me-o,

dum discússi-o vé-ne-rit, at - que ven-tú-ra i - ra.

Tutti *mf*
★Quan - do coe - li _____ mo - vén-di sunt

rall. II *a tempo*
et _____ ter - ra. V. Di - es il - la, di - es i - rae

ca - la - mi - tá - tis et mi - sé - ri - æ, di - es ma - gna

et a - má-ra val - de. † Dum vé - - -

- - ne - ris ju-di - cá - re

sæ - cu - lum per i - gnem.

Ré - qui-em æ-tér-nam do-na e - is Dó - mi - ne;

et lux per-pé-tu - a lú - ce - at e - is.

Repeat *"Libera"* to *"Tremens"*

518

Responses

AT THE ABSOLUTION: after the "Libera"

1st Chorus (Tutti)   2d Chorus

Ký-ri-e e-lé-i-son. Chri-ste e-lé-i-son.

1st & 2d Chorus (Tutti)

Ky-ri-e   e - - lé-i-son.

Cel.
Pater
Noster
(secreto)

Cel.: ℣. Et ne nos indúcas in tentati - - ó-nem.

Choir: ℟. Sed líbera nos a _____ ma - lo. For Visitation

Cel. ℣. A porta _____ in-fe-ri. see note below.

Choir: ℟. Erue Domine ánimam _____ e - jus.

For Visitation: (or ánimas e-ó - rum).
℣. Requiem aeternam dona eis _____ Dó-mi-ne.
℟. Et lux perpétua lúceat _____ e - is.

(b) ℣. Requiéscat in pa - ce.(b) ℟. Amen.‖ *recto tono*

(c) ℣. Domine exáudi   me - am. (c) ℟. Et clámor meus
oratiónem   ad te véni-at.

(d) Cel. ℣. Dominus Vo-bis-cum   (d) Choir: ℟. Et cum Spiritu tuo.
Cel. Oremus...etc.
(e) . . . . . Per Christum
Dominum nostrum.(e)Choir: ℟. A-men.

"In Paradisum" or "Ego sum" with Benedictus — follow.(See Program.)

Note: For Visitation add after "Sed libera nos a malo" etc.
℣. In memória aetérna erunt justi.
℟. Ab auditióne mala non ti-mé-bunt.

519

270-k Benedictus
Canticum Zachariae

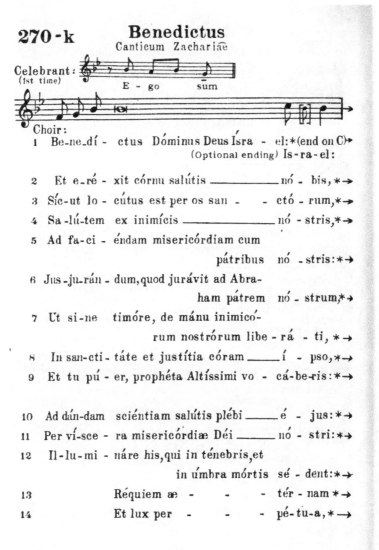

Celebrant: (1st time)

E - go sum

Choir:

1 Be-ne-dí - ctus Dóminus Deus Ísra - el:＊(end on C)➤
(Optional ending) Is-ra-el:

2 Et e-ré - xit córnu salútis _____ nó - bis, ＊→

3 Síc-ut lo - cútus est per os san - - ctó - rum,＊→

4 Sa -lú-tem ex inimícis _____ nó - stris,＊→

5 Ad fa-ci - éndam misericórdiam cum
pátribus nó - stris:＊→

6 Jus-ju-rán - dum,quod jurávit ad Abraham pátrem nó - strum,＊→

7 Ut si-ne timóre, de mánu inimicó-
rum nostrórum libe - rá - ti, ＊→

8 In san-cti- táte et justítia córam _____ í - pso,＊→

9 Et tu pú - er, prophéta Altíssimi vo - cá-be-ris:＊→

10 Ad dán-dam sciéntiam salútis plébi _____ é - jus:＊→

11 Per ví-sce - ra misericórdiæ Déi _____ nó - stri:＊→

12 Il-lu-mi - náre his,qui in ténebris,et
in úmbra mórtis sé - dent:＊→

13 Réquiem æ - - - tér - nam ＊→

14 Et lux per - - - pé-tu-a, ＊→

Second Psalm Tone

1 quia visitávit, et fécit redemptió -

nem plé-bis sú - æ.

2 in dómo Dávid pú - - - e - ri sú - i:

3 qui a sǽculo sunt, prophe - - tá-rum é - jus:

4 et de mánu ómnium qui o - dérunt nos:

5 et memorári testaménti sú-i sán -cti:

6 datú - - - - - rum se nó - bis:

7 servi - - - - - á-mus íl - li.

8 ómnibus di - - - - é-bus nó - stris.

9 prǽíbis enim ante fáciem Dómini

paráre ví-as é - jus:

10 in remissiónem peccató - - rum e - ó - rum:

11 in quíbus visitávit nos, óri - - ens ex ál - to.

12 ad dirigéndos pédes nóstros in ví - am pá - cis.

13 dona (e - i)
e - is Dó-mi-ne.

14 lú - - - - - - ce - at e - is.
(e - i).

Choir repeats Antiphon "Ego Sum" in its entirety

(See next page)

Antiphon - Ego Sum

Responses   Vatican Antiphonale

SECOND MODE

CHORUS

mf E - go sum* re-sur-ré-cti-o et vi - ta: qui cré-dit

in me, et - i - am si mórtu-us fú-e-rit, vi-vet: et o - mnis

rall.

qui vi-vit et cré-dit in me, non mo-ri-é-tur in ae-tér-num.

1. CEL. Ky-ri-e e-lé-i-son (In any Key suited to the Celebrant's voice)

1. CHOIR   Chri-ste e-le-i-son (Choir proceeds) Ky-ri-e e-lé-i-son.

2. CEL.   Pater noster (in silence, ending with:)
           Et ne nos inducas in tentati - - - ó - nem.

2. CHOIR — *Sed líbera nos a* _____ *má - lo.*
3. CEL. — A pórta_____ ín-fer-i.
3. CHOIR — *Erue, Domine, ánimam*_____ *é - jus.*
4. CEL. — Requiescat in _____ pa - ce.
4. CHOIR — (Recto tono) *A-men.*
5. CEL. — Domine, exáudi oratiónem _____ me-am.
5. CHOIR — *Et clamor meus ad te* _____ *vé-ni-at.*
6. CEL. — Dominus Vobiscum _____
6. CHOIR — *Et cum Spiritu tuo* (recto)
7. CEL. — O remus — ending with "Per Christum Dominum no-strum."
7. CHOIR — (Recto) *Amen*
8. CEL. — Réquiem ǽtérnam dona ei,_____ Dó-mi-ne.
8. CHOIR — *Et lux perpétua lúceat*_____ e - i.

9. CHOIR

9. CHANTERS   Re-qui-és-cat in pa - ce.

A - men.

10. CEL.   (in a lower pitch) Anima ejus et animǽ
            ómnium fidelium defunctórum, per mi-
            sencordiam Dei requiescant in pace
10. CHOIR   (in the same pitch-Recto) — *A-men.*

522

In Paradisum

Ant.VII

In pa - ra - dí - sum ★ de - dú - cant te
An - ge - li: in tú - o ad - vén - tu sus - cí - pi - ant
te Már-ty - res, et per-dú-cant-te in ci - vi - tá-tem
sán - ctam Je - rú-sa-lem. Chó - rus An - ge - ló - rum
te sus - cí - pi - at, et cum Lá - za-ro quon-dam
páu-pe - re ae - tér - nam há-be-as ré-qui-em.

The Mass of the Angels*
(Missa de Angelis)
(VIII- In Festis Duplicibus 5)
with Credo No. 3

Kyrie

Vatican Graduale
Transcribed by
N. A. Montani
XV - XVI Century

Gloria

XVI Century Melody

Fifth Mode

Celebrant   *mf* Choir I *

Gló-ri-a in ex-cél-sis De-o   Et in ter-ra pax

ho-mi-ni-bus bó-næ vol-un-tá-tis. Lau-dá - mus te.

Be-ne-dí-ci-mus te.   Ad-o-rá - mus te.

Gló-ri-fi - cá-mus te.   Grá-ti-as a-gi-mus ti - bi

pró-pter má-gnam gló-ri-am tu-am. Dó-mi-ne De-us,

Rex coe-lé-stis De-us Pa-ter o - mní-pot-ens.

Dó-mi-ne Fi-li u-ni - gé-ni-te Je - su Chri-ste

✶ To obtain contrast and observe the traditional Antiphonal manner of rendition it is suggested that the choir be divided; one section singing the portions indicated by ① the other the portions de-signated by ②.

273

Credo
III

Fifth Mode
(Optional)

(De Angelis
XVII Century Melody)

Credo in u-num De - um. Pa-trem o-mni-pot-én-tem,

fa-ctó-rem coe-li et ter-ræ, vi - si - bí - li - um

ó - mni-um, et in-vi - si - bí - li-um.

Et in u-num Dó-mi-num Je - sum Chrí-stum,

Fí-li-um De-i u-ni-gé-ni-tum. Et ex Pa-tre

na - tum an-te ó-mni-a sǽ - cu-la.

528

a tempo
II
mf
Cru - ci - fí - xus ét - i - am pro no - bis:

pp
sub Pón-ti-o Pi-lá-to pas-sus, et se-púl - tus est.

I a tempo
p
Et re-sur- ré-xit tér-ti- a di - e, se-cún-dum

II
f
Scri-ptú-ras. Et a - scén-dit in cœ - lum: se-det ad

mf I
déx-te-ram Pa - tris. Et í - te-rum ven-tú-rus est

p f
cum gló-ri- a ju - di-cá-re vi-vos, et mór-tu - os:

II a tempo
p
cu-jus re-gni non e-rit fi-nis. Et in Spí-ri-tum

p p
San-ctum, Dó - mi-num, et vi - vi - fi - cán-tem:

Sanctus and Benedictus*

274

Sixth Mode   XI Century

San - - ctus,* San-ctus, San - - ctus

Dó - - mi-nus De-us Sá - - - -

ba-oth. Ple-ni sunt cœ - li et ter - ra gló-ri-a

tu - a. Ho-sán-na in ex-cél - - sis. Be-ne-

dí - ctus qui ve - nit in nó-mi-ne Dó - mi-ni.

Ho-san - - na in ex-cél - - - sis.

* The "Benedictus" is sung after the Elevation.

531

275   Agnus Dei

Sixth Mode   XV Century

A - gnus De - i, qui tol-lis pec-cá-ta mun-di: mi-se-ré-re___ no - bis. A-gnus De - i, qui tol - lis pec-cá-ta mun - di: mi-se-ré-re___ no - bis. A - gnus De - i, qui tol-lis pec-cá-ta mun - di: do-na no-bis___ pa - cem.

For "Ite Missa Est" and "Deo Gratias" see No. 259 - 13- ⓔ

532

Vespers in honor of the Blessed Virgin Mary

276

(Can be sung in place of the proper Vespers of the day)

From the Vatican Antiphonale
Transcribed by N. A. M.

Celebrant

℣. De-us in ad-ju-tó - ri-um me-um in-tén - de.

Choir

℟. Dó-mi-ne ad ad-ju-ván-dum me fe-stí - na.

Gló-ri-a Pa-tri, et Fí-li-o, et Spi-rí-tu-i San - cto.

Sic-ut e-rat in prin-cí - pi- o, et nunc, et sem-per,

et in sǽ-cu-la sæ-cu-ló-rum. A - men. Al-le-lú - ia.

★ *From Septuagesima to Easter the following is sung instead of the Alleluía.* rall.

Laus ti - bi Dó-mi-ne Rex ae-tér-næ gló-ri-ae.

533

First Antiphon and Psalm
276-a

Third Tone (a ending)

Dum es - set____ rex * in ac-cú-bi-tu su-o,   nar-dus →

Dixit

1 Di-xit Dóminus   Dó-mi-no me-o:* →

2   Donec ponam ini - -   mí - cos tu-os,*

3   Virgam virtútis tuæ

                     emíttet Dómi-nus   ex   Si-on:*

4   Tecum princípium in die

                     virtútis tuæ in splendóri-bus san-ctó-rum:*

5   Jurávit Dóminus, et non pæni-té - bit   e - um:*

6   Dominus a   dex-tris tu - is,*

7   Judicábit in natiónibus, im-plébit ru - í-nas:*

8   De torrénte in   vi - a bi-bet:*

9   Glória   Patri, et Fí-li - o,*

10   Sicut erat in princípio, et nunc, et semper,*

534

me-a de - - dit o-dó-rem su-a-vi-tá-tis. Al-le-lú-ia.

Dominus (Psalm 109)

1 Sede a déx - - - -	tris me - is:__
2 scabéllum pédum	tu-ó - rum.
3 domináre in médio inimicórum	tu-ó - rum.
4 ex útero ante lucíferum gé - -	nu-i te.__
5 Tu es sacérdos in aetérnum secúndum órdinem	Melchí-se-dech.
6 confrégit in die iræ su - - -	æ re - ges.
7 conquassábit cápita in terra	mul-tó - rum.
8 proptérea exaltá - - -	bit ca - put.
9 et Spirítu - - - -	i San - cto.
10 et in sǽcula saeculó - -	rum.A - men.

Repeat Antiphon
Dum Esset

276-b

Second Antiphon and Psalm

Fourth Tone (A)

Chanter   Choir

Læ-va e - jus * sub cá-pi-te me-o, et déx-te-ra⟶

Laudate

1 Lau-dá- te pú - - - e - ri Dó-mi-num: * ⟶
2 Sit nomen Dómini____ be-ne-dí - ctum, *
3 A solis ortu usque_____ ad oc-cá - sum, *
4 Excélsus super omnes gen-tes Dó-mi-nus, *
5 Quis sicut Dóminus Deus
   noster, qui in ⌜ al-tis há-bi-tat, *
6 Súscitans a_____ ter-ra ín-o-pem, *
7 Ut cóllocet eum_____ cum prin-cí-pi-bus, *
8 Qui habitáre facit stéri-lem in do - mo, *
9 Glória Pa - - tri, et Fí-li-o, *
10 Sicut erat in princípio, et nunc, et sem - per, *

(Eastertide a.t. add) *rall.*

il - lí - us   am-ple - xá - bi-tur me.   Al - le - lú -ia.

pueri (Psalm 112)

1 laudá - - -	te no - men Dó-mi-ni.
2 ex hoc nunc, et_____	us-que in sǽ-cu-lum.
3 laudábi - - -	le no-men Dó-mi-ni.
4 et super coelos_____	gló-ri - a e - jus.
5 et humília réspicit in coe -	lo et in ter - ra?
6 et de stércore_____	é - ri - gens páu-pe-rem:
7 cum princípibus_____	pó-pu - li su - i.
8 matrem fili - - -	ó - rum lae - tán - tem.
9 et Spi - - - -	rí - tu - i San - cto.
10 et in sǽcula sæ - -	cu-ló - rum. A - men.

Repeat Antiphon
Læva Ejus

Third Antiphon and Psalm
276-c

Third Tone (b)

Nigra sum sed for-mó-sa,*fí-li-æ Je-rú-sa-lem: íd-e-o di-lé-xit➞

Laetatus

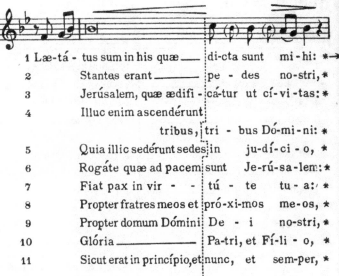

1	Læ-tá - tus sum in his quæ___	di-cta sunt	mi - hi: *➞
2	Stantes erant___	pe - des	no-stri,*
3	Jerúsalem, quæ ædifi -	cá-tur ut cí-vi-tas:*
4	Illuc enim ascendérunt		
	tribus,	tri - bus Dó-mi-ni: *
5	Quia illic sedérunt sedes	in	ju-dí-ci - o, *
6	Rogáte quæ ad pacem	sunt	Je-rú-sa-lem:*
7	Fiat pax in vir - -	tú - te	tu - a:' *
8	Propter fratres meos et	pró-xi-mos	me-os, *
9	Propter domum Dómini	De - i	no-stri,*
10	Glória___	Pa-tri, et Fí-li - o, *
11	Sicut erat in princípio,et	nunc, et	sem-per, *

me rex, et in-tro-dú-xit me   in cu-bí-cu-lum su-um. Al-le-lú-ia.

sum (Psalm 121)

1 In domum Dó - - - | mi-ni í-bi-mus.
2 in átriis tu - - - | is Je-rú-sa-lem.
3 cujus participátio ejus_____ | in id-íp - sum.

4 testimónium Israel ad confiténdum nó | mi-ni Dó-mi-ni.
5 sedes super | do-mum Da - vid.
6 et abundántia dili - - | gén-ti-bus te:
7 et abundántia in túr - - | ri-bus tu - is.
8 loquébar _____ | pa-cem de te:
9 quæsívi _____ | bo-na ti - bi.
10 et Spirí - - - - | tu - i San - cto.
11 et in sǽcula sæcu - - | ló-rum. A - men.

Repeat Antiphon
"Nigra Sum"

539

276-d
Fourth Antiphon and Psalm

Eighth Tone (G)

Jam hi-ems tran-si-it,* im-ber áb-i-it et re-cés-sit: →

Nisi

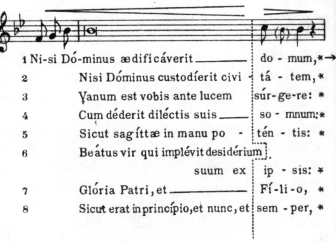

1 Ni-si Dó-minus ædificáverit _____ | do - mum,* →
2   Nisi Dóminus custodíerit civi ⊣ | tá - tem,*
3   Vanum est vobis ante lucem | súr-ge-re: *
4   Cum déderit diléctis suis _____ | so - mnum:*
5   Sicut sagíttæ in manu po - | tén - tis: *
6   Beátus vir qui implévit desidérium ⌉.
                          suum ex | ip - sis: *
7   Glória Patri, et _____ | Fí-li-o, *
8   Sicut erat in princípio, et nunc, et | sem - per, *

sur - ge a-mí-ca me - a, et____ve-ni.　Al -le-lú-ia.

Dominus (Psalm 126)

1 in vanum laboravérunt qui ædí - - | fi-cant e ˞am.
2 frustra vígilat qui cu - - - - | stó-dit e - am.
3 súrgite postquam sedéritis,qui manducátis pa-nem do-ló-ris.
4 ecce hæréditas Dómini,fílii: merces, |fru-ctus ven-tris.
5 ita fílii _____ | ex-cus-só-rum.

6 non confundétur cum loquétur inimícis su|- is in por-ta.
7 et Spirí - - - - | tu - i San-cto.
8 et in sǽcula sǽcu - - - | ló-rum.A-men.

Repeat Antiphon
"Jam hiems"

276-e Fifth Antiphon and Psalm

Fourth Tone

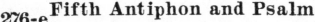

Chanter Choir

Spe-ci-ó-sa fa-cta es * et su-á-vis in de-lí-ci-is →

Lauda

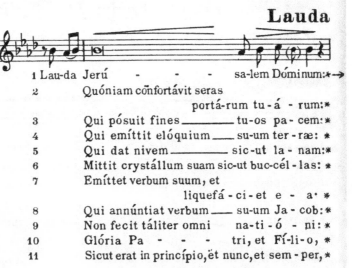

1 Lau-da Jerú - - -	sa-lem Dóminum:⋆→
2 Quóniam confortávit seras	
	portá-rum tu-á - rum:*
3 Qui pósuit fines_____	tu-os pa-cem:*
4 Qui emíttit elóquium____	su-um ter-ræ: *
5 Qui dat nivem_____	sic-ut la-nam:*
6 Mittit crystállum suam sic-ut buc-cél-las: *	
7 Emíttet verbum suum, et	
	liquefá-ci-et e-a· *
8 Qui annúntiat verbum____	su-um Ja-cob:*
9 Non fecit táliter omni	na-ti-ó-ni: *
10 Glória Pa - - -	tri, et Fí-li-o, *
11 Sicut erat in princípio, ét nunc, et sem-per, *	

The Celebrant sings the Capitulum:
After which the Choir sings ——→

The Hymn "Ave Maris Stella" is then sung (see No. 201)
after which the following versicle and response are sung:
** →
For the Second Vespers the Antiphon to the Magnificat
is then intoned by a Chanter (or the Celebrant) and contin-
ued by the Choir.

542

tu - is,   san-cta De-i Gé-ni-trix. Ál - le - lú - ia.

Jerusalem (Psalm 147)

1 lauda De - - - um tu-um Si - on.

2 benedíxit fíli - - - is tu-is in te.
3 et ádipe frumén - - - ti sá-ti-at te.
4 velóciter cur - - - rit ser-mo e - jus.
5 nébulam sicut_____ cí - ne-rem spar-git.
6 ante fáciem frígoris ejus quis sus-ti-né-bit?

7 flabit spiritus ejus,_____ et flu-ent a - quæ.
8 justítias et judíci - - - a su-a Is-ra-ël
9 et judícia sua non mani - - fe-stá-vit e - is
10 et Spi - - - - rí - tu - i San - cto
11 et in sǽcula sæ - - cu - ló-rum. A - men.

Repeat Antiphon
"Speciosa"

℟. De-o grá-ti-as.__

**
℣. Dignáre me laudáre te Virgo sacráta. (T.P. Alleluia)

Choir ℟. Da mihi virtútem contra hostes tu - os. _____
(Eastertide) Da mihi virtútem contra hostes tuos. Alle - lú - ia. _____

543

276-f

(For the Solemn Version of the Magnificat see No. 216)
The version given below is the simple setting.

Antiphon

Ad
(In II.

Chanter
Choir

Be-á - tam me di-cent * o-mnes ge-ne - ra-ti - o-nes,

1 Ma-gní-fi - cat *

2 Et ex-sul - távit spíritus _____ me - us *
3 Qui-a re-spéxit humilitátem ancíllæ ___ su - æ: *

4 Qui-a fe-cit mihi magna qui _____ pot-ens est: *
5 Et mi-se-ricórdia ejus a progénie in pro-gé-ni-es *
6 Fe-cit pot-éntiam in bráchio _____ su - o: *
7 De-pó-su-it poténtes de _____ se - de, *
8 E-su-ri-éntes implévit _____ bo - nis: *
9 Sus-cé-pit Israël púerum _____ su - um, *
10 Sic-ut lo-cútus est ad patres _____ no - stros, *
11 Gló-ri-a Patri, et _____ Fí-li-o, *
12 Sic-ut e-rat in princípio, et nunc, et sem - per, *

544

Magnificat

Vesperis)

rall. *(Eastertide ƒ add)*

qui-a an-cíl-lam hú-mi-lem___ re-spé-xit De-us. Al-le-lú-ia.

ánima | me-a Dó-mi-num

2 in Deo salu - - - | tá-ri me-o.
3 ecce enim ex hoc beátam me dícent
omnes gene -ra-ti-ó-nes.
4 èt sánctum _____ | no-men e-jus.
5 timén - - - - | ti-bus e-um.
6 dispérsit supérbos mente | cor-dis su-i.
7 et exal - - - - | tá-vit hú-mi-les.
8 et dívites dimí - - - | sit in-á-nes.
9 recordátus misericór - - | di-æ su-æ.
10 Abraham, et sémini e - - | jus in sǽ-cu-la.
11 et Spirí - - - - | tu-i San-cto.
12 et in sǽcula sæcu - - - | ló-rum. A-men.

Repeat Antiphon
"Beatam"

545

Responses after the "Magnificat"
276-g

Celebrant — **Choir**

℣. Dóminus vobíscum. ℟. Et cum spíritu tu-o.

Cel. — **Choir.**

℣. Orémus. *(etc.)* ℟. A-men.

Commemorations follow at this point. Consult "ORDO" for the proper antiphons and prayers which are given in the *"Liber Usualis."*

Cel.

℣. Be - - ne-di-cá-mus Dó - - mi-no.

Choir

℟. De - - o_____ grá-ti-as.

Cel. — **Choir**

℣. Fidélium ánimæ. ℟. A-men. Pater noster (secreto)

Cel. **Choir**

℣. Dóminus det nobis suam pacem. ℟. Et vitam ætérnam. A-men.

After this, one of the Antiphons to Our Lady is sung according to the season "Alma Redemptóris Mater", "Ave Regina", "Regina Coeli", or "Salve Regina." (See Nos. 277 to 280). (Also 202 - 205) also see Supplement.

Four Antiphons in honor of the Blessed Virgin

★ Note: See settings in figured style — Nos 202 to 205.

Alma Redemptoris Mater

Fifth Mode   Gregorian (Solesmes)

Ál - - ma*Re-dem-ptó-ris Má-ter, quæ pér-vi-a

coe-li pór-ta má-nes, Et stél-la má-ris, suc-cúr-re ca-dén-ti,

súr-ge-re qui cú-rat pó-pu-lo: Tu quæ ge-nu-í-sti,

na-tú-ra mi-rán-te,   tú-um sán-ctum Ge-ni-tó - rem:

Vir-go pri-us ac pos-té-ri-us, Ga-bri-é-lis ab ó-re

sú-mens íl-lud A-ve,   pec-ca-tó-rum mi-se-ré - re.

1st Response (In Advent) Et Concépit de Spíritu Sancto.
2nd Response (After Christmas) Dei Génitrix intercéde pro nobis.

278

Ave Regina Coelorum
(Simple Version)

Sixth Mode   (Solesmes)

Response: Da mihi virtútem cóntra hóstes túos.

Regina Coeli
279

Sixth Mode

(Simple Version)

Gregorian
(Solesmes)

Re-gí-na cóe-li* læ-tá-re, al-le-lú-ia: Qui-a quem me-ru-í-sti por-tá-re, al-le-lú-ia: Re-sur-ré-xit, sic-ut dí-xit, al-le-lú-ia: O-ra pro nó-bis Dé-um, al-le-lú-ia.

Response: Quia surréxit Dóminus vere, allelúia.

Salve Regina
280

Fifth Mode

(Simplex)

(Solesmes)

Sál-ve, Re-gí-na,* Má-ter mi-se-ri-cór-di-æ: Ví-ta, dul-cé-do, et spes nós-tra, sál-ve. Ad te cla-má-mus, éx-su-les, fí-li-i Hé-væ.

549

Ad te su-spi-rá-mus, ge-mén-tes et flén-tes
in hac lac-ri-má-rum vál-le. E - ia er - go,
Ad-vo-cá-ta nós-tra, il-los tú-os mi-se-ri-cór-des
ó - cu-los ad nos con-vér-te. Et Jé - sum,be-ne-dí-
ctum frú-ctum vén-tris tú-i, nó-bis post hoc ex-sí-li-um
os-tén-de. O___ clé-mens, O_____ pí - a,
O_____ dúl - cis Vír-go Ma-rí - a.

Response: Ut digni efficiámur promissiónibus Chrísti.

Missa Brevis

A short and easy Mass for Unison Chorus
or Chorus in two or three parts

S. S. A. or T. T. B.

281

Nicola A. Montani

* Numerals in circle indicate sections of the Choir singing in alternate style.
This manner of rendition is recommended when sung by Unison Chorus.

Copyright 1922, by N. A. Montani

551

Repeat from beginning
(Kyrie) to 𝄐 Fine

Gloria

282

Celebrant "Gloria in excélsis Déo:"

Choir *Moderate*

Nicola A. Montani

Et in ter-ra pax ho-mí-ni-bus bó-næ vo-lun-ta - tis. Lau-dá - mus te. Be-ne-dí - ci-mus te. A-dor-rá - mus te. Glo-ri-fi - cá-mus te. Grá-ti-as á-gi-mus ti - bi pró-pter má-gnam

* See note at foot of the first page of the Mass.

554

555

556

GOSPEL
RESPONSES

Celebrant — Choir

℣ Dó-mi-nus vo-bís-cum. ℞ Et cum Spí-ri- tu tu - o.

Celebrant — Choir

℣ Per ómnia sáecula sae-cu-ló - rum.   ℞ A-men.
(Per Christum Dóminum nostrum.)   (A-men.)

At the
Gospel

Celebrant — Choir *With animation*

℣ Dóminus vobíscum ℞ Et cum Spí-ri-tu tu-o

Priest

℣ Sequéntia sancti Evangélii se-cún-dum Jo - án-nem.
                                   Matthǽ-um.
            or "Se - cúndum Lu-cam."
                                   Marcam.

Choir

℞ Gló - ri - a   ti - bi Dó - mi - ne

557

283   Credo*

Missa Brevis

Celebrant: Unison Two or Three part Chorus

"*Credo in unum Deum*"   (equal voices)

Andante Maestoso   Chorus   Nicola A. Montani

Pa-trem o-mni-po - tén - tem, fa-ctó-rem cœ - li et ter - ræ, vi - si - bí - li - um ó - mni - um, et in - vi - si - bí - li - um.

Et in u-num Dó-mi-num Je - sum

559

Sán - cto. (Solo or Chanters) Et in-car - ná - tus est de
II or III

pp

Spí - ri - tu Sán - cto. Ex Ma - rí - a Vir - gí -

ne: Et hó - mo fá - ctus est. Organ

Andante moderato

Cru - ci - fí - xus ét - i - am pro nó - bis sub

566

Responses after the Credo:

Celebrant: Dóminus Vobíscum.

Choir: Et cum Spí-ri-tu tu-o.

Celebrant: Orémus, etc.

Choir proceeds with the proper Offertory of the day, after which, (if time permits) a fitting and appropriate Offertory Motet may be sung.

RESPONSES AT THE PREFACE
For Solemn Feasts, Sundays, etc.

Celebrant

To be sung in any key convenient for the Celebrant unaccompanied Choir ⏵*pp*

Per ó-mni-a saé-cu-la sæ - cu-ló-rum. ℟ A - men.

Celebrant Choir *pp*

℣ Dó-mi-nus vo - bí - scum. ℟ Et cum spí-ri-tu tu - o.

Celebrant *pp* Choir *pp*

℣ Sur - sum cór-da. ℟ Ha-bé - mus ad Dó-mi-num.

Celebrant

℣ Grá-ti - as a - gá - mus Dó-mi-no Dé -

Choir *pp*

o no-stro. ℟ Di - gnum et ju - stum est.＿

At the end of the Preface (which concludes with the words:"Sine fine dicéntes") the Choir immediately sings the"Sanctus."

284 Sanctus

Nicola A. Montani

Sán - ctus,— Sán - ctus,— Sán -

- - ctus— Dó-mi-nus Dé-us Sá - ba - oth.

Plé-ni sunt cœ-li et ter - ra glo-ri-a tu-

a.— Ho-sán-na in ex - cél-sis, Ho-sán-na in ex-

cél-sis, Ho-sán-na in ex - cél - - - sis.

570

Benedictus

(Solo Voices)

285

Nicola A Montani

Be-ne-dí-ctus qui vé - nit, qui vé-nit in nó-mi-ne Dó-mi - ni, qui vé-nit in nó-mì-ne Dó-mi - ni. Ho-sán-na in ex-cél-sis, Ho-sán-na in ex-cél-sis, Ho-sán - na in ex-cél - - - sis.

571

RESPONSES TO THE PATER NOSTER

Per ó-mni-a sǽ-cu-la sæ-cu-ló - rum. ℞ A- men.

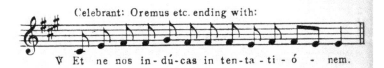

℣ Et ne nos in - dú-cas in ten - ta - ti - ó - nem.

℞ Sed líb - er - a nos a ma - lo.
Here there is a slight pause. *(No singing or playing.)*

BEFORE THE AGNUS DEI

Celebrant: Per ómnia saeculórum.(as above.)
Choir: A-men.(as above.)

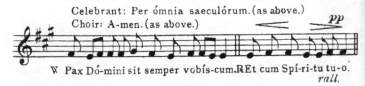

℣ Pax Dó-mini sit semper vobís-cum.℞Et cum Spí-ri-tu tu-o.
rall.

Proceed immediately to the Agnus Dei.

Agnus Dei

286

Moderato

(I) Solo

A - gnus De - i, qui tol - lis pec - cá - ta

Tutti *Faster*

mun - di: mi - se - ré - re

(II) *a tempo*

no - bis. A - gnus De - i, qui

Solo

tol - lis pec - cá - ta mun - di:

574

SUPPLEMENT

TO THE

Saint Gregory Hymnal
and
Catholic Choir=Book
(Melody Edition)

Edited and Arr. by Nicola A. Montani, K.C.S.S.

A Collection of Gregorian and Ambrosian Chants, Liturgical Hymns
and Motets, in Polyphonic and Homophonic style
(with Approved Texts).

Approved by the Music Committee of the Society of
St. Gregory of America, September, 1941

Publishers

THE ST. GREGORY GUILD, Inc.

1705 Rittenhouse Square, Philadelphia, Penna.

NIHIL OBSTAT

JOSEPH A. M. QUIGLEY

Censor Librorum

Philadelphia, October 3, 1940

IMPRIMATUR

+ D. CARD. DOUGHERTY

Archiepiscopus Philadelphiensis

Philadelphia, October 4, 1940

ALPHABETICAL INDEX

SUPPLEMENT TO THE ST. GREGORY HYMNAL AND CATHOLIC CHOIR-BOOK

287

ASPERGES

XIII Century

Sung on Sundays during the year except in Eastertide.

(❋ Note:) On Passion and Palm Sundays the "Gloria Patri" is omitted and repetition is made from the "Asperges me" to the Psalm.

Sic - ut é-rat in prin-ci-pi-o, et nunc, et sem-per,

et_ in sáe-cu - la sæ-cu - lorum. A - men.

a tempo *tutti*

A - sper - ges me, Do - mi - ne, hys-só -

po, et mundá__ bor: la - vá - bis me,

et __ sú - per ni - vem de__ al-bá - bor.

RESPONSES

Celebrant	1	Osténde nóbis, Dómine, misericórdiam	tu - am.
Choir	1	Et salutáre tuum da	no - bis.
Celebrant	2	Dómine exáudi oratiónem	mé - am.
Choir	2	Et clámor meus ad te	vé - ni - at.

Celebrant 3 Dóminus vobíscum. Choir 3 Et cum Spí-ri-tu tu-o
Celebrant 4 Prayer ending with,
"Per Christum Dóminum nostrum." Choir 4

A-men

288 VIDI AQUAM
From Easter Sunday to Pentecost inclusive

Eighth Mode Celebrant (first time) 10th Century

Vi - di a - quam * e - gre - di - én - tem de tem - plo, a lá - te - re dex - tro. Al-le - lú - ia: et ó - mnes, ad quos per - vé - nit a - qua i - sta, Sal - vi fa - cti sunt, et di - cent, al - le-lú - ia, al - le - lú - ia.

580

Ps.117. Con-fi - té - mi-ni Dó-mi-no quó-ni - am bo-nus: ✳

quó - ni - am in saé-cul-um mi-se-ri-cór - di - a e-jus.

Glo-ri - a Pa-tri et Fi-li- o, et Spi-rí - tu -

i San-cto. ✳ Sic - ut e - rat in prin-cí -pi- o, et

nunc,et semper, et in sáe-cu-la sae-cu - ló - rum. A-men.

Chorus repeats from beginning"Vidi Aquam" to *Fine.*

RESPONSES

Cel. 1 ℣. Osténde nobis, Dómine, misericórdiam tuam. Al-le-lú-ia.
Choir 1 ℟. Et salutáre tuum da nobis. - - - - - Al-le-lú-ia

Celebrant 2 ℣. Dómine exáudi oratiónem me-am.
Choir 2 ℟. Et clamor meus ad te ve-niat

Celebrant 3 ℣. - - Dó - mi nus vo - bís - cum.
Choir 3 ℟. Et cum Spí - ri - tu tú - o.

4

Cel.Prayer ending with, Per Christum Dóminum nostrum. Choir 4 A-men.
The Introit Proper to the Feast is sung as the Priest proceeds toward
the foot of Altar. 581

289 The Ambrosian "Gloria"

FOURTH MODE

Ambrosian Chant

582

De-us Pá-ter o-mni-pot-ens. Dó-mi-ne Fi-

Tutti

li u-ni-gé-ni-te, Je-su Chri-ste

Dó-mi-ne Dé-us, A-gnus De-i,

Fí-li-us Pá-tris. Qui tól-lis pec-cá-ta mún-

di: mi-se-ré-re no-bis.

Qui tól-lis pec-cá-ta mún-di

sú-sci-pe de-pre-ca-ti-ó-nem no-stram.

Qui se-des ad déx-te-ram Pá-tris, mi-se-ré-re
no - bis. Quó-ni - am tu so-lus san-ctus.
Tu so-lus Dó-mi-nus. Tu so-lus Al-tis-si-mus,
Je-su Chri-ste.
Cum Sán-cto Spi-ri-tu, in gló - ri-a
Dé - i Pá-tris. A - men.

II (or Tutti until the end)

I   II

pp Tutti

Broader
Allargando molto,

a tempo

Allargando

290

CREDO
I

VATICAN GRADUALE
XI Century
Transcribed by N. A Montani

Fourth Mode

Celebrant
Cre-do in un-um De-um.

I Choir
Pa - trem o-mni-pot-én-tem, fa - ctó-rem cœ-li et ter - ræ, vi - si - bí - li-um ó-mni-um,— et— in-vi-si-bí-li - um.

II
Et in u - num Dó-mi-num ___ Je-sum Chrí-stum, Fí - li-um De i u - ni-gé - ni - tum.

I
Et ex Pa-tre na-tum an - te ó-mni-a sǽ-cu la

585

De-um de De - o,   lu-men de lú-mi-ne, ____

Dé- um ve - rum de   De - o   ve - ro.

Gé- ni-tum, non fa-ctum, con-sub-stan-ti - á-lem Pa-tri

per quem o-mni-a fa- cta sunt.   Qui pro-pter nos hó -

mi-nes, et pro-pter no-stram sa-lú tem de-scén-dit de cœ-lis

Et in-car-ná-tus est de Spí-ri-tu San-cto ex   Ma-

rí - a Vír- gi - ne: Et   ho-mo fa- ctus est.

Cru-ci-fí-xus ét-i-am pro no-bis: sub Pón-ti-o

Pi - lá - to   pas - sus, et se-púl-tus   est.

Et re-sur-ré-xit tér-ti-a di-e,   se - cún-dum

Scri-ptú-ras.   Et a-scén-dit in cœ-lum: se - det

ad déx-te-ram Pa-tris.   Et   í - te-rum ven-tú -

rus est cum gló-ri-a _____ ju-di-cá-re vi - vos,

et mór-tu - os: cu -jus re-gni non e-rit-fi ‑ nis.

II Et in Spí-ri-tum San-ctum, Dó-mi-num, et vi-vi-fi-cán-tem·

qui ex Pa-tre Fi-li-ó-que pro-cé-dit. Qui cum Pa-tre et

Fí-li-o si-mul ad-o-rá-tur, et con-glo-ri-fi-cá-tur:

II qui lo-cú-tus est per Pro-phé-tas. Et u-nam san-ctam ca-thó-li-

cam et a-po-stó-li-cam Ec-clé-si-am. Con-fi-

te-or u-num ba-ptí-sma in re-mis-si-ó-nem pec-ca-tó-rum.

II I-II Et ex-spé-cto re-sur-re-cti-ó-nem mortu-ó-rum. Et vi-tam

f tutti ráll. ven-tú-ri sǽ-cu-li. A men.

Rorate Coeli

291

FIRST MODE

Solesmes
Acc. by N. A. M.

Chanters (first time)

Ro - rá - te coé - li dé - su - per,   et   nú - bes

plú - ant jú - stum. 1. Ne i - ra - scá - ris Dó - mi - ne, ne

Chorus repeats "Rorate" etc.

úl - tra me - mí - ne - ris in - í - qui - tá - tis: ec - ce cí - vi -

tas Sán - cti fá - cta est de - sér - ta Si - on de - sér - ta

_mf_

fa - cta est: Je - rú - sa - lem de - so - lá - ta est:

do - mus san - cti - fi - ca - ti - ó - nis tú - ae,   et

gló - ri - ae tú - ae, u - bi lau - da - vé - runt te

Chanters

rall

pá - tres nó - stri. 2. Pec - cá - vi - mus, et fa - cti su -

Chorus repeats "Rorate" etc.   589

mus tam-quam im-mún-dus nos, et ce-cí-di-mus

qua-si fó-li-um u-ni-vér-si: et i-ni-qui-

tá-tes no-strae qua-si ven-tus ab-stu-lé-runt nos: ab-

scon-dí-sti fá-ci-em tu-am a no-bis,____

et al-li-si-sti nos in ma-nu in-i-qui-

Chanters

rall. a tempo

tá-tis no-strae. 3. Vi-de Dó-mi-ne, af-fli-cti-ó-

Chorus repeats "Rorate" etc.

nem po-pu-li tu-i et mit-te quem mis-

sú-rus es: e-mít-te Á-gnum do-mi-na-tó-rem

590

tér - rae, de pé -tra de-sér-ti ad mon-tem fí -

li -áe Si - on: ut áu-fe-rat i -pse ju-gum ca-

rall Chanters

pti - vi -tá - tis no-strae. 4.Con-so-lá - mi - ni,

Chorus repeats "Rorate" etc.

con-so-lá,- mi - ni, pó -pu - le me - us

ci -to vé -ní - et sa-lus tu - a: quá-re moe-ró -

re con ·sú - me-ris, qui - a in -no - vá - vit

p *mf*

te do - lor? Sal - vá - bo te, no-li ti -

mé-re,— é - go e-nim sum Dó-mi-nus Dé-us

rall

tu - us, Sán-ctus Ís - ra - el, red-ém-ptor tu - us.

Chorus repeats "Rorate" etc.

292 Venite Omnis Creatura

Ambrosian Chant - XI Century Ms.
Acc. by N. A. M.

Ve - ní - te o-mnis cre - a - tú - ra

ad-o - ré-mus Dó-mi - num,

qui il - lú - xit nó - bis:

quem prae-di-ca - vé -runt pro-phé-tae a Mó - yse

us - que ad Jo - án - nem Ba - ptí-stam.

Hó - di - e ap-pá - ru - it Chri - stus, De - us

de De - o, lú - men de lú - mi - ne.

Resonet In Laudibus

293

Motet for Two-part, three-part or four-part Chorus

C. Jaspers
Edited and arr. by N. A. M.

294 **Dies Est Laetitia**

For Unison, 2-part or 3-part Cho.
S.S.A. or T.T.B.

Traditional Melody
Arr. by N.A.M.

1. Di - es est lae-tí - ti - a, In or-tu re - gá - li, Nam pro-cés-sit
2. In ob-scu-ro ná-sci-tur Il-lu-strá-tor so - lis, Stá-bu-lo re-
3. Chri-ste, qui nos pró-pri-is Ma-ni-bus fe-cí - sti, Et pro no-bis

1. hó-di - e Clau-stro vir-gi - na-li, Pu-er ad-mi - rá-bi - lis,
2. pó-ni-tur Prin-ceps ter-rae mo-lis; Fa-sci-á - tur dé-xte-ra
3. ím-pro-bis Na-sci vo-lu - í - ste: Te de-vó-te pó-sci-mus;

1. Vul - tu de-le-ctá-bi-lis, In hu-ma-ni-tá - te; Qui in-ae-sti-
2. Quae af-fí - xit sí - de-ra, Dum coe-los ex-tén-dit; In-ge-mit va-
3. La - xa, quod pec-cá-vi-mus; Non si-nas pe-rí - re; Post mor-tem nos

Allarg. marc.

1. má-bi-lis Est et in - ef - fá-bi-lis In di-vi-ni-tá - te.
2. gí - ti-bus, Qui to-nat in nú-bi-bus, Dum fulgur de - scén - dit.
3. mí-se-ros, Sed te-cum ad sú-pe-ros Jú-be-as ve-ní - re.

Adeste Fideles*

295

For 3-part Chorus S.S.A. or T.T.B.

Trditional Melody
Arr. by N.A.M.

1. Ad - é - ste fi - dé - les, lae - ti, tri - um -
2. De - um de De - o lu - men de
3. Can - tet nunc i - o, Cho - rus An - ge -

1. phán - tes: Ve - ní - te, ve - ní - te in Béth - le - hem.
2. lú - mi - ne:____ Ges - tant pu - él - lae ví - sce - ra.
3. ló - rum;____ Cán - tet nunc au - la coe - lé - sti - um.

1. Na - tum vi - dé - te Ré - gem An - ge - ló - rum, Ve-ní-te, ad-o-ré-mus, ve-
2. De - um.____ Ve - rum Gé - ni-tum, non fa-ctum: Ve-ní-te, ad-o-ré-mus, ve-
3. Gló - ri - a, gló-ri - a in ex-cél-sis De - o: Ve-ní-te, ad-o-ré-mus, ve-

1. ní - te, ad - o - ré - mus, ve - ní - te, ad - o - ré - mus Dó - mi - num.
2. ní - te, ad - o - ré - mus, ve - ní - te, ad - o - ré - mus Dó - mi - num.
3. ní - te, ad - o - ré - mus, ve - ní - te, ad - o - ré - mus Dó - mi - num.

* For Unison or four-part arrangement see No. 158

Jesu Dulcis Memoria

296

For 3 part Chorus — S.S.A. or T.T.B.

A CAPPELLA

Joseph A. Murphy

Andante moderato

Je-su dúl-cis me-mó-ri - a, Dans vé-ra
Nil cá-ni-tur su-á-vi-us, Nil au-dí-

cór - dis gáu-di - a:___ Sed sú-per mel et
tur___ ju-cún-di - us,___ Nil co-gi-tá-tur

sen - ti-
Fi - li-

ó-mni - a, E-jus___ dul-cis prãe-sén-ti -
dúl-ci - us, Quam Je-su De - i Fi-li-

A - men,
a. A - men, a - men.
us.
a - - men.

Attende Domine

297

Fifth Mode
Chanters 1st time
Choir 2nd time

Gregorian-Solesmes

At - tén - de Dó - mi - ne,   et mi - se - ré - re,

qui - a pec - cá - vi - mus ti - bi.

Repeat "Attende," etc.

Chanters

1. Ad te Rex sum-me, ó-mni-um re - dém - ptor,
2. Déx-te - ra Pá - tris, lá - pis an-gu-lá - ris,
3. Ro - gá-mus, De-us, tu-am ma-jes-tá - tem:
4. Ti - bi fa - té - mur, cri-mi-na ad - mis - sa:
5. In - no-cens ca - ptus, nec re - pú-gnans du - ctus,

1. ó - cu-los nó-stros sub-le - vá-mus flen - tes:
2. vi - a sa - lú - tis já - nu - a cœ - lé - stis,
3. áu - ri-bus sa-cris gé - mi - tus ex - aú - di:
4. con-trí-to cor-de pán-di-mus oc - cúl - ta:
5. tés - ti-bus fal-sis, pro ím - piis da - mná - tus:

1. ex - aú - di, Chri - ste, sup-pli-cán-tum pré - ces.*
2. áb-lu - e no - stri má - cu - las de - lí - cti.
3. crí-mi-na no - stra plá - ci - dus in - dúl - ge.
4. tú - a Re-dém-ptor, pí - e - tas i - gnó - scat.
5. quos red-e - mí - sti, tu con-sér - va, Chri - ste.

*"Attende" etc. repeated after each verse.

597

O Bone Jesu

298

For three-part chorus of equal voices: S. S. A. or T. T. B.

A cappella

G. P. da PALESTRINA

Ed. & Arr. by NICOLA A. MONTANI

May be transposed
one half tone higher

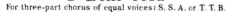

★ Small notes to be taken only if the choral resources permit.

Arr. Copyright 1940, St. Gregory Guild, Phila., Pa.

An arrangement for four-part chorus will be found at No. 256

598

Vere Languores Nostros 299

For 3-part Chorus S.S.A. or T.T.B. a cappella

A. Lotti, ✝ 1740
Arr. by N. A. M.

600

Ingrediente Domino 300

For Unison, two, or four-part Chorus
S. A. T. B.

Nicola A. Montani

Moderato

1. In - gre-di - én - te Dó - mi - no in
2. Cum-que au - dís - set pó - pu - lus, quod

san-ctam ci - vi - tá - tem, He - bræ-ó - rum
Je - sus ve - ní - ret, Je - ro -

pú - e - ri, re-sur - re - cti - ó - nem
só - ly - mam, ex - i -

vi - tae pro-nun - ti - án - tes.
é - runt ób - vi - am e - i.

Cum rám-is pal - má - rum, Ho - sán - na cla -
Cum rám-is pal - má - rum, Ho - sán - na cla -

má-bant in ex - cél - sis, — in - ex - cél - sis.

301 ## Jesu, Salvator Mundi

Motet for three-part Chorus
S. S. A. or T. T. B.
a cappella

Menegali-Montani

Je - su, Sal - vá - tor mun - di, tu - is fá - mu - lis

súb - ve - ni, quos pre - ti - ó - so sán - gui - ne,

quos pre - ti - ó - so san - gui - ne red - e - mí - sti.

Regina coeli

302

For Unison 2-part or 4-part Chorus

Moderato con anima Melchiorre Mauro-Cottone
Chanters (Soprano or Tenor) Edited and arr. by N. A. M.

Re - gi - na coe - li, Re - gi - na coe - li lae - tá - re. Al - le - lu - ia, Al - le - lu - ia, Al - le - lu - ia.

Unison or Semi Chorus S. and A. or T. and B.

Qui - a quem me - ru - í - sti, Qui-a quem me - ru - í - sti, qui - a quem me-ru - i - sti por - ta-re.

Al-le-lu - ia, Al-le-lu-ia, Al-le-lu - ia.

604

Juravit Dominus   303
Tu es Sacerdos in Aeternum

Motet for Ordination — First Mass or Sacerdotal Jubilee

Andante maestoso   Nicola A. Montani

* In Eastertide insert Alleluia in place of Secundum etc.

MOTET FOR FIRST MASS OR JUBILEE

304   Tu es Sacerdos

For Unison, Two-part (S. A. or T. B.) or 3-part Chorus
Equal Voices (S.S.A. or T.T.B.)   Aloys Desmet

Edited by N.A.M.

606

* Sing "Alleluia" in place of "in aeternum" in Eastertide.

305

PONTIFICAL CEREMONIES
MUSICAL PROGRAM FOR THE CONSECRATION
OF A BISHOP

ORGAN PRELUDE

1. **PROCESSIONAL**—Ecce Sacerdos (**246**) or Sacerdos et Pontifex (**244**)
2. **Presentation** etc.
3. **INTROIT - KYRIE - GLORIA - GRADUALE (TRACT OR SEQUENCE)**

   CONSECRATION CEREMONIES

   LITANY OF THE SAINTS (224) To "Ut ómnibus Fidélibus" etc. After the insertion of three Invocations the Litany is resumed.
4. RESPONSES TO THE **PREFACE** (FERIAL TONE) (**259-8**)
5. VENI CREATOR (**199**)
6. **UNGUENTUM IN CAPITE (305-a)** ECCE QUAM BONUM (**305-b**) UNGUENTUM.
7. **ALLELUIA** (or the last verse of Tract or Sequence) **DEO GRATIAS** (or BENEDICAMUS DOMINO).

   RESPONSES TO THE PONTIFICAL BLESSING (**259-11**)
8. **TE DEUM (264)**—"FIRMETUR" (**305-c**)
9. **VERSICLES AND PRAYER ("DOMINE EXAUDI"** etc. *Et. Clámor méus ad te véniat* V. DOMINUS VOBISCUM R. *Et cum Spiritu Tuo)*
10. **PONTIFICAL BLESSING (259-11) RESPONSES by the Choir as indicated.**
11. **AD MULTOS ANNOS** (NO RESPONSE).
12. **CHRISTUS VINCIT (310) FAITH OF OUR FATHERS (126)** or **HOLY GOD (39)**.

    RECESSIONAL.

305a Unguentum In Capite

1st time intoned by the Consecrator (unaccompanied)
2nd time (after the Ps."Ecce") sung by Chorus accompanied (ad lib.)

Gregorian
Acc. by N. A. M.

Un-guén-tum in cá - pi-te,* ____

quod de-scén - dit in bár - bam,

bár-bam ___ Á - a - ron,

quod de - scén - dit in ó - ram ves-ti -

mén - ti e - jus: man-dá-vit

Dó - mi-nus be-ne - di-cti-ó - nem

rall.

in ___ saé-cu - lum.

Proceed to Psalm "Ecce quam bonum"

Ecce Quam Bonum   305b
Psalm 132

FOURTH PSALM TONE

1. Ec-ce   quam bó-num et | quam ju- cún - dum *(1-B)*
2.   Sicut unguén - | tum in cá - pi - te *(2-B)*
3.   Quod descéndit
    in oram vesti- | mén- ti e - jus *(3-B)*
4.   Quóniam íllic
    mandávit Dó-
    minus bene- | dí - cti- ó - nem *(4-B)*
5.   Glória Pá - | tri, et Fí- li- o, *(5-B)*
6.   Sicut érat in
    princípio, et | nunc, et sém - per, *(6-B)*

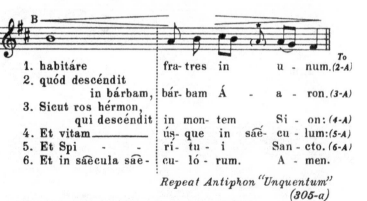

1. habitáre | fra- tres in u - num. *(2-A)*
2. quód descéndit
    in bárbam, | bár- bam Á - a - ron. *(3-A)*
3. Sicut ros hérmon,
    qui descéndit | in mon- tem Si - on: *(4-A)*
4. Et vitam_____ | ús- que in saé- cu - lum: *(5-A)*
5. Et Spi - - | ri- tu - i San - cto. *(6-A)*
6. Et in saécula saé- | cu- ló - rum. A - men.

Repeat Antiphon "Unquentum"
(305-a)

★ To be sung only for the dactylic form as indicated.

611

305c   Firmetur Manus Tua

1st time Consecrator sings (unaccompanied)   Acc. by N.A.M.

Fir - mé - tur ma-nus tu - a,* ___ et ex-

al - té - tur déx - te - ra tú - a: jus - tí -

- ti - a et ju - dí - ci - um prae-pa-rá - ti -

o se - dis tu - a. Glo-ri - a Pa-tri, et Fí-li-o,

et Spi - rí - tu - i Sán-cto, Sic-ut é - rat

in prin - cí - pi - o, et nunc, et sem-per,

et in sae - cu - la sae-cu - ló - rum, A-men.

Repeat "Firmetur" to ⌒

306

PONTIFICAL CEREMONIES
MUSICAL PROGRAM FOR THE INSTALLATION
OF A BISHOP

1. Organ Prelude (Ad libitum)

2. Processional **"Ecce Sacerdos" (246)** or **"Sacerdos et Pontifex" (244)**.

3. Here the Bulls are usually read.

4. The **"Te Deum"** follows (**No. 264**).

5. The administrator sings the versicles **"Protector noster."** etc. (**No. 244**). The Choir responds **"Et respice,"** etc. **Amen** at the end of the prayer. The Bishop is enthroned.

6. Here the clergy make their obedience. The Organ plays or motets are sung.

7. The Antiphon versicle and response of the titular of the Church are sung by the Choir, to which the prayer (Oration) is added by the newly installed Bishop. (Antiphon, etc., from Lauds if in the morning, otherwise from 1st Vespers). (See **Ordo** and consult with the pastor and Master of Ceremonies). Chant is given in **"Antiphonale Romanum"** or the **"Liber Usualis."**

8. Pontifical Blessing **No. 259-11.**

8. Solemn Mass usually follows. See Liber Usualis or the Graduale for the Proper of the day.

9. **Recessional**—"Christus Vincit" (**No. 310**) or similar appropriate Motet may be sung at the close of the Ceremony.

10. Organ Postlude (ad libitum).

307

PONTIFICAL CEREMONIES
PROGRAM FOR THE CHOIR AT THE VISITATION
OF A BISHOP

(Where the complete Ceremony is carried out)
1. Responsory "**Ecce Sacerdos**" (**246**) or **Sacerdos et Pontifex** (**244**). (The **Te Deum** is not sung.)
2. The Versicles and responses "**Protector noster,**" etc. (**244**) are sung.
   (N.B.) The Antiphon, versicle, etc. of the titular of the Church is not prescribed, thus the Pontifical blessing, "**Sit nomen Domini,**" etc. (**259-11**) will follow the Oration after the versicles.
3. Mass may be celebrated.
   After the Sermon, another blessing is given.
4. Responses to the Blessing (Pronounced by the Bishop on this Occasion).
   BISHOP: *Précibus et méritis beátae Maríae semper Virginis, beáti Micháelis Archángeli, beáti Ioánnis Baptistae, Sánctorum Apostolórum Petri et Páuli et ómnium Sanctórum, misereátur véstri omnipotens Déus, et dimissis peccátis véstris, perdúcat vos ad vitam aetérnam.*
   CHOIR—R. **Amen.**
   V. Indulgéntiam, absolutiónem et remissiónem peccatórum vestrórum tribuat vóbis omnipotens et misericors Dominus.
   R. **Amen.**
   The Bishop continues:
   Et benedíctio Dei omnipoténtis Pátris †. et Fílii † et Spíritus † Sáncti descéndat súper vos et máneat semper.
   R. **Amen.**
5. ABSOLUTION FOR THE DEAD. (After the Mass.)
   The "**De Profundis**" is recited by the Bishop and clergy with the "**Kyrie eleison, Christe eleison,**" etc. as given for the Absolution (See page 519).
   (If there is no Cemetery attached to the Church the following ceremonies are carried out in the Church:)
   During the Procession to the Cemetery or to the Catafalque the Ant: "**Qui Lazarum**" (**No. 308**) is sung in its entirety. On arrival at the cemetery (or at the Catafalque in the center of the Church) the "**Libera me Domine**" is sung. All the responses are sung as indicated after the "**Libera**" Page 519 (plural form). After the Bishop has sprinkled and incensed, the choir chants "**Kyrie eleison,**" etc., to which the Bishop adds the versicles and prayers, and **Requiem aeternam,** etc. The Chanters sing: **Requiescant in pace. R. Amen.** See Note below.
   The visitation of the Church follows. Then, Confirmation, if it is to be given. Benediction of the Most Blessed Sacrament concludes the Function. (See program for Confirmation **No. 247**).
   NOTE: For the Visitation add after the response "Sed libera nos a malo" (p. 519)
   V. **In memoria aetérna erunt justi.**
   R. **Ab auditióne mala non timébunt.**

614

Qui Lazarum 308

For Unison or two-part Chorus (S. A. or T. B.)

Andante (not too slow)   Nicola A. Montani

Qui Lá-za-rum re-su-sci-tá - sti,

mo-nu-mén - to fóé - ti-dum:

a mo-nu-mén-to fóé-ti - dum:

Piu vivo   *Calmo*

Tu e - is, Dó-mi-ne do-na ré-qui-em

rall.   *Fine.*

et lo-cum in-dul - gén - ti - ae.

a tempo

V. Qui ven-tú-rus es ju-di-cá-re ví-vos et

Calando allarg.

mór-tu-os, et saé-cu - lum per í - gnem.

Repeat from sign ⊕ "Tu eis", to Fine ⌢

309 Veni Creator Spiritus

For two-part, 3 or 4 part Chorus

D. Thermignon
Edited and arr. by N.A.M.

Andante moderato

1. Ve - ni Cre - á - tor Spí - ri - tus,
2. Qui dí - ce - ris Pa - rá - cli - tus,
3. Tu sep - ti - fór - mis mú - ne - re,
4. Ac - cen - de lu - men sén - si - bus
5. Hos - tem re - pel - las lón - gi - us
6. Per te sci - a - mus da Pá - trem,
7 (a) Dé - o _____ Pá - tri sit glo - ri - a,
7 (b) Dé - o _____ Pá - tri sit glo - ri - a,

1. Men - tes tu - ó - rum ví - si - ta:
2. Al - tis - si - mi do - num De - i,
3. Dí - gi - tus Pa - tér - naê déx - te - rae,
4. In - fún - de a - mó - rem cór - di - bus,
5. Pa - cém - que do - nes pró - ti - nus:
6. No - scá - mus at - que Fi - li - um,
7 (a) Et Fi - li - o qui - a mór - tu - is
7 (b) E - jus - que so - li Fí - li - o.

1. Im - ple su - pér - na gra - ti a, Quae
2. Fons vi - vus, i - gnis ca - ri - tas, Et
3. Tu ri - te pro - mis - sum Pa - tris, Ser -
4. In - fír - ma no - stri cor - po - ris Vir -
5. Duc - tó - re sic te prae - vi - o Vi -
6. Te - que u - tri - ús - que Spi - ri - tum Cre -
7 (a) Sur - réx it, ac Pa - rá - cli - to, In
7 (b) Cum Spí - ri - tu Pa - rá - cli - to Nunc

1. tu__ cre - á - sti pé - cto - ra.
2. spi - ri - ta - lis ún - cti - o.
3. mó - ne__ di - tans gút - tu - ra.
4. tú - te fir - mans pér - pe - ti.
5. té - mus ó - mne nó - xi - um.
6. dá - mus ó - mni tém - po - re.
7 (a) sae - cu - ló - rum sae - cu - la.
7 (b) et per o - mne sae - cu - lum

8. A - men, A - men.

A - men, A - men.

617

310 Christus Vincit! Christus Regnat! Christus Imperat!

Acclamations as sung in Rome on the occasion of the Election
and the Coronation of Pope Pius XII and as rendered at Solemn
Functions; at the Reception of Archbishops or Bishops. Also for
Jubilees, Te Deums or other Festival occasions.

Arranged by
Nicola A. Montani

For Unison, two, three or four-part Chorus
Chanters sing 8 meas. Cho. repeats.

Chri-stus Vin-cit! Chri-stus Re-gnat!

Chri-stus Vin-cit! Chri-stus Re-gnat!

Chri-stus, Chri-stus Im - pe-rat!

Chri-stus, Chri-stus Im - pe-rat!

Chanters
Chant (free rhythm)

Pi - o   sum-mo Pon-tí-fi-ci, et u-ni-ver-
Le-ó - ne   sum-mo "
Be-ne - dí-cte sum-mo "

sá-li Pá-tri; Pax vi-ta, et sa-lus per-pé-tu-a.

Refrain *Maestoso*

I
II
III

Chri-stus Vin - cit! Chri-stus Re - gnat!

S.
A.

Chri-stus Vin - cit! Chri-stus Re - gnat!

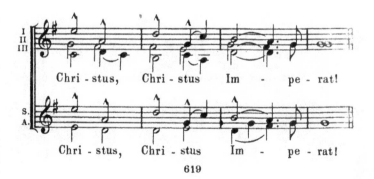

I
II
III

Chri - stus, Chri - stus Im - pe - rat!

S.
A.

Chri - stus, Chri - stus Im - pe - rat!

619

Chanters Solo voices
*Insert Name of Cardinal, Archbishop, Bishop or Abbot

*Thó - mae, Re-ver-en-dís-si-mo Ar-chi-e - pí-sco-po,
*Jo - an - ni, Re-ver-en-dís-si - mo E pí-sco-po,
*Gu-gliél-mo, Re-ver-en-dís-si - mo Ab-bá - te,
*Moy - se,

This can be omitted at will

et ó-mni cle-ro e - i com-mí -so: pax vi -ta,

Maestoso

et sá-lus per-pé-tu-a.   Chri-stus Vin-cit!

Chri-stus Vin-cit!

Chri-stus Re-gnat! Chri-stus, Chri-stus Im - pe-rat!

Chri-stus Re-gnat! Chri-stus, Chri-stus Im - pe-rat!

620

Chanters (Solo voices)

Tém-po-ra bo-na vé - ni - ant, pax Chrí-sti

vé - ni - at, __ Re-gnum Chri-sti vé - ni - at!

Best effect when sung in Unison

Tutti

Chri - stus Vin - cit! Chri - stus Re - gnat!

Chri - stus Vin - cit! Chri - stus Re - gnat!

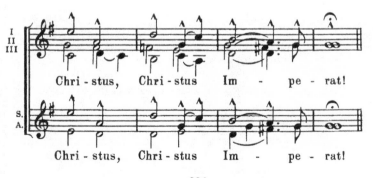

Chri - stus, Chri - stus Im - pe - rat!

Chri - stus, Chri - stus Im - pe - rat!

311 Cantate Domino Canticum Novum

For Unison, Two, Three or Four-part Chorus

Psalm 95

Vincent d'Indy

Edited and arr. by N. A. Montani

Allegro moderato (with spirit)

SOP. I
SOP. II
or Alto
in 4 pt.
Chorus

Can - tá - te Dó - mi - no cán - ti - cum no - vum: Can-

★ ALTO

Can - tá - te Dó - mi - no cán - ti - cum no - vum: Can-

★ Alto when sung by 3 part chorus S.S.A.

tá - te Dó - mi - no ó - mnis ter - ra.

tá - te Dó - mi - no o - mnis ter - ra.

(Chanters) Soprano or Tenor or Semi-Chorus

Slower

mf

rall.

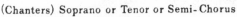

Quó - ni - am ma - gnus Dó - mi - nus et lau - dá - bi - lis ni - mis.

Can-tá-te Dó-mi-no cán-ti-cum no-vum, Cán-ta-te

Can-tá-te Dó-mi-no cán-ti-cum no-vum, Cán-ta-te

Dó-mi-no o - mnis ter - ra.

Dó-mi-no o - mnis ter - ra.

Quo-ni-am ter-ri-bi-lis est su-per-o-mnes de - os.

An-nun-ti - á - te   in - ter - gen-tes,

An-nun-ti - á - te   in - ter -

gló-ri-am   e - jus,   gló - ri-am   e - jus.

gen-tes,   gló-ri-am   e - jus, gló-ri-am   e - jus.

Chanters (Soprano or Tenor)

Piu lento   *molto rit.*   *Tempo I*   Tutti

Dó-mi-nus áu-tem coelos fecit.   Organ   Can-tá-te Dó-mi-no

Can-tá-te Dó-mi-no

poco rit. *a tempo*

cánticum novum, Cantáte Dó-mi-no,   o-mnis ter-ra. A-men.

poco rit. *a tempo*

cánticum novum, Cantáte Dó-mi-no,   o-mnis ter-ra. A-men.

624

Ave Maria

For three-part Chorus of Equal Voices
S.S.A. or T.T.B.

Nicola A. Montani

SOPR I or TEN. I — A-ve Ma-ri - a,

SOPR II or TEN. II — A-ve Ma-ri -

ALTO or BASS — A-ve Ma-ri -

gra-ti-a ple - na,_____ Do - mi-nus te-cum:

a,_____ gra-ti-a ple - na, Do-mi-nus te-cum:

a,_____ gra-ti-a ple - na, Do-mi-nus te-cum:

626

nunc et in ho - ra mor - tis

nunc et in ho - ra mor - tis

nunc et in ho - ra mor - tis

no - strae. A - men,

no - strae. A - men,

no - strae. A - men,

A - men. Organ.

A - men. Organ.

A - men. Organ.

* The portion between the signs 𝄌 may be omitted or used as an organ interlude.

Ave Maria 313

For 2 or 4 part Chorus S.A. or T.B. or S.A.T.B.

L. Bottazzo
Adapted and Arr. by N.A.M.

314   Ave Maris Stella

For Unison or four-part Chorus

Petrus Damiani, +1072
Arr. by N.A.M.

Andante moderato

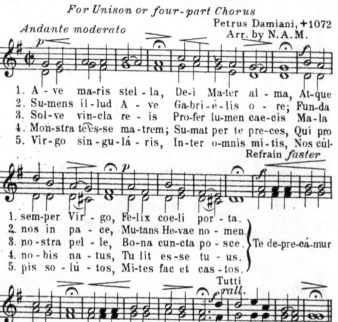

1. A - ve ma-ris stel - la, De-i Ma-ter al - ma, At-que
2. Su-mens il-lud A - ve Ga-bri-é-lis o - re; Fun-da
3. Sol-ve vin-cla re - is Pro-fer lu-men cae-cis Ma-la
4. Mon-stra te es-se ma-trem; Su-mat per te pre-ces, Qui pro
5. Vir-go sin-gu-lá - ris, In-ter o-mnis mi-tis, Nos cúl-

Refrain faster

1. sem-per Vir - go, Fe-lix coe-li por - ta.
2. nos in pa - ce, Mu-tans He-vae no - men.
3. no-stra pel - le, Bo-na cun-cta po - sce. ⎫
4. no-bis na - tus, Tu lit es-se tu - us. ⎬ Te de-pre-cá-mur
5. pis so - lú - tos, Mi-tes fac et cas-tos. ⎭

Tutti
rall.

au-di nos; et Fi-li-o commén-da nos, O Vir-go Ma-rí - a!

6.	**7.**
Vitam praesta puram,	Sit laus Deo Patri,
Iter para tutum,	Summo Christo decus,
Ut vidéntes Jesum,	Spirítui Sancto,
Semper collaetémur.	Tribus honor unus.
Ref. Te deprecámur, etc.	Ref. Te deprecámur, etc.

MOTET FOR BENEDICTION OR GENERAL USE

Jesu Deus, Amor Meus   315

Traditional Melody
Arr. by N. A. M.

Adagio

TEN. I & II

1. Je - su De-us, a-mor me-us, cor-dis ae-stum
2. Cre-do, Je-su quod re-vé-las O ae-tér - na
3. Spe-ro, Je-su quam lar-gí-ris pec-ca - tó - rum
4. A - mo Je-su bo - ni -tá-tem Tu-am su - per
5. Je - su De-us cor-dis me-i, Me-a vo - ta

1. im-pri-me, U-rat i-gnis, u-rat a-mor,
2. ve - ri - tas! Ju-va men-tem con-fi-ten-tem,
3. ve - ni - am, spi-ro vi - tae, quam par-ti - ris,
4. ó - mni - a, cun-cta há-bent va - ni - tá - tem,
5. re-spi-ce cre-do, spé-ro, a - mo Je - sum,

1. cor-di flam-mam sub-ji-ce, cor-di flam-mam súb-ji-ce!
2. tu-ta est si ád-ju-vas, tu-ta est, si ád-ju-vas!
3. sem-pi-tér-nae gló-ri-am, sem-pi-tér-nae gló-ri-am!
4. Prae te spér-no ré-li-qua: Prae te spér-no ré-li-qua.
5. A - mo su-per ó-mni-a, A-mo su-per ó-mni-a.

316   O Deus, Ego Amo Te

For Unison, two, three, or four-part Chorus

Andante religioso
For 2 part Chorus

XVIII Cent. Melody
Revised and arr. by N. A. M.

1. O De-us, e - go a - mo te,— Nec a-mo
2. Ex crucis li-gno ger - mi - nat, Qui pec-tus

For 3 part Chorus

1. O De-us, e-go a-mo te
2. Ex cru-cis li-gno ger-mi-nat,

te ut sal-ves me, Nec quod qui te—— non di - li-
a - mor oc-cu - pat, Ex pan-sis un - de bra-chi-

per - e - unt.
ar - ri - pes.

gunt,   Ae-ter-no i - gne per - e - unt.
is,   Ad te a - man-dum ar - ri - pes.

Ecce Panis Angelorum 317

BONE PASTOR

G.B.Polleri
Arr. by N.A.M.

Ec-ce pa-nis An-ge-lo-rum, Ec-ce pa-nis An-ge-lo-rum, Fa-ctus ci-bus vi - a - to-rum, fa-ctus ci-bus vi - a - to-rum; Ve-re pa-nis fi-li - o-rum, Non mit-ten-dus ca-ni-bus. Bo-ne pa-stor, pa-nis ve-re, Bo-ne pa-stor, pa-nis ve-re, Je-su, no-stri mi - se-re-re, Tu nos pa-sce, nos tu - e-re mi-se - re-re, Tu nos pa-sce, nos tu - e-re; Tu nos bo-na fac vi-de-re, In ter-ra vi-ven - ti-um. A-men.

318

Panis Angelicus

For three-part Chorus equal voices
(S. S. A. or T-T. B.)
A Cappella

(C. Casciolini?)
Jacopo Tomadini, 1820-1883
Arranged by N. A. Montani

1. Pa - nis an - gé - li - cus fit pa - nis
2. Te tri - na Dé - i - tas u - ná - que

hó - mi - num, fit pa - nis hó - mi - num; Dat pa - nis
pó - sci - mus, u - ná - que pó - sci - mus, Sic nos tu

cóe - li - cus fi - gú - ris tér - mi - num, fi - gú - ris
ví - si - ta, si - cut te có - li - mus, si - cut te

tér - mi - num: O res mi - rá - bi - lis!   O res mi -
có - li - mus: Per tu - as sé - mi - tas,   per tu - as

rá - bi - lis! man - dú - cat Dó - mi - num, man - dú - cat
sé - mi - tas duc nos quo tén - di - mus, duc nos quo

Dó - mi - num pau - per, ser - vus, pau - per, ser - vus, et
tén - di - mus, Ad — lu - cem, ad lu - cem quam — in -

hú - mi - lis, et hú - mi - lis, et hú - mi - lis.   A - men.
há - bi - tas, in - há - bi - tas, quam in - - - há - bi - tas.

* Interpolated

635

319   **Panem Vivum**

For Unison, two, three, or four-part Chorus
Slowly (Unison or 2-part Chorus)   Arr. by N.A.M.

O Sacrum Convivium 320

D. L. Perosi

O sá - crum con - vi - ví - um in quo Chri-stus sú - mi-tur; re - có - li - tur me - mó - ri - a pas-si - ó - nis e - jus: mens im - plé - tur grá - ti - a, et fu - tú-rae gló-ri - ae no - bis pi - gnus da - tur, da -

Eastertide and Corpus Christi only (T. P.)

Fine. For the Year

tur. *Al - le - lu - ia, Al-le-lu - ia. tur.

★ Alleluia omitted during Lent.

321   Tantum Ergo-A

For Three-part Chorus Equal Voices
S.S.A. or T.T.B.

D.L.Perosi
Arr. by N. A. Montani

Sop. I or Ten. I

Sop. II or Ten. II

1. Tán - tum er - go Sa - cra - mén - tum Ve - ne -
2. Gè - ni - tò - ri, Ge - ni - tó - que Laus et

Alto or Bass

re - mur cér - nu - i: Et an - tí - quum do - cu - mén - tum
ju - bi - lá - ti - o: Sá - lus, hó - nor, vír - tus quó - que

Novo - ce - dat rí - tu - i:— Prae - stet fi - des sup - ple -
Sit et be - ne - dí - cti - o:— Pro - cé - dén - ti ab u -

mén - tum Sén - su - um de - fé - ctu - i. A - men.
tró - que Com - par sit lau - dá - ti - o.

Tantum Ergo-B

D. L. Perosi

Sostenuto

1. Tán-tum er-go Sa - cra - mén-tum Ve-ne -
2. Ge - ni - tó - ri, Ge - ni - tó - que Laus et

re - mur cér-nu - i: Et an - ti-quum
ju - bi - lá - ti - o: Sá-lus, hó-nor,

Allarg. molto

do - cu - mén - tum No-vo ce - dat rí - tu -
vír - tus quó - que Sit et be - ne - dí - cti -

a tempo

i: Práe-stet fi - des sup - ple - mén - tum.
o: Pro - ce - dén - ti ab u - tró - que

Largo

Sén - su - um de - fé - ctu - i. A - men.
Com - par sit lau - dá - ti - o.

639

323   **Tantum Ergo**

CHORALE

Nicola A. Montani

3rd Mode

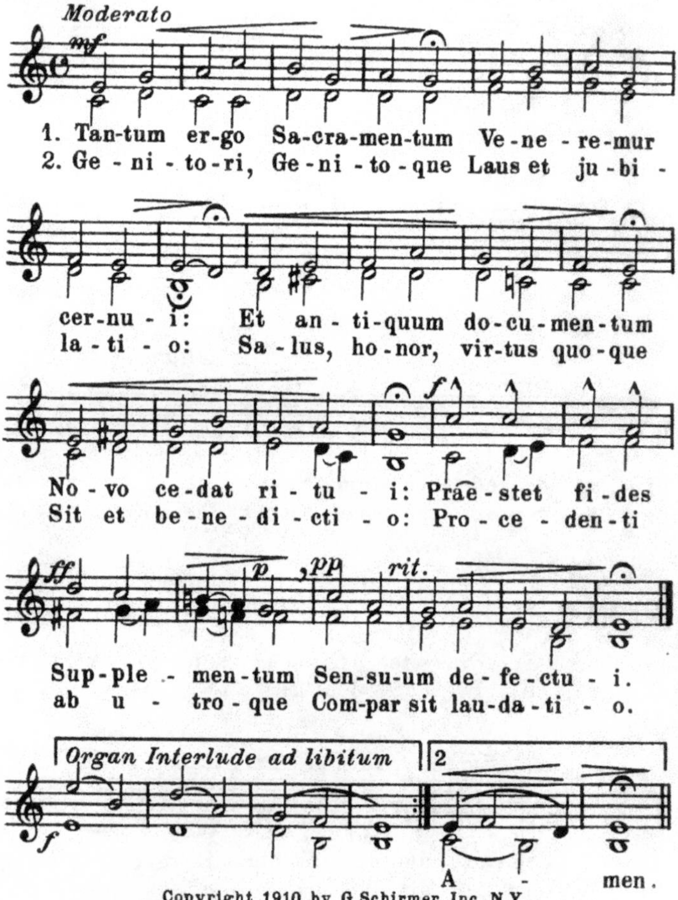

Moderato

1. Tan-tum er-go Sa-cra-men-tum Ve-ne-re-mur
2. Ge-ni-to-ri, Ge-ni-to-que Laus et ju-bi-

cer-nu-i: Et an-ti-quum do-cu-men-tum
la-ti-o: Sa-lus, ho-nor, vir-tus quo-que

No-vo ce-dat ri-tu-i: Prae-stet fi-des
Sit et be-ne-di-cti-o: Pro-ce-den-ti

Sup-ple-men-tum Sen-su-um de-fe-ctu-i.
ab u-tro-que Com-par sit lau-da-ti-o.

Organ Interlude ad libitum   2

A-   men.

Tantum Ergo

E. M. Sullivan

Andante religioso

1. Tan-tum er - go Sa-cra-men-tum, Ve-ne-re-mur
2. Ge - ni - to - ri, Ge -ni - to - que, Laus et ju - bi

cer - nu - i: Et an ti - quum do - cu -
la - ti - o: Sa - lus, ho - nor, vir - tus

men-tum No - vo ce dat ri tu - i:
quo - que Sit et be - ne - di - cti - o:

Prae - stet fi - des sup - ple - men-tum Sen - su -
Pro - ce - den - ti ab u - tro - que Com - par

um de - fe - ctu - i.
sit lau - da - ti - o.

A -

men, A - men.

★ Cut may be made ad libitum from ✠ to ✠

325

TANTUM ERGO
Spanish

Fifth Mode

Version given by Dom Suñol

1. Tan-tum ér - go. Sa-cra - mén - tum _____
2. Ge - ni - tó - ri, Ge - ni - tó - que _____

Ve - ne - ré - mur cer nu - i: Et an - tí - quum do - cu - mén - tum
Laus et jú - bi - lá - ti - o,   Sa - lus, ho - nor, virtus quo - que

No - vo ce - dat rí - tu - i: _____
Sit et be - ne di - cti - o: _____

Prae-stet fi - des sup - ple - mén - tum _____
Pro - ce - dén - ti ab u - tró - que _____ *rall.*

Sén - su - um de - fé - ctu - i.   A - men. _____
Com-par sit lau - dá - ti - o.

Responses:

During the year   Eastertide

Cel.   Panem de coelo praestítisti | e - is. | e - is. Ál - le - lú - ia.
Choir   Omne delectaméntum in se ha- | bén-tem. | béntem. Al-le-lú - ia.

Cel. Prayer ending with:
"Per Christum Dominum   nostrum."   Choir; A men.

Tantum Ergo

Albert J. Dooner

Moderato

1. Tan-tum er - go Sa - cra - men - tum,
2. Ge - ni - to - ri, Ge - ni - to - que

1. Ve - ne - re - mur cer - nu - i:
2. Laus et ju - bi - la - ti - o:

1. Et an - ti - quum do - cu - men - tum
2. Sa - lus, ho - nor, vir - tus quo - que

1. No - vo ce dat ri - tu - i: Præ - stet
2. Sit et be - ne - di - cti - o: Pro - ce -

1. fi - des sup - ple - men - tum Sen - su - um de -
2. den - ti ab u - tro que Com - par sit lau -

1. fe - ctu - i. A - - men.
2. da - ti - o.

327 Adoremus and Laudate Dominum

Sixth Tone   No. 11   Arr. by N. A. M.

Chanters (first time)   (Solesmes) Gregorian

Ad - o - ré - mus   in   ae - tér - num

San - ctís - si - mum   Sa - cra - mén - tum.

A *Tutti*

1. Lau-dá - te Dóminum   ó-mnes gen - tes:
2. Quóniam confirmáta est
     super nos miseri-cór-di-a e - jus;
3. Glória   Pa-tri, et Fí-li-o;
4. Sicut erat in
     principio, et nunc, et sem - per;

B

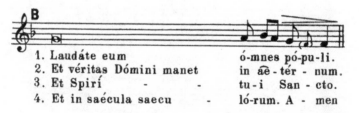

1. Laudáte eum   ó-mnes pó-pu-li.
2. Et véritas Dómini manet   in ae - tér - num.
3. Et Spirí -   -   tu-i San - cto.
4. Et in saécula saecu   -   ló-rum. A - men

All Repeat "Adoremus"

My Song of Today 328

(O HOW I LOVE THEE, JESUS)

Words by Saint Therese
of the Child Jesus
The Little Flower of Jesus*

Music by
Nicola A. Montani

1. Oh how I love Thee Je - sus! my soul as-
2. But if I dare take thought_____ of what the
3. O sweet-est star of' Hea - ven, O Vir - gin

1. pires to Thee, And yet for one day on - ly my
2. mor-row brings It fills my fic-kle heart_with
3. spot-less blest_____ Shin-ing with Je-sus' light_____

1. sim - ple pray'r I pray, Come reign with-in my heart,
2. drear-y dull dis-may, _ I crave in-deed' my God,
3. guiding to Him our way, _Moth-er be-neath thy veil,

1._Smile ten-der - ly on me_____ to - day, dear
2._The cross and suff'rings to-day_____ to - day, dear
3._Let my tired spir - it rest_____ for this, dear

1. Lord, to - day_____ to - day, dear Lord, to - day.
2. Lord, to - day_____ but on - ly for to - day.
3. Lord, for this_____brief pass - - ing day.

Copyright, 1925, St. Gregory Guild Inc., Phila., Pa. International Copyright

* The complete Novena to the Little Flower of Jesus, with Hymns, Litany
and Prayers, is published in separate form by the St. Gregory Guild Inc

645

329 Christ the Lord Hath Risen

PRCESSIONAL

Tr. from the German
XII Cent.

XII Century Melody
Harmonized and Arr. by N. A. M.

Maestoso

1. Christ the Lord hath ris - en
2. Christ to rend a - sun - der
3. Christ, our Vic - tor - gi - ant

1. From His three-day pris - on; Meet it is to
2. Chains that kept us un - der, Sa - tan's yoke was
3. Quells the foe de - fi - ant: Let the ran-somed

1. make mer-rie, Je - sus will our sol-ace be.
2. slain of yore; Now He lives to die no more.
3. peo - ple sing Glo - ry to the Ea-ster King.

Al - le - lu - ia, Al - le - lu - ia,

no rit.

Al - le - lu - ia, Al - le - lu - ia.

O Sacrament Most Holy 330

INVOCATION   Ch. Gounod
Arr. by N. A. M.

With devotion

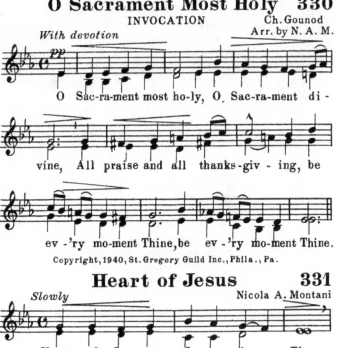

O Sac-ra-ment most ho-ly, O, Sac-ra-ment di -

vine, All praise and all thanks-giv - ing, be

ev -'ry mo-ment Thine, be ev -'ry mo-ment Thine.

Heart of Jesus 331

Nicola A. Montani

Slowly

Heart of Je - sus I a - dore Thee:

Heart of Ma-ry, I im - plore thee: Heart of Jo-seph,

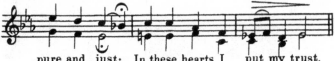

pure and just; In these hearts I put my trust.

332 My God, My Father, While I Stray
(THY WILL BE DONE)

Traditional

Slowly and with devotion

A.H.Troyte
N.A.Montani

1. My God my Fa-ther, while I stray
2. Though dark my path and sad my lot,
3. What though in lone-ly grief I sigh
4. Re-new my will from day to day,

1. Far from my home in life's rough way;
2. Let me be still and mur-mur not;
3. For friends be-loved no long-er nigh,
4. Blend it with Thine, and take a-way

1. Oh teach me from my heart to say:
2. Or breathe a pray'r di-vine-ly taught,
3. Sub-mis-sive still would I re-ply:
4. All that now makes it hard to say,

1. "Thy Will be done," "Thy Will be done!"
2. "Thy Will be done," "Thy Will be done!"
3. "Thy Will be done," "Thy Will be done!"
4. "Thy Will be done," "Thy Will be done!"

Hymn to the Infant Jesus of Prague 333

Text by a Carmelite Nun*

Music by Philip A. Bansbach

mf *Andante* (Unison or two-part)

1. O sweet In-fant Je-sus, we hail Thee Our
2. Thy Right Hand is raised high to bless us, The
3. O sweet-est Child Je-sus we love Thee, Our

1. Sav-iour, our God and our King! The Word in our flesh dwell-ing
2. world in Thy Left Hand doth lie; Then how can we fail, Lord to
3. lives mir-ror Thine ev-'ry day In mer-cy and jus-tice to

1. with us Our hearts all a-dore as we
2. ha-sten To Thee when e'er sor-row is
3. oth-ers, For then Thou will heed when we

1. sing. Though Thou art the great God of__ Heav-en, We
2. nigh? Dear In-fant of Prague, hear our pray'r For-
3. pray. Lit-tle King, we all trust in Thy good-ness Our

1. ex-iles on earth for a-while Re-joice in the sweet con-so-
2. get not Thy prom-ise so true That when we but hon-or and
3. needs now we place in Thy care. We know Thou wilt hear us and

1. la-tion The light of Thy heav-en-ly smile.
2. love Thee, Thy bless-ings are lav-ished a-new.
3. help us, And let us Thy great bless-ings share.

* Copyright

334 Hail, Holy Queen Enthroned Above

SALVE REGINA COELITUM

Traditional

Allegretto

Philip A. Bansbach

1. Hail, ho-ly Queen, en-thron'd a-bove, O Ma-ri-a! Hail,
2. Our life our sweet-ness here be-low, O Ma-ri-a! Our
3. To thee we cry, poor sons of Eve, O Ma-ri-a! To

(1) Sal - ve Re-gi - na coe-li-tum, O Ma-ri-a! Sors
(2) Ad te cla-man-us ex-su-les, O Ma-ri-a! Te

1. fount of mer-cy and of love, O Ma-ri - a!
2. hope in sor-row and in woe, O Ma-ri - a!
3. thee we sigh, we mourn and grieve, O Ma-ri - a!

(1) u - ni-ca ter-ri - ge-num, O Ma-ri - a!
(2) nos ro-ga-mus sup-pli-ces, O Ma-ri - a!

1-3 Tri-umph all ye Cher-u-bim; Sing with us, ye

(1-3) Ju - bi-lá - te Ché-ru-bim, ex-sul-tá - te

1-3 Ser-a - phim; Heav'n and earth re-sound the hymn:

(1-3) Sé - ra - phim, Con-so-ná - te pér-pe-tim:

1-3 Sal - ve, Sal - ve, Sal-ve Re - gi - na!

(1-3) Sal - ve, Sal - ve, Sal-ve Re - gi - na!

Hymn to Christ the King 335

Joseph Michaud

Maestoso

1. Praise we Christ; the King, The strength of all the
2. Grant us Thy law to   keep, Teach us Thy cross to
3. From the great judg-ment seat May'st Thou in jus-tice

1. strong, To whom a - lone all   ho-ly deeds And
2. bear, And thus re - turn Thy love_____ Here
3. say   That we too kings may be,_____ And

Chorus

1. all great works be - long.
2. and in realms a - bove.   O   Praise,   O
3. share Thy Throne with Thee.

Praise be to Thee, our Lord and King. King.

TO CHRIST THE KING

336 Great King of Kings

J. G. Hacker, S.J.   J. Kreitmaier S.J. (adapted)

Solemnly

1. Great King of Kings and Lord of Lords,
2. Thy claim to King-ship was con-firmed
3. "Thy King-dom come!" shall be our prayer,

1. Rul - er of all cre - a - tion, Whose roy-al right and
2. When, to our earth de-scend-ing, Thou didst re-deem our
3. Souls to Thy serv-ice lead-ing, Till all the world is

1. sov-ereign sway Ex-tend to ev - 'ry na-tion.
2. fall - en - race To share Thy reign un - end - ing.
3. won to Thee And heeds Thy ten-der plead-ing.

Refrain (Two beats in measure)

Thee, God's A-noint-ed, hail we our King;

Pledg-ing al - le - giance, trib-ute we bring;

allargando

Firm in our faith to Thee we cling!

A Priestly Heart, the Sacred Heart 337

English Version by the Rev. Henry Barth,
O.M.Cap. B.Mus.

I. Mitterer
Edited by N. A.M.

Allegro cantabile

1. A priest-ly Heart the Sa-cred Heart, For
2. A priest-ly Heart the Sa-cred Heart, Its
3. A priest-ly Heart the Sa-cred Heart, Our

1. sins of men the bur-den bear-ing, Seek's ev-'ry-where. in
2. heav-y cross a sad life stor-y, It takes the weight of
3. souls' sal-va-tion its de-sire___ For souls it suf-fered

1. lov-ing care To bring back home the sheep when err-ing.
2. hu-man guilt And gives in turn ce-les-tial glor-y.
3. pain and death With love for souls 'tis all a-fire!

mf

1-3. O Sa-cred Heart with love be-nign, Make

1-3. of our hearts Thy al-tar shrine May we one day with hearts like

allarg.

1-3. Thine Be ho-ly priests, Oh Heart Di-vine! vine!

★ Seminarians sing · *one day*; priests sing: *always*.

Music by permission of Canisianum, Innsbruck. Austria . Copyright 1929 by
Rev. Dominic Meyer, O.M. Cap., S.T.D.   By permission of the copyright owner
★★ For jubilee of a Priest insert "his heart"
★★★ For jubilee of a Priest insert "he always "
★★★★ For jubilee of a Priest insert "by a holy Priest"

The Revised Edition of

The St. Gregory Hymnal

and

Catholic Choir Book
With Supplement
Compiled, Edited and Arranged by

NICOLA A. MONTANI
K.C.S.S.

PUBLISHED IN THREE DIFFERENT EDITIONS

The Complete Edition. *Organ Accompaniment*
or for four-part chorus, S.A.T.B.
Containing all the music and full text — 640 pages : bound
in blue cloth — gilt lettering — Octavo size

The Singers' Edition - *Melody Edition*
Containing one line of music (2 voices) (S. A. or T. B.) and
the complete text conveniently arranged so that every syl-
lable appears under the proper note. (666 pages. Bound in
blue cloth) — smaller size than the complete edition

The Word Edition - *Book of Words*
Containing the text only — with complete set of indices —
octavo size — (160 pages) bound in heavy and durable paper.
(Especially adapted for Sodalities, Schools and Societies.)

Publishers
THE ST. GREGORY GUILD, INC.
1705 Rittenhouse Sq., Philadelphia, Pa